PRAISE FOR *CHARLIE-316*

"*Charlie-316* is a taut and tense look behind the thin blue line. In a world where the truth is malleable and honor is a tattered banner, justice is as elusive as a ghost. Zafiro and Conway guide us through this world with unflinching honesty and sure handed skill. If you liked *The Force* you will love *Charlie-316*." —**S.A. Cosby, author of *Blacktop Wasteland***

"A hard-hitting police conspiracy tale turned on its head, *Charlie-316* bristles with authenticity and rich detail. Conway and Zafiro deliver an engrossing socio-political drama that packs plenty of action and intrigue, while asking the difficult questions. Corruption, conspiracy, and compromise frame the downfall of a perfect cop. And Wardell Clint is the most nuanced, fascinating detective I've read in a very long time. This one tackles tough issues and will leave no reader indifferent. Compelling." —**James W. Ziskin, Anthony and Macavity Award-winning author of the Ellie Stone mysteries**

"Riveting and compulsively readable, *Charlie-316* is an ambitious book about many things including honor, the murkiness of politics, corruption, and a good man searching for the truth. Any fan of Don Winslow's critically-acclaimed *The Force* needs to be searching out and reading this book." —**Dave Zeltserman, author of *Small Crimes***

"In *Charlie-316,* Conway and Zafiro, two master storytellers, have punched a hole in the blue wall in this compelling tale that offers the reader a no-holds barred, insider's view of corruption in a mid-sized American city." —**Charles Salzberg, author of *Second Story Man***

D0925826

CHARLIE-316

Colin Conway | Frank Zafiro

Charlie-316

Cover design by JT Lindroos

ISBN: 978-1-7368543-7-2

Original Ink Press, an imprint of High Speed Creative, LLC
1521 N. Argonne Road, #C-205
Spokane Valley, WA 99212

This one is for our dads,
David S. Conway and Frank Scalise

CHARLIE-316

For God so loved the world
that He gave His only begotten Son,
that whosoever believeth in Him
should not perish,
but have everlasting life.
—John 3:16

The public weal requires that men should
betray, and lie, and massacre.
—Michel de Montaigne, philosopher

SUNDAY

Everything we hear is an opinion, not a fact.
Everything we see is a perspective, not the truth.
—Marcus Aurelius, Emperor of Rome

Chapter 1

Tyler Garrett slid behind the wheel of the patrol car and shut off his overhead lights. Ahead of him, the car he'd stopped a few minutes ago pulled tentatively back into the roadway and headed on its way. The driver had been a grocery clerk, just off shift, and she'd drifted through a stop sign on her way home. Garrett had given her a friendly warning. He didn't write tickets to working people.

Garrett reached for the microphone and depressed the button. "Charlie-three-sixteen, I'm clear."

"Three-sixteen, copy," came the dispatcher's reply.

He put the car into gear and drove with the air conditioner cranked and the windows down. It was a habit he developed over the years to better connect with his environment. He wanted to be able to feel, hear, and smell the neighborhoods as he drifted through them looking for crime.

Garrett smiled as an image of Marvel's Luke Cage popped into his mind.

"Yeah, I'm Power Man," he muttered to himself. "A regular crime fighting machine."

He guided his patrol car through East Central Spokane, a neighborhood just south of Interstate 90. It was an eclectic mixture of black and white, with a growing Russian population. Spokane was a predominantly pale city but East Central bucked the trend. Almost everyone he knew either grew up in or had connections to the neighborhood. Even though he no longer lived in that part of the city, it was a personal mission to keep watch on this neighborhood.

DJ Khaled's "I'm the One" softly played while he drove. Garrett whispered the words and bobbed his head, his eyes scanning for any illegal activity. With a light ding, a call for service popped up on the Mobile Data Computer to his right. A quick glance told him it was a noise complaint between two neighbors on the South Hill, Spokane's wealthiest part of town. Garrett shook his head. He planned to take a break in a few minutes to stretch his legs. He didn't want to listen to some Richie Rich complaining. Let someone else take it, he thought.

He hooked his finger over the top of the ballistic vest that was underneath his uniform and tugged it down. While he sat in the car, the vest had a habit of riding up until it touched his throat. Most of the time, it didn't bother him much. However, on a hot August night, the vest was a nagging irritant that threatened to put him in a foul mood.

It was shortly after midnight and vehicle traffic had thinned out in the neighborhoods. A white male rode a BMX bike across the street in front of him, a TV balanced precariously on the handlebars. He considered stopping him, but knew it almost certainly meant some sort of paperwork. If the guy didn't have an arrest warrant, then either the TV or bike was stolen.

Or both.

Garrett grinned. If he had a nickel for every scraggly white guy riding a BMX while carrying a TV in Spokane…

A Chrysler 300 lurched out onto Thor Street from Ninth, cutting him off. Garrett tapped his brakes to slow his car. It was the second time Garrett had seen the car tonight. It was hard to mistake it with the front-end damage and the spare tire running on the front left. The Chrysler immediately turned west onto Eighth without signaling, cutting off a newer pick-up truck headed in the opposite direction. The Chrysler accelerated, its engine roaring in the quiet of the night.

Garrett turned in front of the now stopped truck and caught the eye of the BMX rider. Both the driver and the cyclist were watching so Garrett accelerated to catch up with the Chrysler which was doing its best to avoid him. The engine of his patrol car whined as he gained ground for several blocks.

Garrett grabbed his microphone and keyed it. "Charlie-three-sixteen, a traffic stop."

"Three-sixteen," a radio dispatcher responded. "Go ahead."

"A white Chrysler 300 at Greene and Eighth," Garrett said, before he phonetically read the letters of the license plate. "Code Four."

"Greene and Eighth. Code Four," the dispatcher repeated, verifying his instruction that a back-up officer was not needed.

Garrett activated his emergency lights, and, for a moment, the Chrysler accelerated before its brake lights flashed on and off several times as the driver tapped his brakes. The Chrysler continued the length of the block, his speed consistent.

He'd seen this many times before. The guy was deciding whether to run.

"Don't do it," Garrett muttered. "Just pull over."

The car turned right when the street ran into Underhill Park. Garrett keyed his mic. "Charlie-three-sixteen, he's still rolling. We're at the park."

"Copy, Sixteen. Charlie-three-twelve to back?"

Officer Ray Zielinski's gravelly voice immediately responded to the request for back-up. "Twelve, copy."

The Chrysler suddenly pulled over and stopped on the right side of the street. The park was on the opposite side of the street and an older home with a for sale sign stood on the right. Garrett immediately parked his car behind the Chrysler and hopped out, watching for signs that the driver might run into the park where he had played as a child. He keyed his shoulder mic at the same time. "Sixteen, we're stopped. Still Code Four."

"Copy, Sixteen. Charlie-three-twelve, disregard."

Zielinski clicked his mic in response.

The driver exited the car and turned to face Garrett. A tall, skinny white man, he wore only knee length shorts and tennis shoes. A single thick gold chain hung around his neck. Highlighted in blue and red by the splashing rotator lights of Garrett's patrol car were various tattoos that covered his body.

"What is your problem, man?" the driver yelled.

"Get back in your car," Garrett ordered him.

The driver waved his hands around as he yelled. "You think you can do anything? The mighty five-oh. I ain't afraid of you. You can't do nothing to me. Why keep pretending?"

Ty dropped his hand onto his Glock and repeated, "Get back in your car. Now!"

"I'm not taking this anymore!" the driver yelled and reached behind his back.

Garrett unsnapped his holster and freed his Glock.

A shot rang out and the window in his driver's door exploded. Garrett's mind froze for a split second. He hadn't seen the driver fire, but instinctively, he pointed his gun at him.

A second and third shot rang out. He snapped his head to the right in the direction of the shots. They were coming from the vacant house.

Ambush!

The realization hit him hard. A surge of adrenaline seemed to explode through him. He dropped behind the driver's door and took a deep breath to steady himself. Training kicked in as his mind immediately switched into tactical mode.

Two points of fire, he thought quickly. The car and the house. They had him triangulated. Garrett's mind raced and came to one immediate decision. Eliminate one threat *now*.

More shots cut through the night as rounds thudded into the patrol car. Glass exploded and rained down around him.

Remaining crouched, Garrett quickly scooted out from behind the door and fired two shots at the driver. At least one round found the target as the driver collapsed to the street.

Ty moved to the back of the car and arose slightly above the trunk section. He fired three quick shots into the house before dropping below the cover of the car. Without hesitation, he moved toward to the hood section of the car. As he shuffled along in a crouch, he changed magazines, keeping his weapon fully loaded just as he'd been trained. At the front tire, he raised back into view, prepared to fire. Garrett realized no more shots were being fired from the house. An eerie silence had descended upon the neighborhood.

He became keenly aware of the whirring of his emergency lights above him when he heard a screen door slam in the distance. Then it slammed a second time.

Garrett stood and sprinted toward the house, seeing a six-foot-fence that bordered both sides of the house as he ran. He knew not to scale it and come face-to-face with a potential shooter. Instead, he leaped on the porch in a single step. He steadied himself and kicked the door. It opened with a splintery explosion at the handle.

From behind the house, an engine revved loudly. Garrett raised his weapon and hurried through each room, prepared to find a shooter waiting for him in the dark. With each step, he was convinced there'd be a flash of light and the bite of lead. Sweat poured down his forehead and into his eyes. He wiped it away with his left hand and kept his gun trained on the threat areas as he moved through the small house. His radio crackled but he ignored it. No one waited in any room, and there was no furniture to hide behind. The house was completely vacant.

When he got to the rear of the house, the back door stood open. He burst through the screen door which slammed shut behind him. At the edge of the yard, the fence gate was open and he could hear a car racing down the alley.

Garrett sprinted across the grass and into the alley. He could see the red of taillights at the far end of block. He raised his Glock and his finger tensed, but he didn't fire. He didn't know what else was at the end of the block and knew better than to send a round into an environment like that.

Ty Garrett lowered his weapon and felt his heart pounding against his chest. He was suddenly aware that he was drenched in sweat. His ballistic vest felt like it weighed a ton. The lights from his patrol car danced in the sky above the house but didn't reach the alley.

He stood in the quiet of the alley's darkness, wondering what in the hell had just happened.

Chapter 2

Officer Ray Zielinski pulled into the convenience store at Sprague and Freya. Another six hours of his shift remained and without coffee, it was going to be brutal. Hell, *with* coffee it would still be brutal.

He had to stop working so much extra duty, he told himself, but knew it was a fruitless admonition. He needed the money, plain and simple. Two divorces, three kids, and always living on the edge of what his income could support had brought him to this point. Six months ago, he decided he had to get a handle on it, so he sold the house that he had somehow miraculously kept in the last divorce and moved into a small apartment. He lived frugally, and that made a difference, but it wasn't like he could force either ex-wife or the kids to do the same. So, he worked the extra duty gigs, providing police presence at banks, stores, and special events. The pay was good, but the hours were…well, they were brutal.

Zielinski put the car in park and started to roll up the windows when heard the sound of pops in the distance. His first thought was fireworks. They were illegal in Spokane but still inescapable around the Fourth of July. By August, though, most people were over them, even the kids.

More pops.

"Not fireworks," Zielinski muttered. He recognized the sounds now for what they were. Gunshots.

Irritated, he put the car into drive and rolled the windows back down. Coffee would have to wait. He made his best guess as to the origin of the shots and drove in that direction. He didn't bother with his lights or siren. It wasn't like gunshots in

East Central were an everyday event, but it wasn't necessarily uncommon, either. Especially during the summer months.

He drove, listening and knowing what was coming next. It only took another thirty seconds.

"Charlie units, I have a report of shots fired in the East Central area," the dispatcher broadcasted. "Two separate complainants."

"East Central, huh?" Zielinski shook his head. "Way to narrow it down."

A second later, a thought struck him. He reached for the mic, but before he could, the dispatcher came back on.

"Charlie-three-sixteen, a status check?"

Radio silence followed.

"Charlie-three-sixteen, what's your status?"

No reply.

"Hell!" Zielinski punched the accelerator. His patrol car lurched forward, the engine answering with a throaty roar. Out of habit, he reached down and hit his lights and siren and activated his dash camera, all in one quick motion. Random shots didn't merit an emergency response. An officer in danger did.

He raced southbound. Traffic pulled to the side of the road as he approached. He hooked a hard right and made a beeline for Underhill Park. As he approached, he slowed slightly, trying to envision which way Garrett's traffic stop might be oriented. He didn't want to pull onto the street into the line of fire if this was where the shots came from.

Before he could decide, he ran out of street and turned onto the road that ran along the park. He immediately saw a police cruiser with its overhead lights engaged, its headlights illuminating a Chrysler.

Zielinski killed the siren as he screeched to an abrupt stop to the right of the other patrol car. His left hand found the spotlight and flicked it on, further bathing the Chrysler in a curtain of brightness. With his other hand, he keyed his mic.

"Charlie-three-twelve, on scene with Sixteen."

"Copy, Twelve. Advise on further units."

Zielinski popped open his door. His eyes swept the scene, immediately spotting the shattered windows and bullet holes in Garrett's patrol car.

"Twelve, keep them coming. This is where the shots came from."

He dropped the mic and exited his car, drawing his Glock and using his door as cover. "Ty?" he called out.

No answer.

Zielinski clenched his jaw. He glanced up at the suspect vehicle, scanning for suspects, both inside and around the car. He saw none, but the driver's door stood open.

Maybe the guy rabbited, he thought. *Threw shots and ran.*

Zielinski felt a sinking sense of dismay. If the suspect fired on Garrett, was he...?

Keeping low, Zielinski quickly moved to the trunk of Garrett's patrol car. He peeked around the driver's side, his dread heightening. An officer down was every cop's worst nightmare. The driver's seat and the nearby ground was empty, except for shattered safety glass scattered on the pavement.

He moved up to the driver's door, his eyes still scanning. Then he saw the still form crumpled on the ground by the suspect vehicle. Motionless. Even at this distance, Zielinski could see the bright red smear of blood against the pale white skin.

He reached for his portable radio and brought it to his lips. "Charlie-three-twel—" he began, but the screech of feedback from being too close to Garrett's patrol car radio interrupted and overwhelmed him.

"Charlie-three-twelve, say again."

Zielinski flicked off his portable and picked up Garrett's patrol car mic from its hook. "Three-twelve," he said. "Suspect down. Start medics."

"Copy. And Charlie-three-sixteen?"

"No sign of him yet."

"Copy."

Zielinski heard the uptick in tension in the dispatcher's voice. He tuned her out as she began sending additional units. It was unnecessary. Any police officer within driving distance would be coming now, lights and siren. One of their own was in danger.

"Ty!" Zielinski called out again. He listened, but the only sounds he heard were the whirring and clacking of the patrol car's rotator lights, a dog barking half a block away, and sirens in the distance.

He took a deep breath and let it out. Then he raised his pistol toward the suspect vehicle and advanced. The smart thing to do was to keep the car covered while he waited for back up. With a couple more officers, they could safely clear the vehicle. However, he couldn't wait. He had to find Garrett.

The man lay face down near the rear tire on the driver's side of the car, a bloody red hole in his upper back. Keeping his gun trained on the car, Zielinski knelt and touched his throat to check for a pulse. His own heart was pounding so hard, it took him a moment to discern that the man was dead. Protocol said to cuff him anyway, but Zielinski rejected the idea. Instead, he stood and swept his aim throughout the car, looking for any other suspects.

Empty.

He decided that Garrett must be in foot pursuit with a second suspect, somewhere in the vicinity. He reached for his portable radio to direct units into a perimeter position, but his hand froze.

Officer Ty Garrett walked out of a house directly across the street and headed toward him. He appeared uninjured, his gait confident.

"Ty!" Zielinski shouted.

Garrett raised his hand in reply.

"Are you okay?"

Garrett flashed four fingers at him.

Zielinski felt a temporary wave of relief. He reached again for his radio, turning it back on before saying, "Three-twelve, have units slow their response. Sixteen is with me, and he's fine."

The dispatcher copied. A second later, a couple of the distant sirens suddenly muted, while others remained.

As Garrett approached, Zielinski could see light reflecting off the sheen of sweat that coated Garrett's dark skin.

"Are you okay?" he asked again.

Garrett nodded as he tugged down on his ballistic vest. "Yeah. I'm good."

"Any suspects outstanding?"

Garrett shook his head, then stopped and shrugged. "A car, but it's long gone."

Zielinski raised his radio, preparing to broadcast. "You got a description?"

"Red taillights," Garrett said, his tone dejected.

Zielinski lowered the radio. "What happened?"

Garrett took a deep breath and let it out in a long exhale. He pointed at the car. "This guy jumped out in front of me over on Thor, driving like an idiot. I initiated a stop on him, but he kept rolling until he got here. Then he jumps out, starts yelling at me. He reaches for a gun and starts shooting." Garrett pointed at the house. "So did someone from in there, all at the same time."

"An ambush?"

Garrett shrugged. "It felt like one." He spat on the pavement. "Man, I'm thirsty."

"I've got some water in my trunk."

Garrett patted Zielinski's shoulder and then looked at the driver's body. "He's dead, yeah?"

Zielinski nodded. He didn't mention that the wound was in the back. That was a problem for another day. In the distance, the sirens became more insistent as they got closer.

"I shot him," Garrett said. "After he fired on me. Then I went to clear the house."

Zielinski shook his head slowly in amazement.

"What?" Garrett asked.

"Only you SWAT guys think attack in this situation," Zielinski said. He felt a curious mix of admiration and disapproval at the same time. "You guys are a different breed."

"It wasn't like that. The shots stopped. They ran out the back."

"Still."

Zielinski turned back to the sprawled, still form on the ground. He swept the ground with his flashlight. Something was wrong, and a minute later, he realized what it was.

"Where's the gun?" he asked.

Garrett raised his eyebrows, then pointed to the holstered Glock on his hip. "Right here."

"No," Zielinski said. "Not yours. The driver's gun. Where is it?"

Garrett's eyes narrowed, and he quickly scanned the area.

"I don't see any shell casings, either."

"That's not right." Garrett sounded strange.

Zielinski looked him in the eye, trying to gauge what he saw there. Garrett's expression was a jumbled mixture of confusion, anger, maybe even a hint of panic. "Take it easy," Zielinski said, gently. "Grab your flashlight and help me look."

Garrett nodded and hustled back to his patrol car. Zielinski watched him go. A feeling of dread crept into his gut.

Garrett reached into the patrol car and came out with his heavy-duty flashlight. He started to return, then ducked back into the car. Zielinski saw the tiny, unmistakable red light on the dash wink on, indicating the camera there had just been activated.

He hadn't turned on the dash cam when he initiated the stop.

The dread in his stomach grew.

Garrett trotted back toward him. Wordlessly, they both swept the ground near the car with their flashlights, searching for either a gun or shell casings. They found nothing.

Zielinski gave Garrett a hard look as the yelp and wail of the approaching sirens threatened to drown out their speech.

"Tell me this was a good shoot," he said.

Officer Ty Garrett looked straight at him. "It was a good shoot."

Zielinski didn't reply. There was nothing more to say.

Chapter 3

"Huh?"

"Your phone," she mumbled sleepily.

Cody Lofton lifted up on an elbow and, through the darkness, looked over the young woman at his side. His cell phone vibrated and lit up the room. It was a hot night, so they had fallen asleep without the cover of even a sheet. He reached over the woman, feeling her naked warmth underneath him and grabbed the phone.

The phone's display showed a prefix similar to those cell phones owned by the city. Lofton lay back in the bed and answered, "This is Cody."

"Hey, man, sorry to wake you. It's Dan."

Lieutenant Dan Flowers, Lofton thought. A good officer and one of the few who supported the mayor during his re-election. As the mayor's chief of staff, Lofton had cultivated a beneficial friendship with Flowers over the past couple years. Flowers was a patrol lieutenant and if he was calling him at this hour, it meant nothing good.

"Dan, it's early for a social call," Lofton said, his voice raspy from a night of drinking.

"There's been a shooting. From what we know—"

"Hold on," Lofton said and slipped out of the bed. The woman had seemed to be falling back asleep, but she stirred as he talked, and he didn't want her to hear the conversation any further.

Lofton quickly looked for his underwear in the darkness. Not finding them, he shrugged and quietly walked out of the room, closing the door behind him. "I'm sorry about that," he said. "Go ahead."

"We've had an officer involved shooting. One dead."

"Tell me it's not your officer," Lofton said as he searched for a light. When he finally found a lamp, he switched it on, illuminating the living room of the apartment. He squinted against the light. Potted plants of various types were tucked into corners and a large print of a beach setting hung on the main wall.

"Our guy is fine. Not even a scratch."

Lofton sat on the leather couch with the realization that he should have stopped his night earlier. The after-effects of multiple vodka tonics now pulsated at his temples.

"What do you know about the victim?"

"We've identified him. Todd Trotter. He's known to us."

Lofton pushed up from the couch and walked into the kitchen. "What's that noise?"

"It's the radio. I'm in my car."

"Can you turn it down? It's giving me a headache."

The background noise of the patrol radio lowered. Lofton found a glass in the cupboard and filled it with a bottle of Evian water from the refrigerator. He took a sip and then paced the living room.

"Dan, give it to me straight. I know it's coming fast so if it's not perfect, it will be forgiven. I need as much intel as possible to paint a picture for the mayor."

"Here's the unofficial report. Trotter's a maggot that's been in the system since he could walk and steal," Flowers said. "There's no love lost on our side that he caught a bullet."

Lofton finished the water and put the glass down.

"Who was the officer?"

"Ty Garrett."

"Clara Garrett's son?"

"The same."

"Aren't we presenting him with a lifesaving award in a couple days?"

"Yes."

"How is he?"

"He's a professional. He'll handle it."

For a moment, a sense of relief passed through Lofton and he settled back on to the couch, feeling the leather against his naked skin. He rested his head on the back on the couch and thought about the young blonde in the other room.

He realized both he and Flowers had been silent for several seconds.

"Dan?"

"Yeah."

"You okay?"

"I've stepped over the line by calling you. I might get jammed on this one."

Lofton shook his head. "It'll be fine. If there's any fallout, I'll handle it on my end."

"Okay. Sounds good."

Lofton could tell by his voice something was bothering Flowers. "There's something else, isn't there, Dan? What aren't you telling me?"

"I've given you the official report so far, Cody."

Lofton sat upright. *The official report so far.* He closed his eyes and focused intently on the conversation he just had with Flowers when he realized he missed the one question he should have asked. The question that every municipality is concerned with above all others. "Was it a good shoot?"

"Yeah, it looks like it."

"It *looks* like it? What the hell does that mean?" Lofton's voice raised. "That sounds like hedging."

Flowers cleared his throat. "Cody, we're friends, right?"

"Of course."

"Then I'm telling you this because we're friends. You'll want to get in front of this."

"What do you mean?"

"We always talk about perception versus reality, right? I'm afraid this is going to turn bad on the perception side of things."

"What the hell are you talking about, Dan?"

"Aw, damn, the media is already here. We're going to have trouble containing this story."

"Dan, you're pissing me off. Just tell me what's going on."

"I'm not the coroner and we haven't completed our investigation, so this isn't official, you understand?"

"No kidding. Off the record and all that jazz. Tell me what I need to know so I can do damage assessment."

"It looks like Trotter was shot in the back. And…"

Lofton clenched his jaw, bracing himself. "And what?"

"Well, so far, there's no gun."

"No gun?" Lofton repeated. "What the hell does that mean?"

"Maybe nothing. It's early yet, but in the immediate canvass of the crime scene, we didn't find a gun on or near the suspect."

Lofton stared off into the distance, the throbbing in his temples was at maximum.

"Are you still there?"

Lofton didn't answer so Flowers repeated his question, "Cody? Are you still there?"

"What color is he?"

"What?"

"Trotter," Lofton specified. "Is he black?"

"No, he's not. He's white. Hell, Cody, most of our criminals are white in this—"

"Keep the media away from this," Lofton said.

"I don't under—"

Lofton ended the call. He scrambled for a pen and something to write on. He opened the drawers of the end tables, slamming them quickly when he didn't find what he was looking for. He moved into the kitchen, repeating the same action.

The blonde shuffled into the living room. She stood naked in front of him, her eyes adjusting to the light. "What are you doing?"

At the sound of her voice, Lofton looked up from a kitchen drawer. "I need a pen and something to write on."

"What time is it?"

"Did you hear what I said?" Lofton said, irritation clearly on his face. "I need a pen and some paper."

"Is this how you normally are?"

Lofton rolled his eyes. "Listen, Monica, I—"

The blonde's lip curled. "Monica?"

"It's not Monica?"

She shook her head. "Not even close."

"I'm sorry," Lofton said, waiting for her to blow up.

She shrugged. "It's cool. I don't remember your name either."

Lofton stared at her. "You don't remember my name?"

"Nope."

"Cody Lofton," he said, tapping his chest. "I'm the mayor's chief of staff."

She stared at him.

"That impressed you at the club."

"No, it didn't. I was impressed you were buying drinks," she said, grabbing a backpack next to the couch. She unzipped the bag, pulled out a yellow pad and pen, and tossed them on the kitchen counter. "There you go, Chief."

Lofton grabbed the pad and pen before sitting down on the couch.

"Hey," the blonde said. "When you're done making your notes, you can either come back to bed or let yourself out. Either way works."

Lofton watched her walk away, wondering if he should make an effort to talk further with her. When she closed the bedroom door, he shrugged.

On the notepad, he divided the paper into two columns. The left column was labeled *Threats* while the right column was labeled *Opportunities*. The threats came easily enough. Any police shooting was chock full of them. This one had racial overtones, a missing gun, and a victim shot in the back.

Lofton paused, scratched out the word *victim* and wrote *suspect* instead. Words were always important in framing a narrative to sway public opinion. In this case they weren't just important, they were crucial.

For the next thirty minutes, Lofton scribbled notes on how the road ahead would be perceived regarding Ty Garrett's shooting.

When he was done, he stood and stretched. He'd need to brief the mayor in person on this one. He walked quietly into the bedroom and waited for his eyes to adjust to the darkness before gathering his clothes.

Chapter 4

Captain Tom Farrell sat in his car for a few minutes after arriving at the crime scene. Lieutenant Dan Flowers stood with a corporal near his own vehicle. Flowers gave him an upward nod to acknowledge his arrival but didn't approach the car.

Farrell ran down the list of things he needed to know, decisions he needed to make, and those things he could not forget. An officer-involved shooting, or OIS, was one of the more difficult events for a police leader to handle. There were many moving parts and many different considerations. In a typical shooting, he had to concern himself primarily with the criminal investigation, and realistically, Lieutenant Flowers oversaw that. Major Crimes detectives were good at what they did and had his full confidence. Most of the time, his role was limited to informing the chief of police about the details he learned from Flowers. Occasionally, he took media duty, giving them what amounted to a canned statement.

Not tonight, though.

Tonight, he had to worry about more than just the investigation. The media had already assembled in force at the far end of the outer perimeter. In the aftermath of a controversial shooting in Philadelphia, Farrell didn't doubt they were primed to tear into this one with vigor. Right now, the shark tank looked only marginally larger than usual, but he knew it would grow, especially if what Flowers had told him in their brief phone conversation turned out to be accurate. He imagined the blaring headline now: *Black Police Officer Shoots Unarmed White Victim in the Back!*

It didn't matter. He had a job to do. He had to make sure that Garrett's rights were protected, both criminally and in line with the union contract. Unless Flowers had some different news when they talked, he would need to invoke the OIS protocol. That meant calling the county sheriff's office and requesting that they take the lead in the investigation. The purpose of this was to ensure objectivity and avoid conflicts of interest. Farrell wasn't entirely sure the process accomplished either goal any better than the old system, when they investigated their own shootings, but he recognized the political advantages. It just created a different set of headaches for him, dealing with another agency. Especially one headed by an elected official.

Farrell reached for the door, then realized he had forgotten the most important thing. Officer Tyler Garrett. The man had just been involved in a life and death situation. He needed to make sure Garrett was all right.

"Geez," Farrell muttered in the silence of his car. That should have been his first concern. Garrett was a person, not just another box on his checklist. He wondered if he'd been away from the street for too long, practicing politics instead of policing.

He got out of his car and strode toward Flowers. The corporal standing with Flowers saw him coming and suddenly found something else to do. Farrell didn't take it personally. He knew it wasn't him. It was the bars on his collar. That was all most officers saw.

"Hey, Cap," Flowers said.

"Dan."

"You awake yet?"

"Awake enough. Run it for me."

Flowers glanced down at his steno notepad, then he said, "Not much has happened since I called you. We've locked everything down and established an inner and outer perimeter. Media is contained over there." He pointed down the street.

"How are they?"

"Restless."

"I bet. What else?"

"Well, Corporal DeHaan is taking preliminary photos of the scene. We've kept most everyone out of the inner perimeter once we managed to string some tape, so the scene itself is relatively clean."

"You've been inside the scene?"

Flowers nodded. "Yeah, before I called you."

"And?"

Flowers' expression was grim. "It's like I said. Looks like Trotter was hit in the back."

"Still no gun?"

"No."

Farrell sighed and rubbed his tired eyes. "The gunshot wound to the back I can understand. A shooting situation is a tense, uncertain—"

"—and rapidly evolving situation," Flowers finished, picking up the quote. "Perfectly stated, Cap. Straight out of Graham v. Connor."

"Well, it's true."

"Absolutely."

Farrell chewed on his lip. The shot in the back could be legitimately explained, he knew. It was the missing weapon that bothered him.

"Any ideas on the gun?" he asked Flowers.

"Nothing that isn't pure speculation."

"Then speculate."

Flowers looked around to make sure no one could overhear him. "We're in East Central. Maybe someone grabbed it."

Farrell scowled. "Plenty of good people live in East Central."

"So do plenty of scumbags."

Farrell couldn't argue that point, so he moved on. "How, then?"

Flowers pointed at the small house that Garrett's patrol car was parked in front of. "Someone fired on Garrett from that house. He ran after them and hadn't returned yet by the time

Officer Zielinski arrived on scene. There's a window of time that someone could have grabbed the gun."

"How long?"

Flowers shrugged. "A minute. Maybe a little more."

"That sounds like a bit of a stretch."

"It is, but it's possible. Besides, you asked for speculation."

Farrell nodded slowly. "I did." He looked around the scene. "What else?"

"There are expended casings on the floor inside the house. It's for sale and deserted."

"Okay. Witnesses?"

"None yet, but we're still canvassing."

"Who have you called?"

"I notified the chief right after you. He's on his way."

"How is he not here yet?" The chief lived in a condo in the revitalized area of downtown, all of five minutes away.

"He was at his lake cabin."

Farrell nodded. He'd been to the cabin on Loon Lake for a command retreat less than a month ago. Even accounting for how fast the chief liked to drive, he knew that he probably still had ten or fifteen minutes before his arrival.

"The Union here?"

"Yeah, Dale Thomas is around somewhere. I didn't have to call him, though. Someone else already did."

"Who else did you call?"

"I notified Lofton."

Farrell grimaced. "C'mon, Dan. Did you call the Pope, too?"

Flowers looked slightly hurt. "Lofton's on the notification list."

"It's the chief's job to call the mayor, not yours." Unspoken was that the notification from the chief was better done after he'd been thoroughly briefed. As far as Farrell was concerned, telling everyone and their sister what was going on before the investigators really knew themselves was a recipe for disaster.

"Sorry."

Farrell waved it off. "What's done is done. What else?"

Flowers cleared his throat. "I...uh, I made a preliminary call to county to let them know we might need to invoke the OIS protocol. They're just waiting on official word from you as the duty staff officer."

That one didn't bother Farrell as much. In reality, the decision to invoke was a slam dunk, and Flowers probably saved some time in making the call. It meant that county investigators were probably already awake, dressed and waiting for the official notification.

"Good," he said, smoothing over his earlier disapproval. "Go ahead and make the call."

"I thought you—"

"I need to check on Ty. Where is he?"

Flowers pointed across the street. Officer Ty Garret sat on the concrete steps of a walkway leading from the sidewalk to someone's house. He had a blanket draped over his shoulders and held a bottle of water loosely in his hands. Two other patrol officers stood nearby protectively, giving him his space.

"Do we have peer support en route?"

"Officer Griffin is already here, but Ty didn't feel like talking." Flowers motioned toward the pair of officers near Garrett. "Those two are SWAT, and they're pretty much keeping anyone away who doesn't have business with him."

Farrell raised an eyebrow. "Anyone?" He didn't like the idea that the SWAT officers thought they could sequester Garrett from him. He appreciated how hard that SWAT trained and how good they were at their job, but sometimes the price for having such an elite unit was a corresponding elite attitude. "You're SWAT or you're not, huh?"

"I don't mean it like that," Flowers said. "They're just making sure he has some space, is all."

Farrell understood then. "You got a tactical debrief from him already, right?"

"Yes. That's how I know the basics of what occurred here. Shots fired, direction, number of suspects. I got it all from him, by the book. Even had Thomas there for the whole thing."

"Good." He clapped Flowers on the shoulder. "Call the county, Dan. Invoke the protocol."

"Yes, sir."

Farrell turned to go, then thought of something. "Dan?"

"Yeah, Cap?"

"We need to assign a shadow as host agency for this. Who's up next on the wheel?"

Farrell thought Flowers might need to consult his notes, but obviously he had already thought of this. The lieutenant answered immediately. "Talbott's up. I'll get him down here to liaise with the county detectives."

"Make it happen."

Flowers was already pulling out his phone when Farrell walked away.

The two SWAT officers eyed him coolly as he approached. One had his patrol rifle slung and hung, dangling in front of him on its strap, his right hand poised on the grip. The other stood on the opposite side of Garrett with crossed arms. Farrell recognized both men but had to glance down at their silver nametags to remember their names. Unlike large municipalities, Spokane's SWAT team was a part-time unit with team members spread across every patrol unit. Members jumped at moments like this to gear up and look ready, even when a threat was no longer viable. "Gentlemen," he said. "Thanks for taking care of him."

Neither man answered but both dipped their chins in reply.

Farrell settled onto the concrete step next to Garrett. The patrol officer had been staring at his hands until then. When he noticed Farrell, he stiffened slightly.

"How're you doing, son?" Farrell asked, keeping his voice easy.

"Fine, sir." Garrett's tone was neutral, formal.

"I was told you weren't injured. Is that true?"

"Yes, sir."

"Good. You have everything you need?"

Garrett raised the half-empty bottle of water. "Yes, sir."

"Anything I can do for you?"

Garrett shook his head. "No, sir. I don't think so."

Farrell hesitated, then told him. "Things are going to be all right. We'll get through this. If this was a clean shoot—"

"It was a clean shoot!" Garrett interrupted suddenly and forcefully.

Damn it, Farrell thought. He was making a mess of this. He had to choose his words more carefully.

"I know," he said, holding up a hand to calm Garrett. "Everyone knows who you are, Ty." He used the man's first name even though they had never talked in an unofficial capacity. "We all know what kind of cop you are. We'll stand behind you."

Garrett looked at him for the first time since Farrell sat down. "I didn't do anything wrong, sir. *They* shot at *me*. I—"

"Captain?"

Farrell looked up. Union President Dale Thomas stood nearby. He wore jeans and a rumpled Spokane Police Union sweatshirt, a far cry from his usual suit and tie.

"Yes?"

"Why are you talking to my member about this incident?"

Farrell's jaw clenched. He bit back his first two replies. Instead, he turned to Garrett and patted him on the leg. "Everything will work out."

"Yes, sir."

"Let me know if you need anything."

Farrell stood and headed back toward Flowers. On the way, he purposefully brushed past Thomas. The union president called after him, but he ignored his words. Ever since the union transitioned from having an active-duty officer act as president to hiring a full-time advocate in that role, relations between the administration and labor had worsened drastically. It had reached the point where every meeting was contentious, every action based in legality. Farrell remembered the days when command members and union reps simply talked problems out. Now they went to binding arbitration over everything.

An approaching siren irritated him further. He listened to discern if it was law enforcement or medics. It was one of theirs, he decided. He wondered what kind of idiot ran lights and siren to a static crime scene.

Flowers hung up his phone as Farrell approached. "County is en route."

"Good.

"Talbott on the way, too?"

"Yeah."

"Is there any reason we have to keep Garrett here?"

Flowers considered. "No, I guess not."

"Let's get him a ride to the station, then. Corporal DeHaan can photograph him and collect his uniform and equipment for evidence. Afterwards, get him home to his family."

"All right."

The siren drew closer, then abruptly stopped. Farrell saw a black SUV pull to a stop behind his own Chevy Impala. The license plate read L-100.

The chief had arrived.

"Belay my last," Farrell told Flowers. He knew the chief would want to talk with Garrett before the officer left the scene. "But get it arranged."

"Copy that," Flowers replied.

Farrell walked toward the SUV, clicking off the things in his head that the chief would want to know.

Chief Robert Baumgartner eased his huge frame out of the driver's seat of his SUV. He'd taken the time to dress in his uniform. While the uniform itself wasn't particularly impressive on his doughy body, the amount of brass on display made up for it. The three stars on his collar were prominent enough to reflect even the dim light of the streetlights. Farrell noticed that Baumgartner's hair was neatly combed, and he was freshly shaved. How he managed all of that and still got here so fast was a mystery to Farrell, but it could only mean one thing. The chief intended to address the media.

"Tom, what do we know?"

Farrell spent the next ten minutes carefully briefing the chief on everything he knew about the situation. To his credit, Baumgartner listened almost entirely without interruption, only asking for the occasional clarification. When Farrell had finished, Baumgartner pressed lips together and sighed through his nose.

"This one could be bad," he said. "Especially after the one that happened in Philadelphia."

Farrell didn't reply.

"What do we tell the media?" Baumgartner asked.

"Nothing," Farrell said. "Because we know nothing."

Baumgartner narrowed his eyes. "You just spent the last several minutes briefing me on everything we know, Tom. That's hardly nothing."

"I've filled you in on a very few basic facts that we know, Chief. All of the rest is simply what we are doing at this stage. When it comes to what we know for certain, the answer is virtually nothing."

"I can't go in front of the cameras and tell them nothing."

"Then don't go in front of the cameras."

The chief smirked. "I have to. People need to be reassured and hear that everything is under control, especially after the Philadelphia mess."

"That's Philadelphia. It's clear across the country. It has nothing to do with Spokane."

The chief shook his head. "That's not true anymore, and you know it. When some white cop shoots a black citizen and it looks dodgy, the fact that it happened in Philadelphia barely matters. That's why I need to get in front of the cameras and sooner rather than later. I have to tell them that this isn't Philadelphia. That's the reality of the situation. Tell me what I *can* tell them, not what I *can't*."

"All right." Farrell counted on his fingers one at a time. "An officer made a traffic stop. Shots were fired. One person is dead. The officer is safe and we're investigating. That's it."

Baumgartner sighed again. "A trained monkey could make that statement. There's no meat to it."

"We don't have the meat to this case yet, Chief. Just give them those basics tonight. Or don't say anything."

Baumgartner considered this, then shrugged. "Okay, but I won't be able to put them off for long. If we don't get the facts out there, they'll make something up. Either way, there *will* be a story."

Farrell was well aware of Baumgartner's media philosophy. "We should be in a better position by late morning. I'm sure the mayor's office will want to be in the loop."

"You think?" Baumgartner said, anger flashing in his eyes. "I've already been on the phone with Cody Lofton, his chief of staff."

"I know Lofton."

"He already knew about this when he called me. How is that?"

Farrell hesitated, then lied. "I asked Lieutenant Flowers to notify him, as a heads up. Lofton was supposed to wait until you called with the rest of the details."

Baumgartner glared at him. "Well, he didn't wait, did he? Talking to the mayor is *my* job, Tom." He pointed to the stars on his collar. "That's what these mean. For good or bad, it's my job. Don't do that again."

"No, sir. I won't."

Baumgartner dropped his bluster as quickly as he'd assumed it. "You said you invoked the OIS protocol, right?"

Farrell nodded.

"And assigned a shadow from our department?"

"Yes. Detective Talbott."

Baumgartner shook his head. "We're going to change that."

"Excuse me?"

"Talbott. He's out. We need a different look in that role."

Farrell didn't understand. "I'm sorry, sir. A different look?"

"Yes."

"How do you mean?"

The chief affected an even expression, almost imperious. "I spoke with Lofton, and we both agreed that Detective Clint would be the best fit to shadow the county's investigation."

"Wardell Clint? Are you serious?"

"Do I look like I'm making a joke, Tom?"

Farrell stared at Baumgartner in surprise. "Why?" he asked, but as soon as the words came out of his mouth, he understood.

"It makes sense to have good optics on this one. He's the natural choice. Once you think about it, you'll understand. Make it the party line and get him out here." Baumgartner motioned toward Garrett. "He deserves for us to handle this one perfectly. He's a good cop."

"He is," Farrell agreed, but he knew Garrett was more than that. He was a perfect image of the new SPD. Handsome, college educated, family man, and best of all, black.

"They don't make many like him, do they?" Baumgartner said, watching Garrett sitting on the steps.

"I suppose not."

"I'm going to check on him. Then let's get him out of here, huh? Get him home to his family."

Farrell nodded. "I'll take care of it."

Baumgartner turned and plodded toward Garrett. The two SWAT officers somehow found a way to stand a little straighter as the chief approached. Farrell didn't see Dale Thomas in the immediate vicinity, but that didn't matter. There was no way he was keeping the chief from having his moment with Ty Garrett. If he tried, that'd be his problem.

Farrell's problem was more immediate. He found Flowers and broke the news to him.

"They want Wardell Clint? The Honey Badger?" Flowers shook his head. "Tell me you're kidding, Cap."

"This comes straight from the chief," Farrell said. "Or maybe the mayor. I don't know for sure."

"Talbott is up next on the wheel. It's his turn."

"They don't care about that. They only care about one thing."

Flowers nodded. "Yeah, that he's black."

Farrell stared at his lieutenant, surprised that he had vocalized what Farrell was feeling.

"I mean, I get it and all," Flowers continued, "but come on, Cap. Clint is a bad choice for this kind of thing. Our shadow is supposed to observe and maybe advise a little. They need to be diplomatic for that sort of thing. Clint is basically the opposite of diplomatic."

"I know."

"Not to mention the conspiracy and anti-administration crap he's always spouting. He's—"

"It's done, Dan. There's no profit in us talking about whether it's a good idea or not."

Flowers sulked about it for a few seconds. Farrell didn't say anything. He didn't like having his decisions being made for him at a higher level, either. But that was the way the chain of command worked sometimes.

Who am I kidding? Farrell thought. This wasn't about chain of command. It was about politics, pure and simple.

"Make the call," he told Flowers.

Chapter 5

Detective Wardell Clint didn't check in at the crime scene right away. Instead, he parked on the next block over, and walked. For a while, he stood with the crowd that had assembled at the yellow tape of the outer perimeter, observing what he could, and listening to the stray bits of conversation. The snippets he picked up were largely anti-police but only mildly so. He heard a sense of resignation in the words, as if there was a collective acceptance that the SPD was corrupt when it came to dealing with people of color or poverty. It was just something that had to be endured in Spokane, like cold winters or potholes in the streets.

Clint didn't entirely agree with the sentiment, at least not where it concerned line-level members of the department. The admin was crooked, he knew, and either purposefully in league with the politicians or incompetent puppets of the same. He wasn't sure which, but he did know that most of the cops working the street were solid.

Clint made his way toward where the media was gathered. He stayed far enough away to avoid being recognized and asked questions but close enough to get a sense of the mood. It didn't take long for him to decide that the mood was hungry and impatient. He wondered briefly what story they'd decide to concoct, how they'd spin things. There was really no telling. The media agenda was a fickle one, except that it was usually anti-police. With the Philadelphia shooting, he expected that trend to continue.

He circled around and approached the crime scene from the street where the police vehicles were parked. He scanned the license plates, spotting a couple of county ones. That meant the lead investigators were already here. They were supposed to wait for him to start any formal investigating, but he doubted they would. Not that most county dicks could investigate anything more complicated than a shoplifting anyway.

"Ward!"

He turned and spotted Lieutenant Flowers coming toward him. He stopped in place and waited patiently for his boss to come all the way to him. Life was full of small power struggles, and Clint was determined to win as many of them as possible.

"Don't call me that," he told Flowers when he was close enough.

"Huh?"

"It's Wardell, not Ward. You know this, Lieutenant."

"Oh, yeah. Sorry. I always figured Ward was short for it, that's all. Like my name, you know?"

Clint said nothing.

"It's Dan, short for Daniel," Flowers offered.

Clint didn't reply.

"When did you get here?" Flowers asked.

"Just now. Why?"

"Relax. I just wondered."

"No, I mean why am I here?"

"I told you on the phone. We've got an officer involved and need you to shadow the county."

Clint tilted his head, studying the lieutenant. "What's the angle?"

Flowers gave him an exasperated look but tried to plaster patience over the top of it. To Clint, the expression looked more like he was patronizing him. "Angle?"

"Why am *I* here?"

"You're up," Flowers lied easily.

Clint shook his head emphatically. "No, I'm not. I know how the wheel works. Talbott is up next with Pomeroy after him. Then at least two more after Pomeroy. I caught the call out before last. There's no way I am *up*, Lieutenant."

Flowers took a deep breath. "You're right. The chief asked for you specifically."

"Me? Why?"

Flowers looked uncomfortable. "You're a good fit for this one."

Clint stared at him, thinking. He knew most people didn't like him much. That included the white shirts of command *and* other detectives. It was one reason he didn't have a partner anymore. He didn't care. It took a few years after he got his detective's shield, but finally everyone had come to an understanding that the best approach was to give him a case and let him work it alone. Since results were what mattered most, there was an uneasy peace in this arrangement.

"Are you telling me Talbott can't handle this?" he asked, suspicious.

"He could," Flowers admitted, "but like I said, you're a better fit."

Clint wondered what kind of train wreck they had on their hands, and why he was being lined up to be the patsy, to take the blame. Another Sirhan Sirhan or something. He thought about waiting to find out how bad it was for himself but decided to just ask instead.

"What kind of bullshit is this, Lieutenant?"

"None. The chief asked for you. That's all there is to it."

"I say again, why?"

Flowers seemed to struggle to find an answer. Clint watched him, his mind rifling through the possibilities. He kept coming back to the patsy theory.

Finally, Flowers said, "We need you on this one."

Need?

Clint shifted gears, and suddenly it all made sense. They weren't out to screw him this time. They needed him. That could only mean one thing.

"Who's the shooter?" he asked, but before Flowers could answer, he suddenly clapped his hands together. He immediately harangued the lieutenant. "There are four black officers on this department. I'm one. Tammy Preston is two. She's a sergeant in community services, so I don't guess it's her. That leaves either Bo Sherman or everyone's favorite poster child, Ty Garrett. Which is it?"

"It's Garrett," Flowers admitted.

"What a coincidence. He gets into a shooting, and suddenly the chief wants me involved. I wonder why?"

"There's nothing to wonder about. We all know the reality of the world we live in."

"You all created that world."

"You all?" The patience in Flowers's tone slipped. "Who all?"

"You know who you are," Clint said. "And you know this is bullshit."

Flowers glanced around to see if anyone was listening, then lowered his voice. "It's not. It's strategic, that's all."

"Color it any way you want. We both know the truth."

"Listen," Flowers said. "This is a sensitive situation. The suspect is white."

"Ninety percent of the suspects in this city are white," Clint said. "You know why? Because ninety percent of this city is white. Do the math, Lieutenant. It ain't hard."

"I know the demographics," Flowers snapped. "What I'm telling you is that we've got a black officer who shot a white suspect. It's sensitive."

"More sensitive than when a white cop shoots a black man?"

"No," Flowers said firmly. "Not more. Just different."

"Those differences are only in your head. That's why things are so messed up in this country."

"It doesn't matter!" Flowers snapped. "There's other problems here, too, all right?"

Clint grew suspicious again. "Like what?"

Flower took a deep breath and let it out. "The suspect was hit in the back."

Clint shrugged. "So? It happens all the time. The suspect presents the threat and by the time the officer reacts, he's turned away. Action, reaction. It's physiology. It's physics. It might be a media problem, but it's not a criminal one."

Flowers just stared at him.

"There's more?" Clint asked.

Reluctantly, Flowers nodded. "We haven't found the gun yet."

"You haven't..." Clint dropped off into thought. Maybe they *were* bringing him in to be some kind of patsy. Or were they planning to serve up Officer Ty Garrett as a sacrifice?

He shook his head at that. As much as he saw Garrett as a puppet for the image makers of the SPD, he had to admit the officer had a good reputation. He carried his weight on patrol, answering calls, and he had been a SWAT member for several years. Maybe he was a little too willing to smile for the cameras and be featured in promotional materials, but Clint had learned a long time ago that everyone found a way to get by in this world. If you were black, the way was harder, which meant you had to play along at times.

"Listen, man," Flowers began. "I just need you to watch over the county's investigation. That's it. Make sure they hit every detail and do a good job. Our man deserves nothing less."

Clint mulled it over. If the plan was to sacrifice Garrett or make him a patsy of some kind, Flowers wasn't in on it. Of course, the powers that be could just be manipulating the lieutenant, too.

"This is bullshit," he repeated. "You have a protocol in place, and you all preach sticking to it until it isn't convenient for you anymore."

"Policies are guidelines," Flowers said.

"Yeah, that's what you guys always say when you break it. Funny how it ends up being an ironclad rule when a worker bee like me violates one."

Flower rolled his eyes in frustration. "Why do you have to make everything so hard?"

"I'm only speaking truth."

"Yeah?" Flowers' voice grew hard and anger crept into his tone. "How's this for truth, *Detective?* We've got something in this profession called chain of command. It works like this: the chief makes a decision on how things are gonna be, and he tells the captain, who tells me, who tells *you.* Then you do it."

Clint stared back at him, wordless.

Pointing at him, Flowers said, "Do your job, Detective Clint."

Clint nodded curtly. This was authority, and he understood that perfectly. "Yes, sir."

Flowers gave him a long look, then turned and walked away.

Detective Wardell Clint waited until he was out of hearing range before muttering, "Ofay." Then he went to find the county detectives before they completely tanked the investigation.

Chapter 6

Detective Cassidy Harris crouched down near the deceased. She scanned the body slowly, looking for any meaningful details, trying to catalogue as many small facts in her mind as she could. Photographs would capture the scene, but nothing replaced in-person investigation. She only got a single chance to get it right the first time, and she wanted to do exactly that.

Her partner, Detective Shaun McNutt, stood nearby with his hands on his hips, surveying the scene. She wasn't sure what he was looking at and tried to ignore him. He was an adequate detective, based on what she'd seen over the last six months of working with him, but she got the sense that he was more in love with the idea of being a homicide investigator than doing the actual work. If the choice came between pulling an extra hour following up on a lead or hitting the gym, McNutt was in his Under Armour gear and out the door to All-Fitness quicker than she could say Lou Ferrigno.

Not that pumping all that iron didn't make him nice to look at, she admitted. He knew it, too, and had no problem getting his share of action. The badge was a sex magnet all by itself and McNutt's chiseled physique made things ridiculously easy for him. That's probably why he started trying to get her into bed after their first month or so working together. She imagined that he saw her as a challenge. Someone who wasn't impressed by his badge. That, and the fact that she had a bit of a reputation around the sheriff's office as an ice princess. Which was only a short gossipy step away from lesbian, in her experience. Quite the conquest for his already over-sized ego.

Harris shook her head, forcing herself back on task.

The victim was shirtless, which made it easy for her to examine the bullet wound in his back. Based on the size and clean puncture, she judged it to be an entry wound. The fact that the man was shot in the back didn't necessarily bother her. If he pointed a gun toward the officer, there might be as long as a full second before even someone who was well-trained could react. In that window of time, the victim might duck or turn in a way that presented his back to the officer, who was already shooting. It happened more than people realized and could have happened here.

That's right...could, she reminded herself. *Make no assumptions.*

She kept an open mind but found it difficult to believe that an officer would purposefully shoot someone in the back. Especially given what she knew of Officer Ty Garrett. It wasn't the location of the injury that she found concerning. It was the absence of a gun, or anything that might have been mistaken as a gun.

There was no question that Garrett had been fired upon. The damage to his patrol car was obvious evidence of that. And even though neither she nor McNutt had examined the living room of the house across the street yet, Lieutenant Flowers had informed them that there were shell casings on the floor. Shots had definitely been fired from the inside of the house.

Yet, there were no casings beside the body, or in the vicinity. And no damage on the driver's side, where she would expect it to be if the suspect had fired upon exiting his car.

What did that mean?

"What're you thinking, Cass?" McNutt asked her.

She didn't like it when he called her that. No one else did, and it felt like a forced sort of intimacy, like he was trying to get closer to her than she wanted. If she told him to knock it off, it only reinforced her ice princess image. It was a delicate balance. Close enough for them to work effectively together, and for him not to flex his testosterone over every disagreement, but distant enough to keep him from making an overt move on her. She had a rule about not dating anyone from work, and she wasn't about to break it. She saw where it got other women in her field, and she didn't want to be seen as some kind of trophy, or a punchboard. She was a detective, and she was good at it. *That* was how she wanted to be known, but she let the nickname go.

"No gun," she said.

"Nope."

"Either there was a gun, and someone took it, or there was never a gun in the first place."

"In this neighborhood, I vote someone took it."

Harris didn't reply. There was one place they hadn't searched yet, and that was under the body. There could be a gun there, or something that in the stress of the situation, Garrett might have mistaken for a gun. A knife, a cell phone, even a black wallet might present itself as a weapon, if someone else was shooting at him from the house at the moment he saw it.

"Oh, that's just great," muttered McNutt.

Harris looked up. SPD Detective Wardell Clint walked toward them, staring at them through his thin-framed glasses. As always, he had a slightly wild look in his eyes.

"What the hell is the Honey Badger doing here?" McNutt asked.

"SPD must really want to tank this investigation if they're attaching him to it," she said, hoping she was wrong.

McNutt laughed a little harder than the joke merited.

Clint cocked his head at McNutt as he drew close. "Something funny?"

"Yeah," McNutt said.

"You care to share?"

"Nope."

Clint glowered at him. McNutt glared back.

"You're in my crime scene, Detective," Harris interrupted, rising to her feet.

Clint shook his head. "It's *our* crime scene. I'm your shadow."

Harris exchanged a look with McNutt.

"Fill me in," Clint said.

Harris took a second to collect herself. She didn't like Clint, but she prided herself on being professional. The OIS protocol provided for the host agency to assign a shadow for the purpose of observation and, to a lesser extent, to advise. She didn't have a choice in that, but she wanted to make sure the boundary lines were clearly drawn.

"First, let's be clear," she said. "I'm the lead detective, and Detective McNutt is my second. Your role is strictly—"

"—to observe and advise," Clint interrupted. "I've read the protocol agreement. I'll bet I know it better than you do."

Harris ground her teeth together, exhaling. She knew enough about Clint to know that he'd continue arguing as long as he could, and that he always had to be right. Therefore, she took the path of least resistance, and moved on. "The deceased is Todd Trotter. He's got a long record with a fairly common pattern, starting with juvenile offenses, going from theft to burglary to dope. He—"

"I know Trotter. What else?"

Harris pointed to the patrol car. "Officer Garrett made a traffic stop on him here—"

"I'm not asking you to tell me the obvious. Tell me what I *don't* already know from simple observation."

"You know," McNutt said, taking a half step toward Clint. "It's unprofessional to interrupt. And rude."

"Do you really want to show off for her that bad?" Clint chuckled. "Son, the days of detectives throwing hands at a crime scene are long gone."

McNutt took another step toward him, growling something low and unintelligible.

"Shaun!" Harris snapped. "I got this."

McNutt gave her a sidelong look and took a reluctant step back. Clint watched with an amused smile.

"How about you let me brief you and don't interrupt for two minutes?" Harris asked.

Clint shrugged. "All right, then."

Harris ran down what she knew, keeping things concise and factual. Clint surprised her by remaining silent while she spoke. After she'd finished, he asked, "What's your theory?"

"I don't have one yet."

He cocked his head again. "Of course, you do. What is it?"

Harris shrugged. "It seems to be fairly obvious that it was an ambush."

Clint considered, then shook his head. "That theory stinks."

"Really?"

"Like day old fish, yeah."

"How's that?"

Clint pointed at the car. "He was making a traffic stop. How could the ambushers control that, or whether it even happened?"

"Easy," Harris replied, "if the driver of the vehicle was in on the ambush."

"*If*," Clint repeated.

"Yes, *if*," she said. "You might see a traffic stop as uncertain, but the driver of the vehicle being stopped controls where they stop. If the car was the lure, it could have led him here, stopped very purposefully at this location, and then the accomplices fired from the house."

Clint thought about it. "That's a lot of ifs and a whole lot of wanting to make things fit. I think you're already trying to bend the narrative to your theory. To me, it looks just as likely to be a crime of opportunity."

"Oh, really." Harris couldn't keep the contempt out her tone, even though she knew how unprofessional it sounded. "How's that work, exactly?"

"A couple of bangers or other hardcores hanging out in an empty house. Happens all the time."

She shrugged. He was right about that.

"Garrett stops this car out front," Clint continued, "and they see a chance to take a potshot at a cop. They probably didn't even know the driver. Totally random."

"That's your theory?"

Clint smiled without humor. "No. It's too early to be forming theories. All the same, it's every bit as good as yours."

Harris stared at Clint for a long while. After a few moments, McNutt joined her, though his stare was decidedly more posturing than menacing. Clint just stared back, unflappable. She realized that this was going to be a long, painful investigation if she didn't make sure Clint clearly understood his role early on.

She also realized that if Clint was arguing with her about her theory, she was probably on the right track. That part made her happy.

After a long silence, Clint finally motioned toward the dead body. "We gonna check under him for a gun or what? The pictures have all been taken."

Without a word, Harris knelt down next to the victim, avoiding the small pool of blood that had leaked out. The fact that it wasn't bigger than it was told her that Garrett's bullet had struck the man in the heart, and that it had stopped pumping almost immediately. All things aside, at the distance of fifteen, maybe even twenty yards, it was a hell of a shot.

McNutt knelt on the other side, and together they rolled the body up on its side while Clint stood nearby, watching closely.

All three stared for a long while, even though there was nothing there to look at. No gun, no knife, no wallet. No nothing.

Harris lowered the body back down. She glanced up at McNutt, then at Clint.

"Someone must have grabbed it," McNutt said. "Right?"

Clint didn't answer him, and neither did she.

"Come on," Harris said instead. "Let's keep working the scene."

Chapter 7

Cody Lofton walked into the mayor's office and dropped his notepad on the coffee table between the over-sized leather chair and the matching couch.

He pulled out his phone and moved to the window overlooking Riverfront Park.

He'd gotten a text message earlier from Dan Flowers. *Got my ass handed to me for giving you a heads up.*

Lofton thought about his reply then typed. *It meant a lot that you gave me the head start. Meeting with M in a few. Keep me in the loop.*

A couple moments later, Flowers responded, *Drinks are on you next time.*

Lofton smiled and put his phone back in his pocket.

As the sun broke the horizon, the city was coming to life. He watched as a few cars parked along the street and joggers ran through the park.

He walked to the full-length mirror that stood in the opposite corner of the office, stood in front of it and turned sideways a couple times to admire himself.

After his early morning call with the mayor, they scheduled a meeting at 5:30 a.m. It gave Lofton the opportunity to catch a couple hours of sleep in his apartment, a two-bedroom at The M which overlooked Riverfront Park. The apartments were highly sought after and his position as the mayor's right hand worked in his favor as he was pushed to the top of the wait list. He showered, shaved, and put on a freshly laundered suit with white shirt. He spent extra time picking out his neckwear. He went with a David Fin navy & teal woven silk tie. It took him three attempts to get the knot and length exactly how he wanted it.

He was guaranteed to be interviewed today and he would look his absolute best.

Lofton ran his hand down the length of his tie and smiled as he watched the sun rise.

Someday he would stand in this office and know it would be his.

"Enjoying the view?"

Lofton turned as Andrew Sikes, Spokane's mayor, walked into the office.

Sikes wore a Nike running suit and Adidas tennis shoes. His face was red from exertion and beads of sweat gathered on his forehead. He sucked on a red water bottle. When he was done, he said, "I was able to get a workout in."

"Sir?"

"Today is going to go to hell, but I didn't want to start the day off wrong."

"I'm sure the press will want to hear from you shortly. Did you bring a change of clothes with you?"

Sikes nodded. "In my car. I'll grab a shower when we're done."

Lofton nodded, but inwardly cringed. Sikes was the people's mayor, but he often took that vote of confidence too far. He'd won his first term by identifying with the masses, but he sometimes forgot that perception swayed easily on little things. For example, on the mornings he worked out, he tended to remain red-faced for most of the day. Of all days to skip a work-out, this would have been the one. Lofton was already imagining a red-faced mayor explaining an officer involved shooting. It would present a bad image even before the words were heard.

"Where's Amanda?"

"She'll be here any minute," Lofton said. "Did you talk with the chief?"

"Let's wait for Amanda." Sikes said, walking behind his desk. He dropped down into his chair and took another sip of water.

"Sir, are we going to talk at your desk or on the couch?"

"Here's fine."

Lofton grabbed his pad of paper from the coffee table and walked to the mayor's desk. He took the seat that gave him the best view of the mayor. The remaining seat would put Donahue slightly behind his computer monitor.

Amanda Donahue was the mayor's latest assistant, a twenty-seven-year-old that started a few months ago and was suddenly the center of attention. To his knowledge, the mayor wasn't secretly seeing her, but it seemed Amanda was purposefully trying to make it happen both in how she looked and some of the things she would not-so-innocently say. She'd been an assistant at a local marketing company for a few years before transitioning to the mayor's office. She had no prior government experience, but Lofton knew she had the one thing that he'd never have and the mayor loved being around it.

"Sorry, I'm late," Amanda announced as she hurried in.

Like Lofton, she was dressed impeccably for this hour, but the way she looked would cause anyone to look twice. She wore a black mini-skirt suit with light blue blouse. Her layered bob haircut fell just below her chin. Her legs were high-lighted with new black high heels. Lofton did a double take on the shoes because they had red soles.

She's wearing Christian Louboutin, Lofton thought. Are you kidding me?

Amanda caught him looking at her shoes and she smiled. She then considered the seating arrangement and faced the mayor.

"Can we sit on the couch?" Amanda asked. "It's more comfortable and besides I can't see you very well from this chair."

The mayor pushed out of his seat. "Of course."

Amanda positioned herself next to the mayor on the couch. Lofton sat upright on the edge of his seat, his anger already welling. We're here to discuss an officer involved shooting, Lofton thought, and she's leading the mayor around by the nose. He realized his jealousy and pushed it down.

Amanda pulled out her notepad and nodded to the mayor. "I'm ready when you are."

Sikes winked at her before turning to Lofton. "What have we got?"

"You've talked with the chief and been briefed?"

"Yes."

Amanda raised her hand.

"Yes?"

"I haven't been briefed."

Lofton sighed.

"Bring her up to speed, Cody."

Lofton nodded and retold the story as he knew it. Amanda quickly and proficiently made notes. For the next twenty minutes, she read back several sections until she had the story right. "Okay, I think I've got it."

"Where is Officer Garrett now?" Sikes asked.

"He's been put on three-day administrative leave."

Amanda asked, "Why do they do that?"

Sikes leaned over to her, resting on an elbow, and smiled. "Whenever an officer is involved in a shooting, they get some additional time to go home before they're interviewed. It's part of the contract with the union."

Amanda looked to Lofton before returning her gaze to the mayor. "Is that fair?"

"What do you mean?"

"If someone else was involved in a shooting, wouldn't they have to answer questions right away?"

The mayor shrugged. "Doesn't matter if it's fair. It's the rules of the game."

Amanda nodded, accepting the mayor's simple answer. When she looked down at her notepad, however, her expression remained dubious. It was obvious she didn't like Sikes's response.

Lofton watched her briefly before continuing. "Anyway, we won't have Garrett's account of events until after seventy-two hours. We're playing a waiting game."

"Chief Baumgartner instituted the OIS protocol, right?"

"Yes."

"OIS?" Amanda asked.

Lofton lowered his head. She was killing this process with her stupid questions.

"Officer involved shooting," the mayor said.

"I'm sorry that I'm asking so many questions."

Sikes smiled. "It's okay. You keep on asking." Then he turned his attention to Lofton. "What do you know about the county's investigators?"

"I know their names. That's about it."

"Find out more."

Lofton nodded.

"Who is the department's liaison in the investigation?"

"Detective Clint."

Sikes nodded a couple times and then closed his eyes. When he opened them, he tilted his head. "Ward Clint? That conspiracy nut we have to deal with every time the wind changes direction?"

"Yes, sir."

"Whose bright idea was it to assign Clint to this investigation?"

"Chief Baumgartner," Lofton said, distancing himself from his own recommendation.

"Why would the chief select him? He's had more heartburn with that guy than anybody. It doesn't make sense."

"It does if you take a step back, sir."

Sikes was staring at Amanda's legs when his eyes slowly went back to Lofton. "They picked Clint because he's black?"

"He is the only detective of that ethnicity on the department."

"That's overtly racist," Amanda said. "Is that the position we want to take as the city?"

Sikes sat upright, taken aback by Donahue's statement. "We're not...*racist*."

"It's not racist to assign Clint to the case," Lofton agreed.

"Yes, it is."

Lofton sneered. "Listen, until you know how things work, please keep your opinions in check."

Sikes looked between his chief of staff and his assistant. It was clear he was deciding who to back.

Lofton continued, not giving any ground. "It's not racist, sir. I talked with the chief about it and his plan made total sense. I completely support it."

"Plan?"

"Detective Clint gives the department better options than a Caucasian detective would."

"How's that?

Amanda made notes while Lofton spoke.

"First, it plays better for the media. If they see our detective on scene, it reflects better generally on who is investigating. Second, it paints a better picture for the affected community."

"Affected community," Amanda muttered while making notes.

"Seriously?"

Amanda looked up. "What?"

"We've worked very hard to create constructive dialogue with the black community. They'll want to see one of their own as part of this investigation."

"One of their own," Amanda repeated softly.

"Oh my God, what is your problem?" Lofton asked.

Amanda looked at the mayor and then Lofton. "Your attitude toward minorities is my problem," she said. Lofton knew this was her time to go in for the kill. She was making a power play in front of the mayor, one he'd seen many times before. "I think you're being racist. You're handling this matter according to how it best serves you. You're not thinking for one moment how this truly impacts the community as a whole or the African American community, in particular. I think we need to consider that this could have a damaging effect on them."

"You're joking, right?"

"No," she said, a slight air of superiority coming from her as she sat a little straighter.

"You walk in here with your seven-hundred-dollar shoes and your three-hundred-dollar haircut and you throw around your Ivy League idealism like it's some sort of badge of honor," Lofton said, his anger barely veiled. "Well, princess, I know exactly how this is going to impact our community and that's why I'm trying to get our boss out in front of it. My recommendation is you either get with the program or you take that little-girl naivety somewhere else because we're getting nowhere with your interruptions. You're part of the solution or you're part of the problem. Which is it?"

Amanda struggled to hold back her tears as Mayor Sikes watched her with a fascinated expression, as if wondering if she would cry. When she didn't, he turned back to Lofton. "All right, Cody. You made your point. Clint it is. I won't fight it. What else should we be aware of?"

"Nothing at this stage, sir. We need to get you ready for a press conference. I'll get it scheduled as soon as I run some ideas by you."

Amanda's cell phone vibrated, and she turned it over. She read a text message and then looked around the mayor's office. She stood and walked over to his desk, grabbing the television remote control.

She turned to the flat screen TV on the wall and powered it on.

"What are you doing?" Lofton asked.

"I just got a message to turn on CNN. We're on the news."

Scrolling on the bottom of the television banner was *Spokane, WA - Black Police Officer Shoots White Motorist.*

"What the hell is that?" Lofton was out of his chair and standing in front of the television.

"This is bad, isn't it?" Amanda asked.

"How did they get this so fast?" Sikes said.

"They're getting a local feed. That's a local reporter. Turn it to FOX News," Lofton said.

Amanda pressed a couple buttons and the familiar news channel popped into view. Another news feed ran from a local channel, but the banner on the bottom of the screen was more inflammatory.

Spokane, WA - Black Police Officer Guns Down White Victim.

"Oh, crap," Sikes said.

The reporter stared into the camera, full of gravitas. "Another police related death this morning, this one happening here in Spokane, Washington, and on the heels of a questionable shooting in Philadelphia just days ago."

Cody blanched. He'd been so focused on the local angles of this shooting that he hadn't considered national implications.

"This morning's events are still shrouded in secrecy, as police have yet to make a statement, but our investigative reporting team has uncovered some indications that this shooting may be the mirror image of the one in Philadelphia in which a white police officer fatally wounded a black man. Preliminary reports seem to indicate that the officer in this instance was black, while the man he shot and killed was white."

The reporter signed off, and the anchor handed things over to a morning news panel. Talking heads soon filled the screen and began debating why there wasn't outcry from the minority community about this shooting. "Don't *all* lives matter?" one of the panelists asked.

Lofton glanced at Amanda. "Still think it was racist for us to put Clint on this case?"

"I don't know," she said softly staring at the words on the screen.

"Have we even cleared the scene of the shooting yet?" Mayor Sikes asked.

Lofton said, "No. That won't happen for the rest of the day, at least."

Sikes shook his head and sat down. "How are we going to get in front of this now?"

Lofton walked over to the coffee table and grabbed the list of *Threats* and *Opportunities* he made earlier. "I've got some ideas, sir."

Chapter 8

Ty Garrett was cornered.

He'd put himself into a bad position and they spotted their opportunity immediately. They triangulated him, without effort or extra communication.

There was nothing for Garrett to do but brace for impact. They hit him at the same time, wrapping their arms around his legs, both squealing the same word. "Daddy!"

Garrett leaned down and scooped a kid up in each arm. Jake hugged him around his throat. Molly, the younger and smaller child, waited impatiently for her turn.

Angela Garrett walked slowly into the room, her eyes puffy from a night of mixed sleep and worry. She'd been up and down since Garrett had called her about the shooting.

"It's barely six. Why are you two up?"

Angie moved to the coffee pot. "They can sense something is wrong."

Garrett smiled at his children. "They're not dogs."

"No, they're little people," Angie said. "Jake knew something was wrong when I woke up after your phone call."

"I'm sorry, Ang. I didn't want you to see the news and worry."

The two of them had embraced when he first returned home. That didn't last long until little voices were heard in the other room and Angie broke away to check on them.

As the coffee percolated, Garrett played with his kids, giving them his full attention. When the coffee was done, Angie prepared herself a cup with cream. "Do you want one?"

Garrett nodded. "I'm really fading. The adrenaline is long gone so all I've got left is fumes."

Angie pulled a mug and prepared his coffee with cream and sugar.

"All right, guys, Daddy needs to talk with Mommy for a minute."

Garrett moved into the living room and sat on the couch. Angie joined him, handing him his coffee as she sat.

"Tell me what happened."

Garrett nodded and gave her a detailed explanation of how the events unfolded. His cup was empty long before he was finished.

"You and Ray couldn't find the gun?"

Garrett shook his head.

"You did the right thing, right?"

"Oh, yeah," Garrett said, looking into his empty mug.

Angie grabbed his cup and went to the kitchen. Garrett found the television remote and turned on the local news. As expected, the scene of his shooting was getting heavy play from the local news channels.

The young reporter on the screen stood in front of the police tape, droning on about the nuts and bolts of the event. Garrett was more interested in the background of the scene. He could see two county detectives walking around the white Chrysler. He knew one, Shaun McNutt, from his days in the academy and the occasional crossover patrol call. The other was a female detective he'd never met. For a moment, he thought he'd get a fair shake by McNutt's being assigned to the investigation.

Then Garrett's back straightened, and his eyes narrowed. "Are you kidding me?"

"What?" Angie said, handing Garrett another cup of coffee.

He pointed at the TV with his free hand.

"Who do you see?" he asked.

"The reporter? I don't know his name."

"Look past him. In the background. The four-eyed brother with khakis and collared shirt."

"Who is that?"

"That's Wardell Clint. The detective I've told you about."

"He doesn't like you, right?"

"That self-righteous—" Garrett caught himself before he swore, seeing little faces peeking around the corner. "That self-righteous guy doesn't like anyone."

"What does this mean? Why do you think he was assigned to your case?"

Garrett shook his head. "It doesn't work like that, Ang. All assignments are based on rotation. Next man up sort of thing, so this is luck of the draw."

"Sounds like un-luck of the draw if you ask me."

"Maybe. Besides, the county will be in charge of the investigation. Clint's just shadowing them. He's got no authority in this matter. No way he can stir the pot on this one."

The TV reporter's voice caught Garrett's attention and he turned it up, "To repeat, there was an officer involved shooting shortly after midnight tonight. We've learned unofficially the officer is Tyler Garrett." A photo popped up from the crowd showing Garrett sitting on the front steps with a blanket around his shoulders. Captain Farrell was sitting next to him. Garrett had an angry look on his face and Farrell was slightly taken aback. Someone in the crowd must have taken that photo.

"What was going on in that picture?" Angie said.

Before he could answer, the television displayed his department press photo on the screen. The reporter read his bio and finished by saying, "We've also learned that Garrett is scheduled to be awarded the Lifesaving Medal later this week in a ceremony at the department."

"Can they just announce your name like that?" Angie's voiced was tinged with anger.

Garrett nodded.

"That's not right. Who could have told them that?"

Garrett smiled weakly. "They might have made the connection on their own with that photo. More than likely, someone in the crowd told them it was me. I grew up in that neighborhood. Some of the old timers could easily point me out."

"Let's turn it off," Angie said.

"No. Just go to something else. I want to be distracted for bit. What's on ESPN?"

Angie flicked the channel. As she went past CNN, Garrett stopped her. "What was that? Go back."

She reversed to the cable news channel, and the last of Garrett's smile faded completely.

"We're on the national news?" Angie said, fear now in her voice. "Why do people care?"

Then Garrett realized how everyone else could perceive his shooting. The headline said it all.

Spokane, WA - Black Police Officer Shoots White Motorist.

Angie reached out and held his hand.

Garrett grabbed the remote and turned to MSNBC. They were also carrying a feed from their local news affiliate. The reporter was interviewing citizens, most of them black, about their thoughts on a black police officer being involved in a shooting.

"Maybe now some folks will wake up to what we've been going through," a young black woman said. "The police been killing people a long time."

Garrett lowered his head. "This isn't good."

"I know, baby."

"If this is what the liberal news is reporting…" Garrett turned the channel to FOX News. The banner that was placed on the lower portion of the screen caused Angie to gasp.

Spokane, WA - Black Police Officer Guns Down White Victim.

A panel of talking heads spouted off while video from his scene rolled in the upper right-hand corner of the screen.

The panel was made up of three white men and a white woman. One of the white men was clearly the token liberal. The majority of the panel was focused on the lack of outrage from the black community.

"Where's the outcry?" one man said. "Where are the protests?"

"Wait a second," the token liberal said. "The shooting occurred less than eight hours ago. They're still investigating what occurred. Don't you think they deserve some time to figure things out?"

The loudest of the remaining panel attacked him. "The black community doesn't wait when the victim is black. Look at Philadelphia. They're out in force."

"That's different. The video of that situation clearly shows—"

"The only difference I see is the color of the victim's skin," the blowhard panelist interrupted. "Look, the black community is outraged by what happened in Philadelphia, and maybe they should be. They'll put their hands in their pockets over this one, you watch. They're the first ones to tell us that Black Lives Matter. What about All Lives Matter? When will they support that?"

Garrett shook his head.

The screen switched back to the newsroom and the female reporter.

"We've got a breaking update to this story. Our local affiliate is reporting that the officer in this most recent shooting has been unofficially identified as Tyrone Garrett."

Angie looked at him. "Tyrone?"

On the screen was the photograph of him sitting on the steps with Captain Farrell along with his department publicity photo.

"Again, we repeat. The black police officer involved in the shooting of a white victim has been identified as Tyrone Garrett."

The feed switched back to the panel. The woman on the panel said, "Did you see that photo? Can you put that photo back up?"

The picture of Garrett's brief flash of anger toward Captain Farrell filled half the screen.

The woman shook her head and turned to the television camera. "That is the face of a very angry man. Regardless of color, should a man like that be a police officer in our country?"

Garrett turned off the television.

"I'm sorry, baby," Angie said as Garrett moved toward the bedroom.

He raised his hand but didn't say a word.

Chapter 9

"Give me your tie."

Cody Lofton ran his hand along his ninety-five-dollar David Fin. "Excuse me, sir?"

Mayor Andrew Sikes was getting ready in his office. He'd taken a shower in the basement of city hall and changed into his pants and undershirt. Now, he was finishing dressing in front of the full-length mirror.

"I forgot my tie at home, and I can't show up to this briefing without a tie."

Lofton slowly pulled the tie loose and handed it to Sikes. The mayor quickly tied it and stepped back. The knot was haphazard and the tail too short. Sikes grabbed his jacket, quickly slipped into it and buttoned a single button. "There. Looks good, right?"

Lofton nodded.

Sikes checked his watch. "It's about time."

Almost on cue, Amanda Donahue walked into the office and announced, "Sir. The press has assembled. Chief Baumgartner and his staff are downstairs awaiting your arrival."

The mayor patted Lofton on the shoulder. "Let's go."

The press briefing was initially scheduled to be held in the briefing room at the Spokane Police Department. However, in light of the story breaking nationally, Lofton had suggested a change to the front steps of city hall. The suggestion was easily accepted by Sikes and everyone else had to fall in line with the mayor.

Lofton smiled because he learned early in his tenure how to stage a summer interview in front of city hall. A lectern was placed at the entryway, leaving the mayor and his invitees in the shade. The media and other onlookers were put in the sun. It allowed the mayor a place of cool superiority and the longer the interview went, the more uncomfortable the reporters would get.

The day was scheduled to be in the high nineties with the morning temperature already in the low eighties. Not a cloud was expected. It would be hot on the concrete.

Lofton held open the exterior door and Mayor Sikes walked out and straight to the lectern. He turned and acknowledged Chief Baumgartner and Captain Farrell. Baumgartner looked impeccable as usual while Farrell was showing the effects of strain.

"Thank you for coming here this morning," the mayor began. "As you're aware, there was a tragic event in our East Central community this morning."

The mayor's face was still red from his early morning workout. Even in the shade, it made him look stressed and worried, despite his practiced tone.

While the mayor droned on, Amanda Donahue sidled up to Lofton. "Nice tie."

Lofton reflexively reached for his missing tie and then glanced at her.

He whispered, "I'm sorry about earlier."

"You should be," she said without looking at him.

Lofton straightened and stared straight ahead.

The mayor wrapped up his opening comments. "At this time, I'd like to turn this over to Chief Baumgartner and have him bring you all up to speed."

Baumgartner stepped to the lectern and started his briefing. He was a big man, softening around the middle with age, but it didn't lessen his imposing aura. Baumgartner *was* authority and people naturally deferred to him. Lofton had heard rumors of some his exploits during his patrol days. The tales were meant to sully a man's reputation. None of that stuck to Baumgartner, though. It did the opposite and made him somewhat of a mythical figure. The last of the old-school cops who tip-toed along the line between authority and brutality. While the union might challenge Baumgartner on legal issues, no one challenged him as a cop.

Baumgartner ran through the night's events from the traffic stop to the shooting to the start of the investigation. He praised the sheriff's office for their swift response and initial feedback.

At his direction, Captain Farrell held up a couple of blown-up photographs to show the damage to Ty Garrett's police car. Bullet holes were circled. "As you can see," Baumgartner explained, "the officer's patrol vehicle was struck multiple times by gunfire."

Through the briefing, the chief never once mentioned Garrett by name.

When he was finished, Baumgartner asked the assembled reporters, "Are there any questions?"

A male reporter raised his hand. "Curt May with *The Inlander*. Can you confirm the officer is Tyler Garrett?"

The chief shook his head. "No."

"There are various news organizations reporting that the officer involved was Tyler Garrett. If his name is already out there, why won't you confirm or deny?"

The chief stared at the reporter. "I said no. We'll confirm the officer's identity when it's appropriate."

"Sir," a female reporter raised her hand.

"Shelly," the chief said. Shelly Rand had recently interviewed the chief for a piece on community-oriented policing that was favorable to both the city and the department.

"Sir, why was your officer stopping the victim?"

"Good question. Initially, the traffic stop was for reckless driving. We don't know exactly what that entails just yet. When we do, we will let you know. What we do know is that the suspect vehicle failed to stop when lawfully signaled to do so. When the suspect finally pulled over, that is when the shooting started."

Kelly Davis from the *Spokesman-Review* raised her hand and blurted her question at the same time, "What type of gun was used by the victim?"

The chief nodded. "Good morning, Kelly. I can't share what type of gun the suspect had. We will release all information at the appropriate time. Our investigators are still on scene."

"Was the victim shot in the back?"

The chief grimaced. Lofton caught the tick and was immediately angry. He had coached the chief and mayor prior to the briefing about the media saying victim. He knew they would set traps for them in their questioning. He constantly reminded them to wear a poker face and bluff if necessary. Chief Baumgartner just got caught with a hand full of garbage.

"I can't comment on where the suspect was shot at this time, Kelly. The investigation has just started. I can only confirm that one suspect is deceased at the scene. Beyond that, we are still investigating. I'm sure we will give further briefings shortly to update everyone as the investigation proceeds and we learn more."

"Follow up question," Kelly Davis said. "When will the dash camera video be released?"

"The dash camera recordings of both officers are material pieces of evidence and will be released once the investigation is completed."

"Isn't the police car material evidence, too?" Davis asked. "You've released that. Why are you picking and choosing what to release, Chief?"

Baumgartner opened his mouth to reply but a TV reporter blurted out his question without being called upon. "How does this shooting compare to the one in Philadelphia just a few days ago?"

Baumgartner grimaced a second time. When he spoke, his jaw was set. "It doesn't compare at all."

Mayor Sikes looked at Lofton and jerked his head toward the chief.

Cody Lofton stepped toward the lectern and raised his hand. "Thank you for coming," he said to the reporters. "No further questions. We'll notify you of the next briefing."

Kelly Davis yelled out, "Is it true the victim was unarmed?"

Several television cameras swung to her and then back to the chief. Lofton gently grabbed his arm and escorted him into the lobby of city hall.

Kelly Davis yelled once more, "Chief Baumgartner, is it true that you have not found the victim's gun at this time?"

As soon as they were inside Mayor Sikes yanked the tie from his neck and crumbled it in his hand. He looked to Chief Baumgartner and Captain Farrell. "How in the *hell* does she know that?"

Baumgartner stared at the mayor.

Sikes shoved the tie into Lofton's hands before stalking away with Amanda Donahue on his heels.

Baumgartner and Farrell turned to each other. "Who's talking from our side?" the chief asked.

Farrell gave him a weary shrug.

Lofton stared at his tie. The mayor's sweat was all over the middle of his David Fin. He shoved it in the nearest trashcan and headed up to his office.

Chapter 10

"What on earth are you doing here?" Clara Garrett was surprised to see her son but delighted all the same.

"Just checking on you, Mama."

"Well, get over here and give me a hug." She did her best to make her voice strong and resilient. She knew her son worried about her health.

Ty Garrett leaned down and embraced her. She felt him being careful not to squeeze too hard, like always. Today, he held on a little longer. She smelled the clean scent of his soap and the coffee on his breath. She held on to him, glad to have her boy in her arms.

"Did you sleep yet?"

Garrett pulled away and settled into the chair next to her bed. "Some."

"Couldn't have been more than a couple of hours."

He smiled. "I'm off for the next three days. I'll get some sleep tonight. How are you, Mama?"

She waved his question away. "The same as always. Spend more time in this bed than I ought to, but that's not worth talking about. Let's talk about you instead."

Garrett didn't answer right away. His mother's disease kept her confined to bed most of the time, though he knew the caregivers managed to get her outside in a wheelchair to enjoy the afternoon sun in the warmer months.

"I saw the news," Clara said quietly.

"I figured."

"Are you all right?"

"Fine. Not a scratch."

"Like that comic book you used to read."

He grinned. "Luke Cage."

"He's got nothing on Tyler Garrett," she said. "You're a real-life hero, son."

"Not everyone thinks so, at least not from what I saw on TV this morning."

"Some of it looks bad," she admitted, "but it could be a good thing, too, after everything shakes out."

Garrett looked at her as if she were crazy. "Good?"

She nodded. "Yes. As tragic as this situation is, it might cast a light on an even bigger tragedy, son. Black men in this country have been getting killed by police for decades, and hardly anyone pays attention. If they pay attention to this, even if it is for the wrong reasons, maybe then they start paying attention to the other."

"They're painting me as the bad guy, Mama."

"Some," she allowed. "But in the end, when the facts come out, you'll be a hero. Just like when you pulled that woman off the bridge earlier this year. That's who you are, Tyler. You are your father's son."

An expression of pain flashed across Garrett's face. "I'm nothing like my father. I wish I were."

Clara smiled at him. "Nonsense. You're him, through and through."

Garrett shook his head. "He cared about other people, even more than himself. At least, that's what you told me."

"It's the truth."

"I wish I'd known him better," Garrett whispered.

"You'd have made him proud. He always said that the best way to change the system was from the inside and look at you. Joining the police, making a difference, from inside the system."

"Sometimes I think it's a broken system," he said.

"You're doing your part to fix it."

Garrett sat quietly, shaking his head.

"My son, don't lose confidence in what you are doing. We are put on this planet to serve others. You're serving. Your father believed that, and he lived it right up until his last day."

"What if he was wrong?"

Clara gave him a perplexed look. "How do you mean?"

"What if the best you can do is to make a life for yourself? Protect the ones you love, and get what's yours?"

"That's the police officer and the cynic in you talking now. You can't look at the world that way just because you've seen some terrible things. Or because of what happened last night." She smiled at him. "You're a good man, son. You help people every day. Risk your life. All for people you don't even know. Your father would have been proud of you. I know I am."

Garrett drew a wavering breath, weariness showing through his usually strong demeanor. "I've tried to build a good life," he told her. "To be a good troop. Keep my head above the water line in this job. To work the streets, you know, but not *become* the streets."

"I know it has to be hard."

"Harder than people know," Garrett said, a slight edge in his voice. "And after working so hard, I get into this mess. I did the right thing and yet all these talking heads are all trying to crucify me…"

"The department is on your side," Clara said. "And the mayor, right?"

Garrett nodded. "For now."

She gave him a curious look. "For now? What's that mean?"

Garrett sighed. "I hit him in the back, Mama. I shot that man in the back."

Clara didn't react. "You didn't mean to, I'm sure."

"Of course not. They were shooting at me. It all happened fast."

"Your life was in danger."

"It was."

"Then you did what any reasonable person would have done. You protected yourself."

He took another unsteady breath and let it out. "There's something else. They couldn't find his gun."

Clara remained silent for several long moments. Then she reached out and patted Garrett's hand. "You've always told me that some of the smartest people you've ever met work as police officers," she said. "You work with good people. They will figure out what happened. You don't have to worry."

Garrett let out a short laugh. "I can't do nothing but worry. They're sending cops to jail for doing their jobs these days."

"Only the crooked ones."

"Not always."

"It won't happen to you," she assured him, squeezing his hand for emphasis.

"I wish I had your confidence."

"That's what you need to show," Clara said. "Confidence. You know you did nothing wrong. That's what the world needs to see. A confident, righteous man who did his duty. Show them that."

He nodded slowly. "You're right."

"I'll tell you something else, too. Once you get through this, there could be big things on the other side. Opportunities. People around here haven't forgotten your father's name. Or mine, for that matter."

Garrett gave her a tired smile. "One battle at a time, Mama. Okay?"

She squeezed his hand.

Chapter 11

Detective Wardell Clint adjusted his glasses and stared down at his handwritten notes. His chicken scratch was purposefully difficult to decipher, so that no one else could read his notes. The observations he made before putting together the official report were his business and his alone. He knew his bosses got into his desk when he wasn't around, even though he locked the drawers. Probably other detectives, too. That was why he kept nothing but official documents in his desk. Nothing personal, not even a magazine. When the snooping bastards poked around, all they would find was official reports and his undecipherable notes.

The problem was, even he found the notes hard to read at times. That was the price he paid for vigilance.

Even though this was an officer involved incident, he treated it like any other death investigation. The first question of any such investigation was what kind of death was it? He'd long ago learned to assume every death was a homicide unless the evidence led him elsewhere. It was the least dangerous assumption an investigator could make. If you let yourself believe something was a natural death or accidental, or a suicide, you might miss clues that pointed to homicide. That was a terrible mistake. However, if you started at homicide and the evidence didn't match, instead leading you to a natural, accidental, or suicide, justice was still served. All was well.

Too many cops took shortcuts, in Clint's opinion. They thought they were smarter than everyone else, particularly the criminals. They were well-meaning but arrogant, and they made obvious assumptions, jumped to conclusions, or picked a theory and then sub-consciously bent the evidence to fit that narrative. He wondered if Harris was doing that with her ambush theory.

He thought so. Not that the ambush theory was a bad one, necessarily. Just that she was jumping right to it. He wondered if she had even thought about what kind of death they were looking at.

Not natural, clearly, but accidental? Clint wasn't one hundred percent sure he could rule that out yet. There was no gun on or near the dead man, Trotter. He imagined a scenario in which Trotter gets out of his car after the stop to beef with Garrett, and then gunfire erupts from the empty house. Trotter turns to run and Garrett, believing that Trotter is firing on him, shoots him in the back.

It was plausible, Clint realized. but in legal terms, it was not accidental. Falling off a ladder was accidental. One person killing another person made the death a homicide. Since Trotter didn't shoot himself, that ruled out suicide, too.

Or did it?

Clint hesitated. Suicide by cop had become a common enough event that it should be considered. Maybe Trotter reached like he was going for a gun in order to get Garrett to shoot him.

No, Clint decided. That didn't make sense. Why have the shooter in the house, then?

Or was that just a coincidence?

If so, he thought it was a pretty unlikely one. Suicide by cop *and* an ambush, planned or otherwise?

No, when you walked through the logic, it came down to one thing: the cause of death was almost certainly homicide. And when the medical examiner pulled the bullet out of Trotter and ballistics matched it to Garrett's pistol, it would be a certainty. Unless it wasn't, Clint thought ruefully. He'd studied enough ballistics to know there might be some problems headed their way. No need to go down that rabbit hole until the report returned.

Clint moved on to the next question. Was the homicide justified, negligent, or was it murder?

That one was tougher, and ultimately the prosecutor's office would decide. The investigative team would need to collect and review a great deal of evidence before the answer to that question became clear.

He reviewed more of his notes. There was nothing suspicious in the body location or position. Trotter was struck in the upper left scapula and the bullet must have torn apart his heart, because he died quickly. There wasn't enough blood on the ground for any other explanation to fit, although Clint was curious to see what the M.E. found during the autopsy. He hadn't seen an exit wound when they rolled Trotter onto his side to look for a weapon. That meant the bullet was still inside. If Garrett's hollow point expanded fully and had its trajectory stopped before exiting the body, any bleeding would have been internal. Since the heart stopped pumping, only gravity and air pressure was left to push the blood out. That explained the small amount around Trotter.

Of course, it still didn't explain the lack of a weapon, and that part bothered him.

He pondered that problem. There were two possibilities.

There was a gun.

There wasn't a gun.

He tackled the first. If there was a gun, where did it go?

Clint put his mind to work on the possible scenarios. They came to him quickly.

Some unrelated third party could have stolen it from the scene during the time window in which Garrett was pursuing the other shooter. Guns had inherent value in the criminal world, and this may have been a crime of opportunity.

Maybe it was third party, who stole it to make things difficult for Garrett because he was a cop. Or because he was black.

It was possible there was another passenger hiding in the car, who got out after the first exchange of gunfire, grabbed

Trotter's gun during that same window of time, and fled the scene.

Or maybe Officer Zielinski took it in order to jam up Garrett.

Clint slowed down and looked at each scenario. He couldn't eliminate any of them without further evidence. Some of it might come from the dash camera videos, some from witness statements, and some of it from Zielinski's interview, and eventually, Garrett's.

He wished they could interview Garrett now. He was torn when it came to the three-day rule. He'd heard all of the reasoning behind it, and he knew the union had bargained for it, but as an investigator, he still didn't like it. In what other situation did witnesses get three days to think before making a statement? Much less someone who had shot someone else. They either made a statement when the police asked, or they lawyered up and said nothing. Cops were treated differently.

That was part of the problem, as he saw it. Somewhere along the line, many cops forgot that they were held to a higher standard. Clint believed in a higher calling for law enforcement, that police officers must be better than their fellow people. Too often, though, he saw cops who believed they were better simply because they wore the badge, instead of realizing that because they wore it, they had to constantly strive to be better, to live up to the principles of the badge.

It wasn't easy, Clint knew. Even good men and women struggled. If it were easy, everyone could do it. Not everyone could, though, including some cops.

A life like that was hard, and that is what brought Clint back around to the three-day rule again. If it protected good men and women doing a hard, nearly impossible job from getting screwed over by brass, the media, and the prosecutor, then it was a good thing. It just messed with the investigators who were trying to clear the case.

Clint let the barest of smiles touch his lips. *I guess that's the price you pay for vigilance,* he thought again.

"What're you grinning at, Ward?"

Detective Butch Talbott stood several paces away, watching him.

Clint scowled at him. "None of your business. What do you want?"

"I just—"

"And it's Wardell. You know this."

Talbott raised a meaty hand. "Sorry, man."

"What do you want? I'm busy."

"I know," Talbott said. "That's why I swung by."

"To bother me?"

"No. Why are you such a hard ass?"

"I'm not a hard ass. I'm a hard worker. You should try it sometime."

Talbott's patience slipped. "Whatever. I just came by to tell you I'm sorry you got stuck with the officer involved last night. I was up on the wheel, but—"

"You ain't black."

"Uh, no. I'm not."

"I guess we ain't as color blind around here as we pretend to be."

"I guess not," Talbott said, a little defensively. "It wasn't my choice. I pull my weight."

Clint didn't respond. Despite his earlier jab, he had to admit that Talbott was one of the better workers in the unit. He went out into the field more than most, instead of sitting at a desk and trying to solve a case with a phone and no shoe leather.

Talbott was staring at him, expecting a reply.

Clint said nothing.

Finally, Talbott said, "Since I was supposed to be catching and you got tapped instead of me, if you need any kind of assistance, just let me know."

"Uh-huh."

"Least I can do," Talbott added.

"Uh-huh."

Talbott waited for more, and when it wasn't forthcoming, he switched gears. "Me, Pomeroy, and a couple other guys were just about to head over to Waffles n' More to get a bite and have a team meeting. You want to come along, maybe join us?"

"Not hungry," Clint said, and turned back to his notes.

He sensed Talbott's presence for another few seconds before the big man muttered, "asshole," and walked away.

"Ofay," Clint muttered back absently. He didn't know if Talbott heard him and didn't really care. He doubted the detective would have understood what he said, anyway. The word was a colloquial, derogatory term for white people, specifically the kind who tended to make life difficult for blacks. For Clint, it was a word mired in both race and class, and while every white person he knew wasn't an ofay, he wasn't surprised to find that many were.

Clint focused again on his notes, and the problem of the missing gun. He scratched out the possible scenarios he'd come up with to explain why the gun might have gone missing, then turned to the second possibility.

What if there wasn't a gun? Then what?

His mind exploded with possibilities, but he enforced some mental discipline and slowed things down. One big question loomed under this assumption. Did Garrett *think* he saw a gun? He wouldn't know the answer to that until Garrett's interview. There wasn't anything on or near Trotter that could be mistaken for a weapon of any kind. Of course, all of his explanations for a missing gun could just as easily be applied to a missing knife, wallet, phone, or whatever. If that didn't happen, what did that mean?

Clint narrowed his eyes, thinking. While he thought, he made a few notes, trying to capture the questions and theories now racing through his mind.

Trotter could have reached for something that wasn't there. If Garrett was under the stress of being fired upon, he would have registered that as a threat and shot first. It was a legally defensible action. Clint himself had employed it in his own career on several occasions, though in his case, he'd punched first, not fired. His bosses who reviewed the use of force didn't like it, but Clint figured that was just tough.

No one ever said he or any other cop had to wait to get hit before acting. Whenever he'd seen a suspect balling up his fist or dropping into an aggressive fighting stance, that was enough to tell him what was coming. He always made his move at the earliest opportunity, and never regretted it once, even if the brass objected.

What bothered Clint about civilians was that they didn't understand police work. They saw cop shows on TV and in the movies and thought that made them an expert. It didn't. Every time a cop got into a physical altercation, the clock was ticking. The longer the fight took, the more exponential the danger to the officer became. And every fight was a potential gunfight, because a cop brought a gun to every one.

Therefore, he went at suspects hard. It was the only way. And it was why he was still alive. It was also part of the reason why he didn't get along with the brass and never would. He didn't care. It made him who he was, and it made him a better investigator. It was what allowed him to put himself into the shoes of Officer Ty Garrett, even though the reality was that skin color was one of the few things they actually had in common. Garrett was a favorite son, a poster child, a Dudley Do-Right, and admittedly a decent cop. Nothing special, as far as Clint could see, but definitely above average.

He imagined Garrett making the traffic stop. His stress level would probably be mildly elevated because Trotter didn't stop right away. Clint would have to pull the recording of the radio traffic and listen to see if he was right, but it was a reasonable assumption. When he got a copy of the dash camera footage, he could confirm it.

Clint continued rolling the image of possible events in his mind's eye. Trotter gets out of the car and starts yelling. More stress for Garrett, albeit not a lot. Cops deal with jerks like

Trotter all the time. Then the shots ring out. They strike the patrol car, and shatter glass. At that point, Garrett would have experienced an extreme adrenaline dump, and was probably disoriented. The shots came from the house, which he couldn't have expected. He takes cover and draws his gun.

Then what?

Clint saw it like a movie in his head. Trotter reaching for something. Maybe a wallet? Something that looked to the SWAT-trained Garrett like a weapon, causing him to fire at least two rounds at Trotter. They'd found the one bullet wound on Trotter's back and another round buried in the dash of the Chrysler. Garret could have fired more, but Clint doubted it. A double tap was the most likely tactical response, and if Trotter dropped after that, Garrett would have turned his attention to the house.

The house. A whole other mess to try to unsnarl.

He decided to stick with the gun for now. Having examined the possibility that Garrett saw something he interpreted as a gun and fired in self-defense, there was only one other option to consider.

There was no gun, and Garrett knew it.

Clint had greater difficulty imagining these scenarios. Was Garrett the kind of man who would murder a stranger? He didn't think so. What if he knew Trotter and had some kind of a dispute with him? Clint would have to review Trotter's arrests to see if Garrett figured into any of them, but again, he doubted it. He toyed with the idea of blackmail or other corruption, but the thoughts gained little traction. He'd run down the possibilities, just like the others, but from what he'd seen of Officer Tyler Garrett, he was a police chief's dream. A college educated, good-looking family man who did solid police work. Add to that the value he brought in marketing the department to potential recruits and to the minority community, and Garrett went from gold to platinum. Things like the upcoming lifesaving award were icing on the cake.

All right, Clint thought. *Got the possibilities of the gun covered.* Now he needed the evidence to prove or disprove each of them.

Of course, the missing gun wasn't the only problem. There weren't any shell casings near the car, either. The gun could have been a revolver. That would explain the lack of any expended brass.

A gunshot residue test on Trotter's hands would help solve this mystery, too.

After that, they had to tackle the shooter in the house. He had a feeling that was the fulcrum on which the case would turn.

"Hey, Wardell."

Clint glanced up to see Chief Robert Baumgartner standing nearby.

"Chief," he said, keeping his tone neutral. "Can I help you?"

"I was just stopping by."

Clint stared at him. Just stopping by? The chief *never* stopped by. The man never even used the bathroom in the hallway outside the detective's wing. He had his own washroom in his corner office on Mahogany Row. Something was up. He suddenly wondered if Talbott's lunch invitation had been part of a larger plan, to get him away from his desk so the chief could sneak a look his notes.

"How're things going?" Baumgartner asked.

"They're going fine," Clint replied. Don't tell him anything, he reminded himself. *Not yet. Not until I know and must put it in a report. Until then, it's mine.*

"You need anything?"

Clint shook his head. "Nope."

Less is more.

"The county detectives doing their job?"

Don't reveal anything to the enemy.

"They sure think so," he said.

Baumgartner laughed like they were pals. Like he hadn't been part of the upper admin when they suspended him for breaking that guy's arm outside the Circle K. He wondered how Baumgartner justified that to himself, given how heavy-handed he'd been back when he was a patrol officer. Hell, as Clint heard it, Baumgartner didn't stop cracking skulls until after he made lieutenant.

The brass is the enemy.

The chief seemed to notice Clint wasn't laughing, so his own chuckles tapered off. "Well, I know they're lead, and you're only there to shadow, but keep me in the loop, okay? I don't want to find out about anything from the media first."

"I understand."

"Neither does the mayor."

City Hall is the enemy.

Clint nodded. "You got it."

Baumgartner studied him for a few seconds, then gave him a reassuring smile. "All right, then. Carry on, Detective."

Clint watched him go, moving with surprising agility for a man that big. Something was going on, he could feel it. He didn't know what. Not yet.

Before he could return to his notes, the light ding that accompanied his incoming emails sounded. Clint had long ago marked most of the city users as spam, cutting his emails down to those that were strictly business. He checked this one and saw it was from the county IT evidence tech. It was addressed to Harris and McNutt, while he was cc'd.

The subject line read Dashcam Vids. He opened it. There was a brief, testy message from the IT tech named Toby that read, *Yes, this is all there is.* Below that were two hyperlinks labeled "Zielinski" and "Garrett."

Clint clicked on the first link, labeled "Zielinski." His computer auto-selected the video media player and began playing the clip. He watched as the final few seconds of the previous call were included for context, then there was an abrupt break, and a scene switch. He noted the time and date, pausing the video while he checked the printout of the Computer Aided Dispatch (CAD) log for the call. The time was off by twelve seconds, but Clint thought it likely that Zielinski probably didn't start the camera until after he was underway.

He watched the dash camera view of the roadway in front of Zielinski's car as the officer headed to back Garrett. He heard the dispatcher calling for Charlie-three-sixteen with no reply, though the radio traffic was difficult to hear over Zielinski's siren.

Clint had read that the newest dash cameras provided even more information for the recording, including GPS coordinates and vehicle speed. SPD had long ago purchased the system in use now, and it was definitely low tech, no frills.

Even though he had no way to know the speed, Clint figured Zielinski had to be driving as fast as he felt safe doing. The video looked deceptively slow, as if the officer were out for a Sunday cruise. Clint knew that was the illusion of the camera. If he ran a time-distance formula on what he was looking at, he'd find out Zielinski was going at least fifty, probably over sixty.

When Zielinski dropped his siren, the audio improved drastically. The patrol car slammed to a stop just to the right rear of Garrett's. Clint could see the shattered windows and holes in the side. Zielinski exited the car and left the field of view. A few seconds later, the radio in the patrol car screeched with feedback. Then Zielinski updated dispatch on the situation. Suspect down. No Garrett.

Clint watched as Zielinski reentered the dash camera's field of vision, making his way up to the suspect vehicle. He knelt near Trotter's dead body.

Clint frowned. From the angle of Zielinski's car, he could barely see the bottoms of Trotter's shoes. He couldn't tell if Zielinski took anything, gun or otherwise. Couldn't scratch that theory yet, Clint decided, but Garrett's angle should be more definitive.

Zielinski rose to his feet and cleared the vehicle, then appeared uncertain before seeing something off screen. He called out, "Ty! Are you okay?"

Garrett either didn't reply, or Clint was unable to hear what he said. If he needed to, he could take it to the techs for audio enhancement.

Zielinski advised dispatch that Garrett was all right. By that time, Garrett came into view. He and Zielinski engaged in conversation that became difficult to hear, as they spoke in normal tones. It appeared to Clint that Garrett was telling Zielinski what happened, though.

Definitely going to need audio enhancement on this one, he thought.

Garrett spat, then patted Zielinski's shoulder and then looked down at the driver's body. He said something, and Zielinski nodded. Clint could hear the sirens of approaching police cars.

The two officers spoke for another few seconds, then Zielinski shined his flashlight toward the body on the ground. He asked Garrett something. Garrett pointed to the gun on his hip. They exchanged a few more words, then Garrett nodded and hurried back to his patrol car. He was at the extreme edge of the camera's field of vision when he reached inside the patrol car and grabbed something. He stood, then ducked back into the car for a moment. Then he trotted back toward Zielinski. The two officers searched the ground near the car with their flashlights, obviously searching for either a gun or shell casings. Clint leaned forward again, watching carefully for anything suspicious. He saw nothing.

As the sirens drew closer, Clint noticed Zielinski give Garrett a hard look and say something. Garrett's reply seemed adamant.

More officers arrived, and organized chaos ensued. Ty was escorted away by two other patrol cops. Yellow crime scene tape went up.

Clint hit the fast forward button on the media player, then double fast forward. He watched the investigation in super speed, seeing nothing worthy of slowing for a closer look. He knew he'd have to watch it again at regular speed, but the meat of the recording ended once the third and fourth patrol car arrived.

He exited the video and clicked on the link to Garrett's dash camera. Once again, he saw the final few seconds of the previous incident for context, in which Garrett was walking back to the car on an unrelated traffic stop just a few minutes previous. Then came the break and a new scene. Clint was watching the time and date stamp and was immediately confused by what he saw. The time was already well after what CAD indicated as when Garrett initiated his traffic stop.

"What the hell?" he muttered.

Then he noticed the perspective of the dash camera. It was directed at the rear of the White Chrysler. Officer Ray Zielinski stood near the dead body of Todd Trotter, and Garrett trotted toward them.

Clint watched in amazement as the two began searching the ground for the missing gun or any shell casings. He hit the pause button.

Where's the rest of the video?

He went back to his email and re-read Toby's text. *Yes, this is all there is.* The tech had obviously anticipated that there would be a question about the starting point of Garrett's video. What Clint had interpreted as snotty IT attitude had just been factual information.

He returned to the video, pushing play. He watched as the two men searched the ground wordlessly. Then Zielinski gave Garrett a hard look and spoke. The audio wasn't great, but Clint could make it out.

"Tell me this was a good shoot," Zielinski said.

Garrett didn't hesitate and looked Zielinski straight in the eye. "It was a good shoot."

Clint stopped the video and leaned back in his chair. He didn't bother watching any further, at least not now. There'd be plenty of time to pore over it later, watching for clues that probably weren't there. Right now, he had another question to ponder. He thought about emailing it to Harris, but he didn't trust the email system. Too much access by brass and city hall. Plus, if the question didn't occur to her on her own, then she wasn't worth the tin in her badge.

Instead, Clint looked down at Garrett's official department photo on the left sleeve of his case file. "Why didn't you start the camera?" he asked Garrett's smiling face.

Chapter 12

The door opened and a beautiful, dark-skinned woman in a multi-colored summer dress studied him with suspicious eyes. "Yes?"

"You must be Angie. I'm Dale Thomas."

She ran her eyes up and down his length before asking, "I'm sorry. Who are you?"

"I'm the president of the police union," he smiled. "I wanted to see how your husband was doing."

"Hold on for a minute," she said and gently closed the door.

Thomas turned and surveyed the neighborhood. Ty Garrett lived on the Five Mile Prairie, in an area of recent development. New homes with manicured lawns lined the block. Thomas realized there wasn't a car older than ten years on the street. Garrett was probably pushing his economic limits in this neighborhood.

The door opened again, and Thomas spun around expecting to see Angie. Ty Garrett stood there with a stern look. "Dale. Thanks for coming by."

They shook hands before Garrett waved him inside.

Thomas followed Garrett, stepping down two steps in to the living room where Angie Garrett sat with two small children. A large, heavyset man sat on the edge of the couch. He was in khakis and a club shirt to hide his girth. His black skin shined with the sheen of sweat.

Garrett said, "Dale, this is my pastor, Al Norris."

Thomas nodded. "Nice to meet you, Father."

Norris kindly smiled and said, "Close enough."

Thomas shoved his hands into his pants. He'd worn his newest suit, a deal he'd gotten off the rack at Men's

Wearhouse. He'd taken his tie off before he arrived. It was folded and tucked into the inside pocket of his suit jacket. He knew he looked sharp but felt slightly over dressed next to Ty who was in red shorts and a gray Eastern Washington tank top.

"Want something to drink?"

"I appreciate it, but no. Just came by to see how you were holding up."

"I'm all right."

"What they're doing to him in the media is an absolute travesty," Norris said, shaking his head. He looked up to the television hanging on the wall. It was off, but he knew by Norris's comment they had been watching the coverage. It had turned nasty now that the news of Todd Trotter being shot in the back had been revealed by the media. The rumor of a missing gun made it even worse.

"You should quit watching it," Thomas suggested.

"It's hard to stop when it's you they're talking about," Angie said, the kids squirming on her lap.

"It's fake news," Thomas said, smiling at her. "The channels make up whatever they need to drive ratings. Sensationalism sells."

"It's his life," Norris said, his voice booming in the house.

Thomas nodded, turning his attention to the pastor. "I get it. I've seen this before. Well, nothing to this extreme, but media attention that's gone out of whack. It will get worse before it gets better."

Angie stood with the kids. "I'm going to take them into the other room."

Garrett nodded at his wife and gave her an "I'm sorry" look.

Thomas stepped back to let Angie pass by. With her gone, Thomas took her place on the couch and looked intently at Garrett. "Has anyone from the administration come to see you?"

"No."

"That's good. If they do, don't talk with them. Send them away and call me immediately."

"Why would they stop by? I'm on my seventy-two."

"They know they can't interview you about the incident for three days. No one will even try that. That's hallowed ground. However, there's nothing saying they won't come by and check on you. That's their way of getting their foot in the door to start talking. Lawful deception, if you will."

"Sounds like inviting a vampire into your home," Norris said, shaking his head.

Thomas pointed at the pastor. "That's exactly what it is. They'll want to get in here under the guise of your welfare. Remember, it's not your welfare they care about. It's their own."

Garrett crinkled his nose. "Really?"

"My job is to protect you, Ty, and part of that is telling you the hard truth. To help manage your expectations, so to speak. Do you understand what I'm saying?"

"I guess."

"Then here it is—your shooting doesn't look good."

Garrett quickly stood and threw his hands in the air. "I don't care what it *looks* like. I know what I did was right! I'm tired of hearing what I did was wrong."

"Are you here to help or rile him up?" Norris whispered.

Thomas lifted his hands in defense. "You need to know what the rest of the world thinks, Ty. That includes city hall and your own department. Right now, forces are aligning. Some of those forces are going to protect you and some are going to try to bury you."

"What forces? Who's out to bury me?" Garrett asked with his chin thrust out. Thomas liked that. The man was ready to take on challengers.

"You've watched the news," Thomas said, pointing at the blank TV screen. "You tell me. Are *they* on your side or not?"

Garrett stared at the silent black screen and crossed his arms.

"They're persecuting him in the media," Norris said, wiping his forehead with the back of his hand. "They're talking about him like *he's* the criminal."

"What the world sees is that you shot an unarmed white man in the back," Thomas said. "The guy might be a complete dirtball, but they don't care about that part of the story. It doesn't fit the narrative."

Norris groaned at the expletive and shifted uncomfortably in his seat. Garrett, however remained silent and glared at him. Thomas had made his point.

"Whether the perception and reality are the same, it doesn't matter. It's all perception to those news whores. They'll continue to beat that drum until it becomes reality or viewers stop watching. Hopefully, the latter happens. If this story continues to grow, watch out. Then when the truth comes out, it will be a whimper among all the other noise."

Norris chuckled. "Your pep talk needs some work, son."

"I'm not here for a pep talk, Father. I'm here to protect. Remember that if someone from the administration comes by, okay? They don't care about you as a person."

Norris sniffed. "That's been obvious all day."

"Nobody is defending me to the press," Garrett complained. "Why?"

"That's your administration," Thomas said. It was a cheap shot, but he saw the opening and took it. He knew Chief Baumgartner couldn't, and *wouldn't*, release Garrett's name. However, Thomas's job status as the union president relied heavily upon a base of employees dissatisfied with their employer. Therefore, Thomas took every chance he could get to stoke the fires of animosity toward the administration.

"Why aren't you out there then?" Norris asked.

Garrett nodded. "Yeah, why aren't you?"

Thomas knew this question was coming and rolled with it easily. "You don't want me out there fighting perception. That's a waste of my time and your resources. For one thing, we don't have any facts established yet to stack up against the innuendo they are presenting. For now, that's an administrator's job and one, frankly, that will never end. Even after this event's long been forgotten. My primary duty is to protect your employment status and your rights. I'm here to make sure you don't get screwed during this process. We will address the media if and only when doing so furthers that goal."

"You said the city only cares about their welfare, not mine. What did that mean?"

Thomas nodded and smiled. "See, now, you're thinking. To the city, it's all about money. Never forget that. They're going to be looking at exposure, pure and simple. The first thing they've got to ensure is whether the initial stop was legal."

"It was."

"Second, was the shooting good?"

Garrett stared at him.

"Third, was the investigation carried out in a lawful and professional manner?"

"He's got no control over that," Norris pointed out.

Thomas pressed on. "Fourth, who out there in Trotter's family is going to claim unlawful death?"

"SPD's been dealing with his family for years," Garrett said. "He's a generational turd."

Norris cringed at the description.

"Doesn't matter," Thomas said with a wave of his hand. "What the city is looking at is risk versus reward. Right now, some bean counter in the administration has probably affixed some number to Trotter's death. With each tick off the checklist that number is going to go down until they can get it to something *acceptable*. Even if you've done everything right, the family can still file a lawsuit against you and the city. Depending on the numbers, the city may pay, even if it is go-away money."

Garrett shook his head and dropped into his chair.

"Do you think the city is going to offer me up as a sacrifice?"

"No, I don't."

"Okay."

"That can change, though."

Garrett's eyes slanted. "How?"

"If any of those boxes on the checklist don't get marked off completely."

Ty shook his head. "I'm tired of waiting. I want to talk with someone. Can we get the county detectives in here and get started? That way I can be done with this."

"No, we can't, Ty." Thomas lowered his voice to portray patience and caring. It was something he'd practiced over the years. Garrett was so amped up he was going to be his own worst enemy if he didn't wake up soon. "The waiting period is for your own good. It gives you time to recover before you tell your story."

"Listen to him, Tyler," Norris said.

"Here's my recommendation. Get a pad of paper and go someplace quiet. Make notes. Get your story straight. Understand? Make sure it's exactly as you want to tell it. Not as you remember it, but how you want to tell it."

Norris harrumphed. "Are you saying to lie?"

"No, I am not. However, if you think it's important to mention certain elements, do so. Maybe you realized it was Trotter before you stopped him. That could be an important detail for many reasons. Maybe the last time you had contact with him he had a knife. Who knows? Or maybe you felt your safety was in jeopardy for some reason? Again, who knows? See what I'm saying? Take your time and get the narrative straight in your head."

Garrett nodded. "I get it."

"Be prepared when the detectives get here. They won't be your friends when they show up. Do you understand that?"

Garrett's face lightened.

"You thought they were going to treat you nice because you're all brothers in blue, right?"

"Yeah, I guess I did."

"Don't. This is your life we're talking about. Not theirs. They are investigating a homicide. Even if it was justifiable, it's still a homicide. They are going to do their job. Understand?"

Garrett nodded.

"When you're doing that, if you think of anything that needs my attention, call or text me any time. Understand? It's that important. Day or night, it doesn't matter. I'm here for you. Oh, and when you're done with that exercise, destroy the paper. We don't need the wrong eyes seeing you working out your thoughts and getting the wrong idea. Reality can be affected by perception. Never forget that."

They sat in silence for several moments. Thomas finally stood and said, "I'll get out of here and let you get back to it."

Without making eye contact, Garrett nodded, lost in his thoughts.

Norris smiled at Thomas. "Like I said, son. Your pep talk needs some serious work."

Chapter 13

Detective Cassidy Harris stood in the living room of the small house, staring down at the small chalk circles on the hardwood floor. In her case file were several versions of photos of that same floor. One showed the expended shell casings as they were discovered by SPD patrol. Another set of photos showed the casings with a yellow number placard next to them. A third introduced a ruler into the shot. These photos were taken before the casings were ultimately collected by the crime scene forensics technicians, packaged, and booked into evidence. Harris had already requested multiple lab tests for all of the casings, beginning with fingerprints. Maybe they'd get lucky and whoever ambushed Ty Garrett left a nice juicy thumbprint on one of the rounds while loading it into a magazine.

She could really use a ground ball like that. With Todd Trotter shot in the back and no discernible weapon found on or near his body, her case became even more difficult. An officer involved shooting was already a heavy case to begin with, but when you added complications like the ones she had to deal with here, it only got worse.

McNutt was moderately helpful but being saddled with Clint made matters worse. Most of the SPD investigators she knew were top shelf, but he had a reputation for being difficult, and looking for conspiracies within and without the police department. She didn't know how true that was firsthand, but his obvious contempt for Sheriff's Office investigators was clear to her. She wondered if the fact that she was a woman and the lead added to Clint's resentment.

As if summoned by her thoughts, the front door opened, and Detective Clint stepped through. He didn't bother with a greeting, and neither did she nor McNutt. Without preamble, he asked, "You saw the dashcam videos?"

"Of course."

"And?"

"We need audio enhancement on Zielinski's."

Clint tipped his head forward at her almost reprovingly. "That's your big takeaway?"

She shook her head. "Of course not. Garrett didn't turn on his camera prior to the stop."

"We're missing valuable footage," Clint agreed.

McNutt snorted. "Are you saying someone deleted it?"

Clint turned his gaze to McNutt, unimpressed. "Are you? Is that how you all do it over at the sheriff's office?"

McNutt clenched his jaw, then opened his mouth to reply.

Harris interjected, "If you two are going to keep at this, please go out in the backyard and get it out of your system. We've got work to do in here."

McNutt grinned. "Whattaya say, Honey Badger? Wanna go?"

Clint scoffed. "Don't be ridiculous, son." He turned back to Harris. "I assume your forensics are clean? That the recording wasn't modified?"

"Now who's being ridiculous?" Harris asked. "You're not the only one who can do his job, Clint."

"True enough. The sheriff does hate the chief, so the question is worth asking."

"You have my answer. The question I have is why didn't Garrett turn on his camera?"

Clint shrugged. "We'll have to ask him. Maybe it was purposeful. Maybe he forgot."

McNutt moved closer to the two of them, puffing out his chest slightly. "Why is that even a choice? In our patrol cars, it's automated. A deputy hits his lights, the camera automatically goes on. There's no discretion involved."

Harris had to admit McNutt had a point. She looked to Clint for an answer.

"It's a labor issue," Clint explained. "Years back, when the union bargained with the administration about the implementation of the dash camera system, officer discretion was one of the points they successfully negotiated."

"It's not the way the system is even designed," McNutt said. "Your tech guys would have had to modify it."

"That's what they did. Obviously."

"What's the policy say?" Harris asked. She'd pull the SPD Policy and Procedure herself for the case file but wanted to know now.

Clint shrugged. "I haven't been in a patrol car in twelve years, Detective."

"Yet, you know, don't you?"

He gave her the same amused smile he'd given McNutt the previous day. "I do. It says officers are strongly encouraged to activate the system on every traffic stop or other significant contact."

"Does it say 'shall' or 'may'?" Harris asked. The first was a directive, the second a matter of discretion. It was an important distinction.

"It doesn't say either one. It says 'strongly encouraged' like I said."

She looked over at McNutt. "Sounds like a 'shall' with an escape clause."

McNutt shrugged. He obviously saw this as a dead end now.

"How about your ambush theory?" Clint asked. "Any movement on that?"

Harris couldn't tell if he was being sarcastic or not, so she answered him straight. "The idea holds up. Multiple rounds were fired out the open window from the living room." She pointed at the window and the various chalk circles. "If Trotter was in on the ambush, he could have lured Garrett here for the shooters."

"Why?"

Harris sighed. "How am I supposed to know that at this point? Or ever?"

"It's important."

"No," Harris said, "actually, it's not. I have to figure out *what* happened, *how* it happened, and *who* did it. There's very little in the law about *why*, unless we're talking about premeditation. You know very well how infrequently that gets applied."

"It's still important," Clint argued. "It can lead to breaking the case. And it convinces juries, more than all the rest. You don't answer the question of *why*, and reasonable doubt is only a whisper away."

"That's a prosecutor's problem."

"No, it's ours. Everything the lawyers work with comes from our investigation. We gotta know *why*."

"Fine," she conceded. "Then the answer is I don't know yet? Okay?"

"Fair enough." Clint pointed at the chalk circles. "Based on location, there seems to be two clusters of shell casings. What's your take on that?"

Harris had already noticed this. "Either one shooter who moved position, or two shooters. All of the casings are the same caliber, so it's hard to say just yet."

Clint nodded. "Firing pin and ejector marks will tell you."

"I know, but that takes time at the lab. And in case you haven't noticed, this case is blowing up around us."

"Let the white shirts worry about that," Clint said. "We work the case."

McNutt pointed to Harris and himself. "*We* work this case. You observe."

"And advise," Clint added.

"When asked. And we're not asking."

Clint gave both of them a long look. Finally, he said, "I don't recall reading 'when asked' in the OIS protocol. You want to show me that page, Detective?"

"Listen, you—"

"Enough already." Harris interrupted, frustrated, "If you two can't go five minutes without this macho crap, I'll call the sheriff *and* the chief myself, requesting that both of you get pulled off this case for unprofessional behavior. Are we clear on that?"

McNutt dropped into an angry sulk, but Clint didn't seem affected by her threat.

"I'm only trying to help," he said to her. "And we both want the same thing, right?"

"We do. So, play nice."

Clint shrugged. "What caliber were the shell casings?"

"Forty-five."

"How many?"

"Eleven."

Clint nodded. "Most .45s have a mag capacity below that."

"Not all," McNutt grumbled.

"Not all," Clint agreed. "If we're playing the odds, then that means either two guns or a reload."

Harris thought about it, then put the idea on the shelf. It didn't resolve the mystery of how many shooters were in the house.

Clint had moved on, too. He pointed at the broken jamb on the front door. "Garrett?"

"Has to be."

"Pretty ballsy, charging the house," Clint observed.

McNutt scoffed. "You would think so."

"I do. Because it was. Ballsy, and stupid. He broke cover to do it, and advanced in the open. If the shooter or shooters were still in the house, they could have picked him off easily."

"It was an aggressive move," McNutt said, "and aggression wins fights."

"Sound tactics wins fights, but that doesn't matter. Garrett is SWAT and he's still young enough to believe he's immortal, so I get it. His tactical debrief to Lieutenant Flowers was that no one was in here when he entered."

"That's right," Harris said. "According to Garrett, there was a car out back leaving at a high rate of speed."

"Number of suspects?"

"He couldn't tell. Because it was an officer involved shooting, Flowers couldn't ask him any more than the barest of questions, so we're left with a lot of holes."

"Like the one in Trotter's back," Clint observed.

Harris looked at him closely. "*You* have a problem with that?"

"I have a few problems with this case. No gun on Trotter. The bullet in the back. Whatever happened in this room. *Why* it happened."

"I have the same problems," Harris said. "All we know for sure is that Garrett shot Trotter."

"We don't even know that for sure," McNutt said. "You SPD boys use Glocks, so we won't even be able to match the bullet to Garrett's gun."

Clint gave McNutt a look of mild astonishment. Then he turned to Harris. "Where'd you get this guy? Was it take a gym rat to work day, or what?"

"Go to hell," McNutt snapped. "It's a problem."

Clint shook his head. "It's not."

"Oh, really. Why not?"

Clint sighed. "Son, I have neither the time nor the crayons to explain it to you." He turned to Harris. "Let's talk in the morning and brief each other."

He turned and walked out of the house.

McNutt watched him go, muttering about him. Then he turned to Harris, "I guess he's not as smart as he thinks he is, huh?"

Harris bit her lip, nodding. Then she said, "Uh, Shaun?"

"Yeah?"

"What'd you mean before? About the Glocks?"

McNutt smiled. "You liked that?" He took a half-step closer to her and assumed an instructional tone. "See, Glocks are engineered to strict specifications. Very uniform, very precise and the barrels are polygonal cut. Between the precision of the manufacturing and the polygonal rifling, it's impossible to match a fired round to a specific Glock pistol."

"No, it's not."

"Huh?"

"It's not impossible."

McNutt's eyes narrowed. "Yeah, it is. I read—"

"It's not impossible, Shaun. It takes a lot more time and effort. If our lab can't handle it, we might have to send it to the FBI, but it can be done."

"You sure?"

"Positive." How do you not know this? Harris thought.

McNutt's expression was a combination of chagrin and doubt. "Oh. I guess I haven't read up on it recently."

"No problem," she said, letting him off the hook so he wouldn't pout for the rest of the day. "We'll let the lab worry about lab work. We need to plan our approach. I'd like to be ready to interview Garret when his seventy-two is up."

McNutt rebounded. "First thing we need to do is get Clint tossed off this case. The guy is an anchor."

Harris shook her head. "Not our call."

"I'm telling you, Cass, he's trouble for us."

She ignored his not-so-subtle word choice and the shortened use of her name. He clearly wasn't giving up on his campaign to get her in the sack. "I think we need to start with known associates of Todd Trotter. See who he ran with, get a better picture of him."

"Good idea." McNutt looked around. "And this house, don't you think? Find out who owns it. Maybe they have a connection to Trotter somehow."

"Now you're thinking," Harris said, throwing him a small bone.

McNutt gave her his best devil-may-care grin. "Well, I'm no Honey Badger, but I do have my moments."

"Honey Badger. Where's that even come from?"

McNutt grinned broadened. He seemed happy to dish on Clint. "That funny video on YouTube a few years back, all about how the honey badger doesn't give a damn whether bees are stinging it or if it's going up against a cobra, it still fights on?"

Harris shook her head. "Never heard of it."

"Well, you should google it. It fits Clint to a tee. Total prick, cares about nothing and no one. That's why he should be off this case."

Harris asked, "What about Garrett? Do you know him at all?"

"Sure, we went through the academy together."

"And?"

"Stellar guy. Was a squad leader and everything."

"You cross paths with him on the street?"

"A few times, before I made detective. We'd occasionally end up on the same calls if it was near the city/county border. Things like that."

"How was he?"

"Seemed rock solid to me. Good tactics, good attitude. Took care of business."

Harris nodded, taking in the information and adding it to what she knew of Garrett from his public persona. SPD liked to use him in recruitment and advertising materials.

"I really don't want to mess up his world if we can help it," McNutt added. "Like I said, he's a good troop."

"Then there should be no problem."

"What about you?" McNutt asked. "You never worked around the guy?"

"No, but I've been in the detective's office for a long time." She changed the subject. "Let's go back to the barn, get a list of Trotter's known associates and start running them down."

McNutt flashed her another flirtatious grin. "You got it, Cass."

She didn't respond. It was going to be a long day.

Chapter 14

Cody Lofton loved the basement bar of Churchill's restaurant. It was his place to have a couple drinks with the mayor or other party benefactors and relax for a couple hours. Upstairs was Spokane's finest chop house, but the basement was a classic old-school boys' club. Business and politics were discussed at every table. If those subjects weren't to your liking, you could always move down the street to one of the cheap joints where depression and failure were served on tap.

Occasionally, an attractive woman would enter and mute the conversation. That's exactly what happened when Amanda Donahue walked down the stairs and looked around the bar.

Mayor Sikes waved her over to their table in the corner booth.

"What are you guys doing here?" Amanda said.

"The chief and I were just catching up."

Chief Baumgartner smiled at her, his eyes watery from his second Grey Goose and soda.

"What are *you* doing here?" Sikes asked. It was now clear to Lofton that Sikes' marriage was in jeopardy. He'd have to do something about that. Perhaps a conversation with Sikes's wife about the overly flirty new assistant could snuff out this budding relationship.

Amanda shrugged. "I was just out for drink. I'd heard this was a nice place and thought I should stop by to check it out."

Of course, you did, Lofton thought.

"Cody, hop out and let Amanda scoot in."

Lofton smiled and did as the mayor asked. When he sat again, Amanda was uncomfortably close to him. He could feel the heat of her leg against his. He pushed his Maker's Mark to the side and grabbed his water. Suddenly, he felt the need to be sharp.

The bartender, having caught Amanda's entrance, made a beeline over to their table. "May I get you something, ma'am?"

"I'd like something fruity."

"What do you have in mind?"

"Whatever you suggest. I trust you," she said which sent him away with a smile. The TV above the bar was turned to FOX News, even though the sound was off.

"What are you boys talking about?"

"We were talking about the Garrett situation," the mayor said, focusing all his attention on her.

Lofton winced. Even though Amanda was the mayor's assistant, he didn't want to continue the conversation in front of her. Considering her recent behavior, he no longer trusted her.

"As I was saying," Baumgartner said, retaking control of the conversation, "I got an update from Detective Clint earlier."

"How is the investigation going?" Sikes asked.

"Good. I think."

"What do you mean, you think?"

"Clint's an odd duck. All conspiracy theories wrapped in mysteries. Every morning, he sees ninjas in his cornflakes."

Sikes smiled and looked at Amanda, but she was paying close attention to the chief's words. The mayor's smile faded, and he turned back to the chief.

"Do you think it was wise to pick him as part of the investigative team?"

"I do," Baumgartner said confidently.

Sikes shook his head. "Can you imagine what this would be like if it had been him instead of Garrett?"

The bartender brought a red drink over to Amanda and set it on the table in front of her. "It's a—"

"That's okay," she said. "I'll never remember. Just get ready, though. When this is half empty, bring another."

He smiled and walked away.

The chief cleared his throat before continuing. "Clint broke a suspect's arm once outside a Circle K. This was before I was chief. I was a captain then. Anyway, the former chief thought Clint went too far. I didn't, though. I saw Clint's side and made my opinion heard, but it didn't matter none. Too many others didn't like how he handled the situation. They thought it was excessive. I didn't have the juice to do anything about it. Clint was jammed up, lost days and pay, letter in his file, that sort of thing."

The chief stared into his glass, considering something before he continued. "I may not get his conspiracy theories, but Clint's good police. Once he sinks his teeth into something he's like a dog with a bone, a real case solving son of a—"

Amanda giggled.

"I'm sorry," the chief said, slightly embarrassed. "Maybe I should slow down on these."

"I'm not offended," Amanda said.

"Anyway, Clint said things are progressing and there doesn't appear to be any hiccups beyond what we already know."

"Well, regardless," Sikes said, "we're lucky it was Garrett. We can work with him."

Baumgartner nodded and kicked back his glass, finishing his drink. He lifted the empty glass to signal the bartender.

The mayor sipped his beer. He glanced at Amanda who was still watching the chief, studying him. "Cody," Sikes said, "what did you think of the press conference this morning?"

Lofton shrugged. "I thought it went fine."

"No, you didn't."

Lofton met the mayor's eyes which were now full of maliciousness.

"Tell the chief what you thought of his performance."

Sikes quickly looked to Amanda then over to Baumgartner. Lofton knew exactly what the mayor wanted and why. He took a slow breath, steeling himself.

Baumgartner's eyes slanted, sensing danger.

"You set us back," Lofton said.

"How's that?" the chief asked, his jaw muscles flexing.

"You didn't control the message. The press repeatedly called Trotter a victim."

"And I repeatedly corrected them," Baumgartner said. He raised the empty glass to his lips. Finding no relief, he set it back down and looked expectedly to the bartender.

"No, you didn't," Lofton said. "They said *victim* and you said *suspect*. That's not correcting them. You should have stopped their questioning and immediately challenged them. It was that important. If you've watched the television coverage of the press conference you hear *victim* over and over. Tomorrow, when the newspaper comes out, you'll see *victim* in print. Nowhere are you ever on the record correcting them. We had this exact conversation before the briefing. That was our number one priority. Frame the narrative, I said."

Sikes sat up straighter, a wicked smile forming at his lips. He never looked toward Lofton, instead watching the chief the entire time.

"You worry too much," Baumgartner said, unconvincingly.

Lofton moved his water to the side, grabbed his whiskey and took a sip. He felt the warmth of Amanda's leg against his. "You can never worry too much about the press or social media. You also had the opportunity to confirm Garrett's identity. Why didn't you?"

"Because we don't do that. We have procedure. Maybe if you cared about how things are actually done instead of how things look, you'd understand."

Lofton glanced to the TV before speaking. "Take a look at the TV, Chief. Your super soldier is on the national news. The fact that you denied what everyone already knows makes you look like you're hiding something. What's worse, it makes us, *the city*, look like we're hiding something. If the press thinks that, they're going to start digging. If they can't find anything, they'll dig harder until they find something. I don't want that. I want the press to write their stories and go about their business. I know you don't think my advice is worth much, but it would have helped our situation out a lot. If you haven't figured it out yet, Chief, my job is to protect the city."

Baumgartner's lip curled back. "That's my job as well, you little prick."

"Well, you both work for me," Sikes said with a smile. It was clear he enjoyed the exchange.

The bartender brought Baumgartner's drink to the table and left without a word. The chief lifted the glass and took a quick sip.

Lofton lifted his whisky to his lips and froze. Amanda's hand was on the inside of his thigh and moving slowly upward.

"I appreciate your assessment of the situation today, Cody. That's why I like you," the mayor said, smiling at Amanda. She smiled back at him and lifted her hand a little higher on Lofton's leg.

Lofton put his whisky back on the table. "I think it's time for me to go."

"Where are you off to?" Sikes asked.

"Who knows where this thing is headed," Lofton said, thumbing in the direction of the TV. "I could use a good night's sleep."

Lofton nodded to the chief who glared at him. He was going to have to mend that fence as soon as possible. He should have found a way to be more diplomatic, but the chief had seriously mishandled the briefing that morning. Besides, it was clear when the mayor pitted him against the chief that he wanted blood sport. If he had to choose between a happy mayor who trusted him or an unhappy chief who didn't, the choice was easy.

Amanda's hand was high on the inside of his thigh when he scooted out of the booth. He nodded at the table and noticed the subtle wink from Amanda.

Outside, Lofton stood on the corner, waiting for his Uber to arrive. He couldn't believe that Amanda had made a move on him. She was definitely a hottie, but someone he could never see himself chasing. There was too much baggage with her. Still, it was nice to be pursued by a woman that attractive. His sense of satisfaction was soon replaced with the realization that Amanda had played him perfectly.

She was now alone with the mayor and the chief. He couldn't go back into the bar without looking like a complete moron.

He stomped his foot and shouted into the night, "Damn it!"

Chapter 15

Angie Garrett quietly entered her bedroom. Her husband lay sleeping. "Baby," she said, gently rocking him to wake him from his sleep.

"Hmm?"

"It's time to get up."

"What time is it?

"It's after eight. You told me to wake you."

He'd gone to bed a little more than an hour ago, the recent events finally catching up to him. He only wanted an hour of sleep and then he said he'd try to jump to Angie's "normal" sleep schedule.

She'd left her nursing job once Molly was born. She had talked about going back to work, but they were making do and she enjoyed being a stay-at-home mom. Having him home for a couple days would be nice. She wished it was under different circumstances, though.

Garrett swung his legs off the bed and sat up. He rubbed his eyes and grunted.

"You can stay in bed, if you want," Angie said.

Garrett grunted something she didn't understand before he lurched to the bathroom.

He was always sullen when she awoke him from naps. He'd work himself out of it in a few minutes.

She went out to the living room. The kids were in bed for the night, and it would just be the two of them. She was hoping for a couple minutes to reconnect. Even though she hadn't been apart from him since the shooting except when he visited his mother, they hadn't really talked. She wanted to know how he felt, but he had his wall up.

She'd seen it go up and come down for years. Whenever something bad happened to or around Ty, he'd erect it and barricade himself inside. His true feelings wouldn't come out. The only emotion he'd let escape was anger. After a while, though, he'd let the wall crumble and he'd again become the man she fell in love with years ago. She knew that was the challenge of loving a cop, but she was up to the task.

Garrett walked out of the bedroom, rubbing his eyes with the palms of his hands. "Man, I'm hurting."

"We can go to bed right now," she said.

He smiled at her seductive tone. "Mrs. Garrett, are you trying to seduce me?"

"I am."

"On a normal day, I would, but I feel like garbage. It wouldn't be worth it for either of us."

"Speak for yourself," she said.

"You're naughty," he said and dropped on to the couch next to her. He rested his head on her shoulder.

Her phone vibrated, and she picked it up. "It's Winnie," she said.

"Take it," he said with his eyes closed. "You know how she is. She'll keep calling until you answer."

Angie swiped her thumb across the phone to answer the call. "Hey, sis."

"Have you been on Facebook?"

"No, why?"

"Your address was posted by some hate-monger and it's getting shared."

Garrett overheard the conversation and suddenly sat upright. He walked into the other room and disappeared.

"Why would they do that?"

"I don't know," Winnie said. "Why do any of those people do what they do?"

Garrett walked back into the room with his laptop. He sat next to Angie and turned it on.

"Any person in particular we should search for?"

"Type in Ty's name. I'm sure you'll find it."

Angie ended the call with her sister and leaned over Garrett's shoulder. After he completed the login for his laptop, he called up his Facebook account. On his own wall, even though there were supporting comments, ugly and vitriolic statements had poured in.

"Oh, my God," Angie said, looking over his shoulder. "Who are these people?"

There was one account, Jim SupraMan, who posted Garrett's home address. It even had a Goggle Earth photo of his home attached. The caption read, *Murdering Cop's Address* along with the actual street address.

Garrett followed the link and went to Jim SupraMan's home page and saw several links to news clips featuring coverage of Ty's case. Several of the commenters on his page made comments about losing the safety of their streets due to cops like Garrett. They were careful to avoid overtly racist statements that would get them banned from Facebook, but their intentions were clear.

Garrett called up his settings. It took several minutes to determine how to do it, but he deleted his account.

Angie slid the computer in front of her and followed the same steps. She never bothered to check her feed.

"People are animals," she said, closing the laptop.

"I want you and the kids to go stay with your parents in Kennewick."

"We're not leaving you, Ty," Angie said.

Garrett stood. "This isn't up for discussion. Call your folks. Tell them you're coming down now. Tonight."

Angie said, "I am not leaving this minute. The kids are sleeping."

"This situation is spiraling out of control."

"I understand the situation better than anyone. I'm here with you."

"I'm already stressed out, Ang. Don't add to it, please. Just do what I ask."

She studied him and realized the most loving thing she could do was take the kids and go somewhere safe.

"I'll leave first thing in the morning, okay?"

"Fine."

Garrett stormed into the bedroom. There would be no changing his mind now. She would call her parents and then make the two-hour drive to Kennewick in the morning.

She stood alone in her living room, realizing that Garrett's emotional wall would continue to be up. Maybe going to her parent's house would be best for her, too.

Chapter 16

Clint knocked on what seemed like the one hundredth door of the day. Even so, he kept the weariness at bay that ate at the edge of his consciousness. He didn't have time to be tired. Not yet.

A middle-aged white man opened the door. His eyes narrowed as soon as he saw Clint. He crossed his arms across his chest, letting them rest on the shelf of his protruding belly.

"What do you want, boy?"

Clint ignored the flare of anger that the man's tone evoked in him. Disregarding the "boy" was a little harder, especially since he knew what the man really meant with the decidedly un-subtle code word.

Instead, he flashed his badge. "SPD, sir," he said in an even, professional voice.

The man was unimpressed, though his antagonism seemed to soften slightly, replaced by caution. "I din't call the cops."

"I know," Clint replied, putting away his badge and taking out his steno notepad.

"You know what time it is?" the man asked.

Clint glanced at his watch. "Eight-fifty-two. I'm conducting some follow-up investigation on the shooting that occurred near here last night."

"The one with that black cop?"

"The officer involved shooting, yes."

"That was two blocks away."

"It was. Were you home last night, sir?"

The man gave Clint a suspicious look. "Why? Am I some kind of suspect or something?"

"Not that I'm aware of. Did you see anything out of the ordinary in the neighborhood last night?"

"Oh." The man thought about it, then shrugged. "Can't think of nothing. Neighborhood's gone to hell, though." He eyed Clint, adding, "Lots of the wrong sort of people moving in."

"What sort would that be?"

"Your type, mostly."

Clint nodded slowly, taking a few seconds to push down the desire to smash the ignorant piece of white trash in the face. He could handle that people were racist, whether implicitly or overtly. Hell, the way the government and the media promoted hostility, people didn't even know how racist they were inside. Clint had dealt with this and other similar obstacles his whole life, his whole career, and had learned to cope with it. Though it never failed to make him angry, he learned to contain the anger, channel it. When he got it thrown in his face by a superiority-spouting imbecile while he was trying to do righteous police work on behalf of the very same, it rankled him.

The man watched him during those few seconds, but all he let the guy see was a flat stare. When he felt himself in full control, he pulled a photo of Todd Trotter from his inside jacket pocket and held it up for the man. "You ever see this guy before?"

"No. Who is he?"

Clint replaced the photo and pulled a business card from the side pocket. He held it out to the man. "If you recall anything else that might help, please give me a call."

The man stared at the proffered card but made no move to take it. Then he leaned out of the doorway, turned his head to the side and spat a messy glob onto the concrete porch near Clint's feet. Then he looked back at Clint, dark amusement and a hint of challenge in his expression. "I ain't got nothing to say to the po-lice, and less to say to some nigger."

Then he smiled.

Clint saw it all in a flash. Two quick moves, maybe three if he wanted to hurt the man something extra. Nothing extreme. He'd live, but things might not work so right anymore, and he'd always know when it was going to rain. Every time that happened, he'd think of Clint.

On the tail of that came the rest of the story. The complaint, the discipline, the lawsuit. These days, probably criminal charges. And Clint knew there were plenty of people out there who would revel in the chance to hammer him. He'd learned that lesson long ago, from the arrest at Circle K. That guy was swinging at Clint with hammer fists, which was a lot more than this guy was doing.

In the end, Clint settled for a glare. "You should be careful, talking like that. You might get arrested for hate speech."

The man shook his head adamantly. "First Amendment. Freedom of speech."

"Doesn't apply to hate speech."

"I'm in my own home."

Clint nodded, glancing down. "Who spits on their own floor?"

He turned and walked away while the man struggled for an answer. If he came up with anything, Clint didn't know. He'd stopped listening and moved on to the next house.

An elderly black female answered the next door. Clint relaxed slightly, though he could never completely relax. Vigilance had its price, and he knew potential danger lurked everywhere.

The woman had heard about the shooting. She been home the previous night and hadn't seen anything suspicious.

"The neighborhood is going downhill, though," she confided in him.

"Wrong sort moving in?" Clint asked, glancing to her next-door neighbor's house.

She shrugged. "It's the younger ones, if you ask me. They rent their homes." She said *rent* as if the word were a mild profanity. "They don't buy. When you don't own your own home, well you just don't care for it quite the same way, do you?"

"No, ma'am."

"Is that officer all right?" she asked. "The one that they shot at?"

"He is. Thanks for asking."

She shook her head, clucking her tongue. "How you all do that job, I'll never know. It's gotta be hard."

"It can be." He showed her the photo of Trotter. "Do you recognize him?"

She peered closely through her glasses but eventually shook head. "Should I be watching for him?"

"No, ma'am, but if you see anything suspicious, please give me a call." He handed her a card.

She took it. "I will, and God bless you, sir."

Clint thanked her and moved to the next house.

It was that way for him all afternoon and evening. Some people were helpful, some were hostile. Most were neutral. Clint wasn't exactly keeping track, but he had the sense that there was a mild trend based upon race. Nothing he didn't experience everywhere, and most of it subtle. Porch Spitter was the extreme.

This was the shoe leather part of the job. Sometimes it paid off. Other times, like today, it yielded nothing. However, it had to be done, and he was pretty sure Harris and her meathead partner were too self-important to do it. They'd be running down Trotter's known associates and checking out the house from which the shots were fired. Both were reasonable avenues of investigation, ones he would have taken if he were the lead. A thorough background on Todd Trotter was in order, too. If he pursued any of these primary leads, it would be seen as stepping on the toes of Harris and the county investigation. Canvassing the neighborhood, though? He could do that and remain relatively invisible to them. If he happened onto something, they might be pissed that he was acting independently, but that would be overshadowed by his discovery. Even if he didn't, if they ever got down their priority list to the point where a wider canvass of the neighborhood was in order, the fact that he'd already done it might be welcome news. Canvassing was tedious, unenviable work. Harris and McMeathead would be tired by the time they resorted to expanding the canvass. Clint figured that even if Harris carped about it, she'd be secretly happy it was already done.

He glanced at his watch and saw it was after nine. Most detectives didn't like to knock on doors after eight for routine matters. Everyone in this town seemed to think ten o'clock was damn near criminal. Clint considered, then decided to finish the last two houses and call it a night. In the morning, he could get briefed by Harris. Maybe there'd be some preliminary forensics back. Afterwards, he'd quietly run his own background on Trotter.

At the first house, he got no answer, so he tucked his card in the door near the knob. The second house resulted in a pleasant enough conversation with an elderly white couple, but he learned nothing helpful.

Clint strode purposefully back to his unmarked detective's car. He still drove one of the last of the department's Crown Victoria models. Ford had discontinued the line, which forced departments across the nation to transition to the newer Ford Interceptor, a car that Clint had to admit had sexier lines and handled better. Since patrol put so many miles on their vehicles, and hard miles at that, most of the division had cycled through the remaining Crown Victorias. Meanwhile, most of the investigative division, along with the admin, had transitioned to the Chevy Impala. Clint still drove his trusty light gray Crown Vic. He liked the space in the interior, the rear wheel drive, and he especially liked the power of the V8. You never knew when you'd need that kind of get up and go.

When the admin refused his request for an Interceptor, citing cost and lack of need, his response was to refuse to turn in his Crown Vic. The mileage was over the threshold for rotation, so he had to stand guard over the car every time he took it to the garage to make sure they didn't attempt to seize it and cycle it out.

In the end, he was glad they'd turned him down. The new cars came with too much additional baggage, including GPS trackers. He didn't mind when the mechanics complained about the extra maintenance his car required due to mileage. They could yap all they wanted as long as they changed the oil and kept the thing running. He was going to drive the Crown Vic until it dropped. He hated the idea of the brass tracking his location in real time.

Good luck retrofitting a GPS device into this beast, he thought.

He drove north, avoiding the streets that were under construction. Much of that took place in the evening hours and he didn't feel like being held up. Now that he was finished, the weight of the day's work settled into him. He forced himself to stay alert as he drove, ignoring the constant instances of minor traffic infractions that occurred around him.

The townhouse four-plex afforded him the luxury of a garage, and he parked his police car inside it. The apartment he'd lived in before provided only covered parking, leaving his department car out in the open. Not only did it announce his presence, but it was an easy target for vandals. A garage solved that problem.

He knew greater privacy would be much easier to achieve if he moved out of the city, maybe get ten acres or so and fence it. Clint was a city man, though. This non-descript townhouse on a quiet block on the north side was as close as he was going to get to the woods.

The thin piece of nearly invisible fishing line he used as a door marker was still in place. No one had used this door since he'd left that morning. He went inside, disengaging the security system on the pad next to the door. Then he drew his pistol and made his rounds, checking every room in the townhouse by habit. Everything was secure.

Clint grabbed a beer from the fridge and sat down on the couch. He thought about turning on the TV, but he didn't want to watch what passed for intelligent programming these days. It was all reality TV, which was either completely staged or shameful life-whoring. There was no dignity.

He definitely didn't want to see the coverage of the Garrett shooting. Idiots with uninformed opinions would only frustrate him, whether because of their ignorance of the facts, police process, or flat out biases, or all three. Instead, he stared at the black screen, sipping his Miller High Life and thinking about Ty Garrett.

The case seemed like it could turn into a colossal mess. The black versus white piece was difficult enough, especially on the tail of what looked like a bad white-on-black police shooting in Philadelphia just days ago. When the elements of Trotter being hit in the back and the missing gun were factored, it only got worse. Throw in the media frenzy and the self-concerned politicians, and the end result could be a good cop getting railroaded.

Clint had no particular love for Ty Garrett. The man seemed decent enough, even if he was a little bit of a sellout. And he was the right color, twice over. Blue, and black. As far as Clint was concerned, that was reason enough to do right by him, even if he suspected that if things got too hot, no one else would. They'd sacrifice Garrett if it suited their needs, leaving Clint alone to find the truth.

He was used to being alone.

MONDAY

Wrong is wrong, no matter who does it or says it.
—Malcolm X, human rights activist

Chapter 17

Ty Garrett stood alone in his backyard, sipping a glass of orange juice and thinking about his morning.

He'd seen Angie and the kids off shortly before 7 a.m. Jake and Molly were still sleepy, and Angie wasn't happy about it when he loaded them into their Nissan Murano. However, he wanted them on the road and away from Spokane as quickly as possible.

Before they left, Garrett gave Angie the only gun he had in the house to take on the trip. She hated guns and normally wouldn't have one with her, but she agreed to take the revolver. "Things don't feel normal," he said. "Take it just in case."

He remained in the driveway as she backed the Nissan out, the transmission whining lightly in the early morning quiet. When Angie reached the street, she met his gaze. He raised a hand to her and she nodded in reply. Then she put the car in gear and drove away. Ty stared after them until she got to the corner and turned right. His chest ached at their departure, but he knew it was the best choice. They'd be safe. A little more so since Angie had the gun.

The department had seized his Glock following the shooting, so he was now without a weapon. He'd never been one of those paranoid types who thought everyone was out to get him, but not having either gun in the house suddenly felt odd.

Now that Angie was gone, Garrett finally admitted to himself seeing his address posted on Facebook had scared him.

Not so much for him, but for his family. Ty Garrett wasn't used to being scared and he hated himself for being weak. More than that, he hated those who had made him feel vulnerable. The problem was he couldn't point to one person who did it. And the reality was it didn't matter. Anyone can find anyone. He knew that. It took a computer, a credit card, and less than ten minutes to find essentially whatever someone wanted to know about anyone. Garrett knew this but seeing his address on the screen along with a series of vitriolic statements was unsettling. The idiot who posted his address on Facebook did him a favor. He put Garrett on notice.

Maybe Wardell Clint was right. Everyone is out to get us.

Garrett frowned. Who was *us*, then? The police? Or was this about race?

He walked back into his house, his anger at a boiling point.

"Trotter," he muttered. If he would have just stayed in his car, none of this would have happened. Garrett shook his head. *What about the ambush? Who the hell thought it was a good idea to come after me?*

No one from the department talked to him about the case. He was getting frozen out.

Garrett balled his fists and closed his eyes.

It was his seventy-two that was causing this. Three days of mandatory administrative leave was coiling him up inside. "The waiting period is for your own good," Dale Thomas had said. "It gives you time to recover before you tell your story."

Garrett was starting to believe it was something different. He'd read the news and watched the TV coverage. He wasn't stupid. The seventy-two was so the department and the city could get *their* story together, so they could decide which way to move. They were going to make the decision whether to back him or crucify him.

It didn't matter whether or not he did the right thing, only how it looked.

Garrett opened his eyes and unclenched his fists, his hands shaking with rage.

He knew what he needed to do.

2Pac and Dre's "California Love" pumped through his earbuds. He tried to turn off his thoughts and calm his mind, but no relief was coming.

His feet slapped the asphalt to the rhythm of his breathing. One breath in for every two strides, then one longer breath out for every three strides. He'd learned the breathing trick in cross-country back in high school. It continued to pay dividends anytime he hit the road.

He'd been running for thirty minutes through the various neighborhoods on the Five Mile Prairie. He had no idea how far he would run. He just wanted to sweat until the anger stopped. Unfortunately, it was still there. Touching at the edges of his mind. Whenever he felt a sense of relief creeping in, the anger rushed back in to overwhelm him.

Garrett had committed to running until the fury was gone.

As he ran, he'd occasionally wave at someone leaving for work. No one knew him on the Prairie and they didn't care. They just smiled back and waved. A few said something that he couldn't hear but it was done with a smile.

He liked this part of town. Never once had he gotten crossways with a neighbor. He and Angie could go for a walk and talk with random strangers about nothing in particular. People were nice.

A small Chihuahua stood at the edge of a yard, barking at him. The dog's yap was silent due to Busta Rhymes' "Break Ya Neck" blasting his ears. The dog's owner, a mid-thirties woman in shorts and tank top, shrugged with a smile.

When he had turned to watch the dog, Garrett realized a pick-up was behind him. It was a seventies era Chevy beater. He'd seen a similar truck behind him when he started his run, but it had passed him and drove off. Garrett remembered two men in that truck and an Idaho license plate. It struck him as odd for his neighborhood, but he let it pass. He looked over his shoulder as he ran, and the truck continued to follow him at a crawl.

Garrett's pulse quickened, and he struggled to keep his pace and breathing. He continued running straight until he could turn left and head up another street. The pick-up slowly continued on in the different direction.

He relaxed, but the rage returned. Paranoia was setting in, Garrett realized, and he didn't like it. That wasn't who he was. He was better than that. He wasn't Wardell Clint and didn't want to be him. He made up his mind to contact Union President Dale Thomas and get some answers about the investigation. He was also going to schedule the interview with the county investigators.

A little ahead and to his left, a tawny, medium sized dog sniffed the grass of a front lawn, then curl into the unmistakable tuck of getting down to business. The dog gave Garrett a pained expression, as if pleading with him for a little privacy.

Garrett looked away, focusing on the road ahead of him again.

The Chevy turned the corner up ahead and slowly drove toward him. It drifted across the middle of the road onto his side of the street. Garrett slowed to a halt, waiting. He forced himself to relax, preparing to jump out of the way.

He didn't need to, as the truck stopped, and the driver's and passenger's doors opened. It was definitely the same truck that had passed him at the beginning of his run, right down to the Idaho plates. Garrett immediately realized they had birddogged him the entire morning.

Both were white and young, early twenties, in jeans and work boots. The big one wore a Union Jack T-shirt with cut-off sleeves. His arms were sculpted in the gym. The other wore a camouflaged T-shirt and carried a club. He needed the weapon due to his size. He was small and thin. Camo walked with the cockiness of someone twice his size.

Garrett pulled out his ear buds.

"Ain't you gonna run, boy?" Camo asked.

Union Jack laughed and rubbed the knuckles of one fist into the opposite hand.

Garrett tossed his phone to the ground.

Camo and Union Jack looked at each other and then moved to triangulate Garrett. He didn't wait. He moved between them both with decisiveness, striking Camo twice, with a stiff left jab in the face, and a reverse punch to the mid-section, doubling him up.

Garrett looked over his shoulder as he kicked backward. Union Jack who had been surprised by the sudden attack was stepping forward when Garrett drove a heel solidly into his groin. He dropped immediately.

Garrett faced a hunched over Camo again, grabbed his head and brought his knee up into it. He was so amped up that he didn't hear or feel the nose smash. His entire focus was on the club clattering to the asphalt. The little man slumped to the ground.

As Union Jack struggled to stand upright, his hands covering his groin, Garrett stepped to the side. He took in a deep breath and then kicked the big man in the side of the knee. Union Jack screamed as his leg folded sideways. He tumbled to the ground clutching at his knee. Garrett straddled him, the big man's eyes wide with pain and fear. He grabbed the Union Jack shirt to lift his head off the ground and punched him in the face. When it didn't get the desired result, Garrett slugged him again.

"Screw you!" he yelled down at his face.

The big man's eyes rolled back into his head. Letting go of the shirt, Garrett dropped him to the ground.

When he stood, his ragged breathing slowly returned to normal. Garrett watched the two men laying on the ground and realized the anger was finally gone.

He picked up his phone, put his ear buds back in, and jogged home.

Chapter 18

Cody Lofton sipped his coffee and watched as people occasionally walked by. He sat in the little outdoor area behind Atticus Coffee, enjoying the early morning quiet. The coffee shop was a short walk from city hall, but discreet enough that anyone who mattered wouldn't easily see him. A white letter-sized envelope sat on the small metal table between the two chairs. He placed his coffee on top of the envelope when not drinking.

The morning sun was still rising, and the day would soon be hot. He'd arrived a few minutes early to claim a seat in the shade, placing his guest in the sun. It was a smaller version of the play with the press conference in front of city hall.

However, she was already five minutes late. He wondered if she did it on purpose, just like he chose the seating arrangements. His habit for promptness was well-known.

Lofton smiled, hoping that her tardiness was indeed on purpose to needle him. It was these little games that he enjoyed. My pawn for your bishop, he thought. How could he move the pieces about the board? Often, he didn't know what results he would get. He just wanted to *move* the pieces. More importantly, he wanted to make *people* move.

Lofton grew up poor. He never talked about his family and no longer visited them. His parents were still underprivileged, never achieving what they should have in this life and that disappointed Lofton. He watched his parents scratch and claw for a living, always being foolish with what little money they had, and always at the mercy of someone else. As a child, Lofton promised himself that one day, he would be someone who never was at the mercy of others. He went to college on a scholarship for disadvantaged youth, studied and learned, worked and left. School wasn't play time. He was preparing for battle. Now that he was in the thick of things, he couldn't be happier. His time was now.

The door opened, and *Spokesman-Review* reporter Kelly Davis walked outside, a cup of coffee in her hand. She spotted Lofton and nodded. "It's a beautiful day," she said, sitting at the little metal table, her eyes immediately flashing to the white envelope.

Davis raised her hand to temporarily block the sun from her eyes. She reached into her purse and pulled out a pair of sunglasses. When she put them on, Lofton noticed they were an inexpensive no-name brand. The thought of her living on a budget made him smile.

"Sorry, if I kept you waiting," she said.

"I wasn't waiting. I was enjoying the sunshine."

"Sure," she said with a disbelieving smirk. "You're as high-strung as they come, Mr. Mayor in Waiting."

"Chief of staff," he said, coolly.

"You can fool some of the people, right? I've got my eyes on you."

Lofton didn't like that someone in the press already had suspicions of his mayoral aspirations. He'd have to watch himself more carefully in the future. His smile broadened. "I'm flattered that you're watching me."

"Flirting won't get you anywhere."

"Really?"

"Everyone knows your proclivities toward the twenty-somethings, Cody. In your book, I'm well past my prime."

Lofton continued smiling, but this was another fact he didn't like the world to know about him. Too much personal information was leaking out and he'd really need to pay attention to that going forward.

"Why'd you ask me here?" Davis asked.

Lofton dropped his smile and said, "Can't a guy ask his favorite city hall beat reporter to coffee without it being suspicious?" There was no warmth or charm to it. He didn't even try to sell it. Davis had zinged him with the comments about dating twenty-somethings and mayoral aspirations.

"You've asked me to coffee exactly two times before. Both times were for specific purposes. I'm good with that. We have a ...mutually beneficial relationship. Does that sound about right?"

"Yes."

"Give it to me straight then. Why am I here?"

"The Ty Garrett situation."

Davis nodded. "You mean the shooting of an unarmed victim?"

"Suspect."

"How about we say citizen?"

"No. Let's not. Todd Trotter wasn't a citizen. He was a criminal. He never paid taxes and never contributed to the general welfare of our community. Shouldn't a person have to do that to be considered a citizen?"

Davis sipped her coffee. "I get it now. You need my help to change the message."

Lofton turned away and watched a woman walking with a toddler. "I'm asking you to go easy on it."

Davis laughed. "Why? It's national news now. Besides, how can I help? It's not like the *Spokesman* is going to modulate the national perspective."

He turned back to her. "We need some help reframing the story and it has to start somewhere. I'm asking you to help the city. Your city."

"No," Davis said with a shake of her head. "I'm a reporter. I have ethics."

Lofton sipped his coffee, waiting for her.

Even through the sunglasses he could see her eyes flick to the envelope on the table. "What's in there?"

"This is Todd Trotter's record. Including his childhood arrest record."

"How do you have that?"

The curiosity in her tone was unmistakable. He almost had her hooked. "He wasn't a citizen," Lofton said pointedly.

"I can't argue that point. It's a birthright."

"Fine. He wasn't a *contributing* citizen."

"Are you going to keep repeating yourself, or tell me something useful?"

Lofton leaned closer to her, keeping his voice down. "This is what I'm being told. The traffic stop that Ty Garrett made was a good one. It was part of a larger, ongoing drug investigation in which Todd Trotter was a suspect. We couldn't have that coming out as it would compromise the investigation." He tapped the envelope. "Trotter is dirty. As filthy as they come."

Lofton let the lies flow easily. To him, Trotter was now a means to an end and there was no such thing as not speaking ill of the dead.

"Is it true the gun is missing?"

Lofton smirked. "No. The officers secured it right away. Can you imagine leaving a gun lying around in that part of town? Someone would snatch it up in a heartbeat and use it in another crime within an hour."

"That sounds vaguely racist based upon the part of town."

Lofton waved her accusation away. "Trotter was white. Lots of white people live in that part of town, too. I'm just saying the police have the gun."

"Why not announce it then?"

"Again, this is what I've been told. The gun is very special," Lofton said. "It's unique. It also belongs to someone that's part of the larger drug investigation. The police can tie that gun to them as part of a different crime. The chief doesn't want to announce it and spook them. The police need to keep it quiet. That's why it's hush-hush."

He had planned this argument prior to the meeting. He really didn't like it, but it was better than saying the gun was lost. Besides, he kept saying *the chief* and *the police* so when this blew back on him, and he knew it would at some point, he'd step out of the way and point it to the police department. He'd claim the ambiguous *"they"* gave him bad information. It was always important to have a contingency plan.

"You're telling me they're letting an officer twist in the wind for a drug investigation?"

Lofton nodded. "It doesn't seem right, does it?"

"Why are you telling me this?"

"I've advised the mayor to come out with this information," Lofton said, careful not to say *the truth*. "They are advising him not to go public with it. The mayor didn't really have law enforcement support in the last election, and he wants to change that, so he needs to keep them happy. I believe we need to get some of this out there. Like I said. We need to change the national narrative. It's bad for the city."

"And your officer."

"Him, too."

"Did the mayor ask you to do this?"

Lofton smiled and shrugged, hopefully giving her the right impression without saying anything. He needed plausible deniability over everything now. He knew she had taken the bait with that question.

Davis thought about it while she sipped her coffee. Finally, she sat her cup down and reached for the envelope.

Lofton dropped his hand over it. "This is confidential. You never got it from me."

Her fingers tugged on the envelope, trying to free it from under his hand. He pressed down on it, securing it to the table.

"My name never appears anywhere near this article," Lofton said, his eyes serious.

"I understand," she said.

Lofton lifted his hand, releasing the envelope to her. He stood and smoothed his tie. "Thanks, Kelly," he said, walking away.

She ignored him as she tore open the envelope.

Chapter 19

Clara Garrett stared intently at the television, hanging on every word that came out of the mouths of the assembled panel. She was tuned into a local channel, but the host had made a big deal from the outset that this discussion was being aired on several national channels, including MSNBC and FOX.

The host was a Spokane institution, a man Clara had known from the time he was a young reporter covering events at city hall. She treated him with the same respect as all other media personnel during her tenure as a councilwoman and eventually as council president, but she never trusted him. He always seemed to care more about whether his hair looked good than if he reported accurately.

His producer had assembled a foursome that Clara could scarcely believe were in the same room at the same time. Pastor Al Norris had somehow been corralled into appearing on this show, and she found herself simultaneously disappointed and glad to see him there. To the pastor's right sat a white man with a military haircut. Anger seemed to radiate off of him. On the pastor's left was retired SPD Sergeant Sam Gallico, a bitter and vocal critic of the department. Clara was glad there were some watchdog organizations and self-appointed citizens in place for checks and balances, but it was her opinion that even when he was right about something, he took it too far. To the far left was DaQuan Parrish, who she recognized as perhaps the most prominent black activist in the city. While she believed Parrish was fighting the good fight, her preferred method was peaceful and diplomatic. Parrish was much more confrontational.

"Are you saying that this shooting is being treated differently than other shootings SPD officers have been involved in?" the host asked Gallico.

"Of course, it is," Gallico said. "This Officer Garrett is one of the department's golden children. I have no doubt that the administration will pull out all the stops to protect him."

"What do you base that on?"

"Twenty-five years of experience in the belly of the beast," Gallico intoned.

"Could you be more specific?"

"Sure. They're already going full out to protect Garrett. The chief won't even confirm his identity. Everyone knows who the shooter is, but the big man won't tell the truth about that. What else do you suppose they are hiding? The fact that this victim was shot in the back? Or that there are rumors that he was unarmed?" Gallico shook his head. "This is dirty from jump city, and it is typical. Typical SPD."

"I think there's a bigger question here than possible police corruption," the man with a military cut said. Clara noticed the pair of small metal pins on his collar, one United States flag, one Confederate flag. The name Alan Krakowski flashed below him. "For the last decade, every time a white police officer has shot a black criminal, it has resulted in a massive uproar from black people in this community, and in this country. Now we have—"

"Excuse me," Parrish interrupted.

"Let me finish," Krakowski snapped. "Now we have a black officer shoot an *unarmed* white man *in the back*, and we get nothing but silence from those same people who were jumping up and down before. I'd like to know why." He turned to stare angrily at Parrish.

Parrish wasn't intimidated. "Thank you."

"For what?"

"For being so very typically white," snapped Parrish. He turned to the camera. "This is just another example of white privilege in America. Black men have been dying at the hands of corrupt police for *generations*, and it seems that only black people care about that. But let the police shoot a white man, and suddenly we have a problem?"

"The problem," Gallico said, "is more about the fact this man was unarmed and shot in the back, not that he was white."

"I beg to differ," Parrish said, the words rolling in a smooth tenor. "The shootings I'm talking about have been every bit as questionable as this one, maybe more so. What we have here, if you ask me, is another instance of white people taking from black people. You have a history of it. You've got slavery, first and foremost. Our freedom. Now you're taking our culture, too."

"That's ridiculous," Krakowski interjected.

"I agree. It *is* ridiculous. Ridiculous that you would appropriate our music, our heritage, our heroes. Now, you're trying to take our legitimate pain from us and acting like it's yours as well, just because for once, a white man has died at the hands of a black cop instead of the other way around."

In the brief silence after Parrish's statement, the host prompted Norris. "Pastor, would you like to join the conversation?"

Pastor Norris cleared his throat. "I don't claim to speak for all of black America, but I will speak for much of black Spokane. I suspect my words will resonate with a majority of white Spokane as well."

"Don't count on it," snarled the white man.

"I allowed you to speak," Norris said, firm but polite. "Please do me the same courtesy."

"Say something meaningful then and speak for your own people."

Norris shook his head sadly. He held out a hand toward the man. "Now, see, this is what the problem is in our city, our nation. Too much tribalism. We are all one people, under God."

"Please, Pastor," the host said. "This is an interview, not a sermon."

"You invite a preacher on your show, you might as well expect a sermon," Norris said. "I'll answer the question. Tyler Garrett grew up in East Central. His father was destined for great things before his life was cut tragically short, and his mother took up the mantle after he passed. She was one of the greatest citizens of this city, and she raised that boy right. After he went to college and joined the police, he returned to East Central, to make his old neighborhood safe. He is a good man, doing noble work in a noble profession and all of you are rushing to judge him before any of the facts are in. You should be ashamed of yourself, all of you."

"I'm not the one who should feel any shame," Parrish said. "I've got two hundred and fifty years of history helping me judge."

"The only shame in this situation," snapped the other man, "is that an unarmed white man was shot in the back, and you and all of your people seem fine with it, as long it was a black man that did the shooting."

"That's simply not true," Pastor Norris said.

"It is."

"Pastor," Gallico said, his patronizing tone barely masked, "I believe you when you say Tyler Garrett started out as a good person, but he is inside one of the most corrosive, culturally repugnant pits of an organization I've ever known. It's a department that changes people, who they are, and how they see the world."

Norris pointed at Gallico. "Just because you hate your former brothers, don't spread that poison and sell it as fact."

"That's the point, Pastor. That place *is* poison. Look, maybe Ty did nothing wrong on purpose. Maybe this was all a terrible mistake on his part, but the SPD will not hold him accountable for it. They never do." Gallico counted off several controversial, high profile incidents that Clara knew everyone in Spokane would recognize. "In none of those cases was an officer ever held truly accountable. In every instance, they have avoided justice due to the influence the chief wields within city hall and among the local judges."

"Damn straight," Parrish agreed.

"Maybe that was justice," Norris said quietly. "Cases heard by peers and judged is the very definition of justice, even if you don't like the outcome."

"Trust me, no one is going to like the outcome of this situation," Gallico predicted.

"And no blacks will riot when Garrett gets off scot free," added the other man.

"Why should we?" Parrish shook his head.

The host tried to bail Norris out. "Let's not gang up on the pastor," he said.

"I don't feel ganged up on," Norris said, his tone becoming more confident. "The truth will out, and when it does, I am certain it will vindicate a good man. In the meantime, it is the full intention of the Black Ministers League to unequivocally support Officer Ty Garrett in any way we can." He turned to the host. "I expect you to invite me back on this show with these same guests for an apology once that has happened."

The host didn't miss a beat. "Absolutely!" He thanked his guests and turned to the camera for his outro.

Clara Garrett didn't wait for him to finish. She turned off the TV. The mother in her had growing concern for her son, and the politician in her saw even more danger ahead. It was the parishioner in her that kept her from despairing. Pastor Norris and his fellow ministers weren't giving up on Ty, and those men had tremendous clout within Spokane's black community, poor and rich alike. He would watch over Ty.

Him and God, they would both watch over her son.

Chapter 20

Lieutenant Dan Flowers cleared his throat and rang the doorbell. It took a while before Ty Garrett appeared in the small window, looking at them in surprise. He swung open the door and stood in the threshold. "What's up, Lieutenant?"

"Can we come in, Ty? We need to talk to you."

Garrett hesitated, then moved aside. "Sure."

Flowers stepped through the door, followed by Detectives Talbott and Pomeroy. The three of them stood uncomfortably in the entryway while Garrett closed the door and locked it.

"Come on in," Garrett said, leading them down the two steps into the living room.

Flowers and the detectives followed wordlessly.

"Honestly," Garrett said, "I'm glad you're here. I'm ready to talk."

"Good," Talbott said.

Garrett settled into a chair and motioned for them to sit. "Will Dale be here soon?"

Talbott and Pomeroy exchanged a look.

"You mean Dale Thomas?" Flowers asked.

"Yeah. Is he on the way?"

Flowers cleared his throat. "Uh, are you saying you want a lawyer, Ty?"

"It's standard for shootings, right?"

Flowers understood then. "We're not here for that. You're still on your seventy-two."

Garrett looked confused, then his eyes narrowed. "Then why are you here?"

"Come on," Talbott interjected. "You know why."

Garrett didn't react other than to fix them all with a hard stare. "They sent three of you to investigate a fight? Seems like overkill. Maybe I should call Dale after all."

"Look," Flowers said, "the chief wanted extra attention paid to your assault. That's all. Detective Talbott was next up on the wheel, so he's here. Pomeroy is his partner. They're only allowed to ask you about what happened today. Nothing about your shooting."

"And you?"

"I'm here to make sure that happens. But I've got to ask you now, since you brought it up—do you want a lawyer present?"

Garrett considered for a few moments before shaking his head. "I don't need a lawyer. I didn't do anything wrong."

Flowers nodded his understanding. He motioned toward the detectives to begin their interview.

Pomeroy took out his notepad and flipped it open. "We have a report that you were in an altercation earlier this morning."

"I was attacked, yeah."

"And yet you didn't wait at the scene, or call it in."

"I was supposed to hang around in the middle of the street with the two guys who jumped me? Seriously?"

"All right," Pomeroy conceded. He stroked his drooping mustache. "Not calling it in is kinda odd, though, don't you think?"

"No, I don't."

"No?"

"No," Garrett repeated. "I thought about calling it in, but I changed my mind."

"Why?"

"I figured they got the worst of it."

"I'd say they did. What happened, exactly?"

Garrett took a deep breath and let it out. "I was out for a run when I saw this truck that had been stalking me all morning. They—"

Pomeroy held up his hand. "Wait. Stalking you? How's that?"

"I saw them early on in my run, and then they showed up thirty minutes later for a second time. They might have been back there more than that. I'm not always looking behind me when I run."

"You pay attention to every car you see?"

Garrett scowled. "I'm aware of my surroundings. It comes with the job. Besides, the truck had Idaho plates, so it stood out."

Pomeroy didn't reply. He made a note on his pad, then asked, "What did you say to them?"

"Nothing. They passed me and went around the block before stopping."

"And?"

"There were two of them. The bigger guy had a British flag shirt. The smaller guy wore camouflage. He had some kind of club."

"Were you packing?"

"No. I was on a run."

"Anybody say anything?"

"Yeah," Garrett said, a little angrily. "One of them called me 'boy.'"

"Just 'boy'? Nothing else?"

"I don't remember. Maybe."

"All you heard was 'boy'?"

"Yeah."

"If you don't remember more than that, how do you know they weren't looking for a lost kid or something?"

"Are you serious?" Garrett asked.

"I am. Did they call you by name?"

"No."

"What do you think this was about?"

"He called me 'boy.' That's what it was about. And the shooting."

Flowers held up his hands. "Hold it, gents. Let's keep the conversation just on today's incident, all right?"

"Sure," Pomeroy said.

Talbott stood. "You mind if I use the bathroom?"

Garrett glared at Talbott with a strange expression. To Flowers, it looked like suspicion.

"Is there a problem with you two?" he asked.

After a thought, Garrett shook his head. "No problem. Bathroom's down the hall on the left."

Talbott nodded and looked around. "Nice place," he said as he walked away.

"Real nice," Pomeroy added. "Especially on patrolman's pay."

"What the hell does that mean?"

"Nothing," Pomeroy said. "Except that it's a much nicer place than mine. Or Butch's. How about you, Lieutenant?"

Flowers refused to be drawn into whatever game the detectives were playing. He didn't like it, but how they interviewed Garrett was up to them, as long as they didn't get into anything about the shooting.

"My wife is a nurse," Garrett said, his jaw clenched. "She makes good money."

"I thought she quit working. Didn't I see that on Facebook?"

"It was a temporary leave of absence."

"I thought it was more of a stay home for a few years with the kids sort of thing." Pomeroy shrugged. "I'll have to go look it up."

"Good luck. We deleted our accounts."

Pomeroy raised his eyebrows. "Really?"

"Yeah, people were writing all kinds of nasty stuff. Someone even posted my home address. That's why I sent my family away."

"Where to?

Garrett shook his head. "Doesn't matter. What you should be asking about is the two hicks who attacked me."

"Let's talk about that, then. What happened after they went around the block?"

Garrett described the men getting out of the car and advancing on him. Flowers listened carefully, watching the patrol officer relay events in the same confident way he might describe an on-duty call response. He was methodical and descriptive. Flowers barely noticed when Talbott returned to the room until the detective stood at his side, leaning down to whisper in his ear.

"We've got a problem, Lieutenant."

Flowers could smell the stale coffee on Talbott's breath. He gave the detective a quizzical look. Talbott jerked his head toward the direction he'd just come. Hesitantly, Flowers rose and followed him.

Garrett watched them go, his expression confused. "What are you guys doing?"

"Investigating an assault," Pomeroy answered.

As soon as they reached the bathroom, Talbott pointed at the open cupboard beneath the sink. Flowers immediately saw three small baggies of white powder.

"Damn," he muttered.

"I was looking for a towel," Talbott explained. "And…" he motioned toward the baggies.

"Damn," Flowers repeated.

A moment later, Garrett appeared in the doorway, Pomeroy at his heels. "What's going on?"

No one answered.

Garrett followed their gaze and saw the baggies. His expression hardened. "Those aren't mine."

"Never heard that one before," Pomeroy scoffed.

"They're under your sink," Talbott said. "In your house."

"Those *aren't* mine." He glared at Talbott. "What were you doing snooping through my drawers anyway?"

"I needed a towel to dry my hands. Most people keep towels there."

Garrett looked at the empty towel rack, then back at Talbott. "It's not mine."

"Anybody got a field test kit?" Talbott asked.

"I got one in the car," Pomeroy said. He turned and left.

An uncomfortable silence settled on the three remaining men. Flowers looked at Garrett in disbelief, then down at the baggies again. Finding drugs in Garrett's house was the last thing he expected to come out of this visit.

Pomeroy arrived with field test kit. Carefully, he opened one of the baggies with his folding knife and used the blade tip to scoop a small amount into the test tube. He replaced the tube top, twisted it securely, then crushed the ampoule inside containing the reaction reagent. Pomeroy gave the test kit a couple of rapid shakes, but the action was moot. As soon as the ampoule broke, the tube's content flooded purple.

"Positive for heroin," Pomeroy said, unnecessarily.

Damn, Flowers thought, though this time he managed not to say it out loud.

"You want that lawyer now, Garrett?" Talbott asked.

Garrett said nothing. He studied the purple-filled tube in Pomeroy's fingers, his expression distant.

Chapter 21

Detective Harris hung up the phone and turned her chair around. Behind her, McNutt was playing hunt and peck with a witness statement.

"That was the booking sergeant at jail," she told him.

"Yeah? One of Trotter's knowns get picked up?"

"No."

"Who, then?"

"You won't believe me when I tell you."

McNutt kept hunting and pecking for a little while before he seemed to notice she wasn't saying anything more. He stopped typing and swiveled around to face her, his expression one of cautious realization. "You're kidding me."

"No. Tyler John Garrett."

"For what?" McNutt asked, incredulous.

"Assault."

"Against who?"

"Sarge didn't say, but that wasn't the only charge."

"There's *more?*"

Harris nodded somberly. "Possession of narcotics."

"Possession of..." McNutt trailed off, shaking his head in disbelief.

"With intent to deliver," Harris added.

McNutt dropped his hands to his side and leaned back. "You've got to be joking."

"I am one hundred percent completely serious."

"The sergeant isn't pranking us?"

"It's Mathis. When have you ever known him to have a sense of humor?"

"Wow," McNutt breathed. "Drugs?"

"I know. It's hard to believe."

"That's it, then," he said. "The guy's dirty."

Harris shrugged. "We don't have all the details yet, so let's not jump to conclusions."

"Cass, they *booked* him. They don't just casually book a cop."

"I realize that, but I don't know if this impacts our investigation or not. We need to stay focused on the shooting."

McNutt stared at her. "This changes everything."

She shook her head. "It doesn't change what happened that night."

"Yes, it does. It changes *everything*."

Chapter 22

Detective Wardell Clint slid his gun into the metal cabinet, closed it, and withdrew the over-sized key. He put the key in his jacket pocket and followed the corrections officer down the hall to the interview room. He thought his man might already be there, but the room was empty except for a metal table with two short benches, all of them bolted to the floor.

Clint sat and waited.

Less than five minutes later, the lock on the door rotated and the door swung open. Ty Garrett shuffled in, his wrists cuffed in the front. He saw Clint, and his face registered surprise.

"Five minutes," the corrections officer said.

Clint nodded that he understood, and the guard left.

Garrett took a seat across from Clint, eyeing him suspiciously.

"You all right?" Clint asked. He knew the question was stupid as soon as it left his lips but he felt like Garrett needed to know he cared.

"I'm in jail, *Detective.*"

"They treating you okay, all things considered?"

Garrett seemed to think about it, then shrugged. "They cleared the booking area before they processed me."

"That's something."

"It was terrible. I've been in this place a hundred times, hauling in humanity's worst. Now…" he trailed off, at a loss for words.

"They've got you in isolation, right?" Clint asked. Both men knew how dangerous a place jail would be for a cop in general population.

"Yeah. You know how that goes. There's always crossover. If one of these dogs wants to get to me…"

"Anyone else been to see you?" Clint asked.

Garrett shook his head.

"No lawyer?"

"They won't let me talk to one until right before first appearance tomorrow. Can they do that? I mean, it sounds kinda shady, you know?"

"They can do whatever they want," Clint said quietly. "Like everyone in power."

"You're a bundle of joy. Thanks. What are you even doing here?"

"County hasn't talked to you about the shooting?"

"Not yet. I was still on my three days."

"Now you're here."

Garrett gave Clint an earnest look. "Those drugs were not mine. I swear it."

"How'd they get there?"

"Someone must have planted it."

"Who? Detective Talbott? Pomeroy? Maybe Flowers?"

Garrett didn't answer.

Clint raised his hands, showing his palms. "Hey, man, I want to believe you. I really do. I know this place is full of treachery. I've lived it. You gotta help me out here. I mean, be reasonable."

"Is this an interrogation?"

"Did I Mirandize you, son?"

Garrett shook his head.

"You in custody?"

Garrett held up his cuffs.

"All right, then. Even if this was an interrogation, which it isn't, none of it would be admissible, based on Fifth Amendment requirements."

Garrett watched him, still unsure. Finally, he shrugged. "What do you want me to say?"

"Just help me understand, that's all."

"Understand what?"

"If that brown isn't yours, then how did it get under your bathroom sink?"

"I don't know."

"Is it your wife's?"

Garrett scowled. "Of course not. Like I said, someone must have planted it."

"Like who?"

Garrett turned away, not answering immediately.

"You see my problem, right?" Clint asked. "If I am to believe that you are innocent, and the heroin was, in fact, planted, then I have to accept that one of those detectives or the lieutenant planted it. That one, or all of them, is dirty."

"Lieutenant Flowers isn't dirty."

"That'd be my assessment of him, too. Company man, for sure, but not dirty."

"Pomeroy was with Flowers and me the whole time."

"Talbott, then? You're saying he planted the drugs under your sink?"

Garrett looked away again. "I'm not saying that. I'm just saying someone did."

"But not Talbott?"

"I don't know."

"Let's say it wasn't him. Who else could have done it?"

"I have no idea."

"Speculate."

Garrett sighed, then thought about it. "I was out running earlier. Someone could have planted the drugs while I was out of the house."

"Who could have?"

"Anyone who wanted to. Some jerk posted my address on Facebook, which is how the guys in the truck probably found me."

"Did you lock the door before you left?"

Garrett nodded.

"See any sign of forced entry when you got back?"

"No, but I didn't get a chance to really look around before the detectives came to my house."

"To investigate the assault."

"Yeah."

"The assault they booked you for, in addition to the drug charge."

"It's as bogus as the drugs. Those two guys attacked me. It was self-defense."

"All right," Clint said evenly. "All right."

"It's true."

"I said all right."

"You didn't say it like you believed me."

"Don't be paranoid, son," Clint told him.

Garrett stared at him in disbelief.

Clint returned his stare. Then he said, "We should take a look at your house as soon as you're out on bail. See if there's forced entry."

"You think I'll get out?"

Clint nodded. "You should. You're a first-time offender."

"*I didn't do it!*"

"I didn't say you did. I'm saying that's how the judge will see you. Plus, you've got a long work history and ties to the community. Your in-laws in town, too?"

"No. Kennewick."

Clint waved that away. "That's still in-state. All in all, you're not a flight risk."

"Gee, thanks."

"I'm just laying it out for you."

"What about the shooting?"

"That investigation continues, independent of this." Clint hesitated, then he asked, "Why didn't you turn on your dash camera when you stopped Trotter?"

Garrett gave him a blank look. "I did."

"Not until after the shooting, once Zielinski was there."

"Are you sure?"

"I saw the videos. Zielinski's and yours."

Garrett shook his head and sighed. "I must have forgot. It all…it all happened so fast. The whole thing seems like it happened a year ago."

Clint scratched his cheek, watching Garrett. Compassion was not his bailiwick, but he felt for Garrett. Three days ago, the man's life had been normal. Hell, it had been good. Now everything was upside down for him, and most of it not of his own doing. "Don't worry," he told Garrett. "We'll get it figured out."

Garrett considered. Then he asked, "Why are you helping me?"

"I just want the truth," Clint said.

"I don't believe it. This is one brother helping out another."

Clint shrugged. "Maybe a little. The two aren't mutually exclusive."

Chapter 23

Captain Tom Farrell hung up the phone, waited a moment, then picked up the handset again. He punched in the number for the pager system, then the specific pager, followed by 6666 in the message field. He knew his number would show on the pager with his name and rank in next to it. Four sixes signified Signal 6, which told the recipient to meet him at his office.

Flowers knocked on the partially open door a few seconds later, poking his head in. "You page him?"

"Yes."

Flowers came into the office and took a seat across from Farrell. "You sure you don't want me to handle this? He's my guy."

"You work for me. All of your guys are my guys, too."

"You know what I meant, Cap."

Farrell shook his head. "No, this needs to come from me. It's an inter-agency issue already."

"Fair enough. Did you tell the chief about Garrett yet?"

"Of course."

"And?"

"He was as shocked as I was."

"I'm sure. What's the plan?"

"The plan right now is to let things run their course. This doesn't change the shooting. It's a separate matter."

"Yeah, somehow I don't think the media is going to spin it that way."

"I can't help that."

"It's gonna get ugly. You know that, right?"

"It's already ugly," Farrell said.

"Yeah, but—"

Detective Wardell Clint appeared in the doorway. Without waiting to see if he was interrupting or not, he said, "You paged me, Captain?"

"Yes. That was fast."

"I was at my desk."

"Okay. Come on in."

Clint stepped inside the threshold of the doorway, but no further.

Farrell motioned toward the chair next to Flowers. "Have a seat."

"I'll stand."

Frustration nipped at the edge of his patience, but Farrell kept it out of his voice. "We might be a few minutes. I'd appreciate it if you sat."

Clint seemed to consider, then relented. He took the seat next to Flowers, pointedly shifting it slightly away from the lieutenant. His posture was ramrod straight, and he sat near the edge of the seat. "What can I do for you, Captain?"

"I know you're busy, so I'll get straight to it. Did you contact Officer Garrett over at jail?"

"I spoke with him, yes."

"Did Detective Harris ask you to do that?"

"Not that I recall."

"So, you did it on your own. Why?"

"Because I needed to ask him a couple of questions."

Farrell sighed. "About what?"

"Stuff."

"What kind of stuff?"

"Investigation related stuff."

"Detective, you are flirting dangerously close to insubordination here."

Clint didn't reply.

Farrell considered waiting him out, then decided to forge ahead. "I just took a call from Detective Harris, complaining about you stepping all over her investigation. You do know you're supposed to be the shadow, right? That was made clear to you?"

"My role is clear, sir."

"Good. Then—"

"I am the token black man on this investigation."

Farrell just stared at him. "You didn't just say that."

"Of course, I did. It's the truth." Clint turned toward Flowers. "The lieutenant and I even discussed it on scene. Didn't we, Lieutenant?"

"You're out of line, Clint." Flowers tone was resentful but weak.

"I'm just speaking truth."

"You're peddling paranoid conspiracy hogwash."

Clint cocked his head at Flowers. "Really? We didn't have a conversation about me not being up on the wheel, but catching this case anyway because I was...what did you call it? Oh yeah, a good fit."

"You didn't *catch* this case," Farrell interjected. "It's the county's case. You were assigned to shadow. That means observe, maybe advise if needed. Not conduct independent investigative operations outside of the lead detective's direction. That's what you did when you contacted Garrett at jail. You've probably tainted the investigation."

"Which one?"

"All of them," Farrell snapped. "Let me be clear. I'm ordering you to stand down. Observe the county's investigation, offer advice when they request it, but otherwise do not overstep your bounds again."

"Or what?"

The room grew immediately quiet.

"What did you say?" Farrell whispered.

"I said, or what?" Clint replied in a conversational tone. "I want to know."

Farrell found his voice. "Or you'll be removed from the case, that's what."

"I'm only on the case in the first place because I'm black. Go ahead and pull me off. Great story, huh?" He swept his hand along an imaginary headline. "Black Detective Asks Questions, Ofay Pulls Him Off Case."

"This is *not* about race," Farrell snapped. "It's about rules."

"Captain, it is most certainly about race. Regardless, all I want is the truth. That's my job. To find the truth. That means asking the right questions, not the ones that make people comfortable."

Farrell gave Clint a long, hard look. Finally, he said, "It's not your case. It's Harris's. Observe her investigation. Advise her if needed. Assist if asked, but do not overstep your bounds again, Detective Clint. That is an order. Am I clear, Detective?"

Clint clenched and unclenched his jaw. Then he gave a short nod. "Clear, sir."

"Dismissed, then."

Without hesitation, Clint stood and left the office.

"Freaking Honey Badger," Flowers said, half to himself. "Unbelievable."

Farrell sighed. "Yeah, well we made him that way."

"Huh?"

Farrell nodded. "The department created him."

"No way," Flowers said. "He's always been paranoid and full of conspiracy crap. How did we make him?"

"I'm sure he's always been paranoid to a degree and yeah, he sees conspiracy in every coincidence. I get that. The anti-administration, contrarian, alienated employee part is on us."

Flowers shook his head. "What are you talking about?"

"You remember that Circle K incident he was involved in?"

"Of course. He broke the guy's arm."

"The chief at the time ruled against him on the use of force."

"That wasn't Baumgartner."

"No, Livermore. He was that way with everyone. Had a real empty holster approach to policing."

"I remember. Hugs not drugs."

"Right. Anyway, Clint took the punishment for that. Before it happened, he was a hard charger, and afterward, only slightly less so. I was working at the academy at the time, and a position came open for a defensive tactics instructor. Clint put in for it, and I accepted his application. He was solid tactically and had some martial arts background. But Livermore said no way. He shot it down because he didn't want 'someone like that'—" Farrell made air quotes, "—teaching our new recruits."

Flowers gave Farrell a curious look. "He might've been on to something there, Cap. I mean, he did break that guy's arm."

"He was probably justified, but that's not the point. The point is, he was still engaged. Still trying to be part of the department mainstream. As an entry-level DT instructor, he'd be teaching recruits basic stuff. Wrist locks. Standing and kneeling handcuffing. Nothing crazy. Getting the position would have pulled him back into the fold. Helped him come back from the broken arm thing. Instead, he got his paranoid views reinforced when he was told 'you're in,' then 'you're out.' After that, his anti-administration stance became far more pronounced, his self-righteous attitude more prominent, and he was done. Over the rise. We lost him, but we also created him. Believe it."

Flowers shrugged. "If you say so. All I see is a paranoid detective who hates the admin and is a pain in the ass. You say we made him that way, but I think he was born that way."

"The guy was born a detective. *That's* how he was born."

"That's true, too," Flowers allowed. "He a tenacious son of a bitch, which is great when he's on task. When he's not…"

Farrell didn't reply. He'd done what he needed to do in response to Detective Harris's phone call, but if he was being honest with himself, he was halfway happy that the Honey Badger was on the case.

The other half was full of dread.

Life for Captain Tom Farrell right now was waiting to find out which half won out.

"Hey, Cap?"

"Yes?"

"What the hell's an ofay?"

Chapter 24

Cody Lofton watched the mayor on the phone, red blotches forming on his cheeks that soon grew in to a full flushing of his face. His tie hung loosely around his neck and his collar was unbuttoned. His suit jacket hung on the back of his chair. The mayor's hair was jostled from running his hand through it several times while on the phone.

Lofton heard him say "Uh huh" and "what's that mean?" before he heard the name Garrett.

Whoever he was talking with wasn't giving him good news. He imagined it was Chief Baumgartner, but he wasn't sure.

Lofton pulled out his cell phone and texted Lieutenant Dan Flowers. *Did something happen with Ty Garrett today?*

He held his phone on his lap, so he could see the response.

The mayor stood from behind his desk and turned away from Lofton to look outside.

Lofton grabbed his phone and hurriedly typed out a new text. *M is melting down over something with Garrett.*

"How did this happen?" the mayor demanded.

The lack of response from Flowers was more worrisome than the mayor's ire. The lieutenant was usually timely. He knew how important his intel was to Lofton in keeping ahead of the mayor's shifts in mood. Lofton was deeply indebted to him even though he tried to pay him back with intel that was beneficial to him in the department. Flowers was the one who had given Lofton the Trotter information that he fed to Kelly Davis. Flowers had bigger aspirations than being a lieutenant within the police department. It was a relationship of quid pro quo that had some element of friendship. However, Lofton knew he could never get overly friendly with Flowers, in case he needed to distance himself for some reason.

"When you pull your head out of your ass, Chief, I'd appreciate knowing how this happened!"

The mayor slammed the receiver of his phone down, missing the base. He slammed the receiver down again.

"Amanda!" he yelled, his face almost purple now.

"Sir," Lofton said, "What—"

The mayor pointed at him, his hand shaking. The look on his face told him not to say another word.

"Amanda!" he yelled again, louder. Lofton was sure everyone on the seventh floor had heard him.

Amanda Donahue stepped into the mayor's office with a notepad and pen. She wore a red mini-skirt suit. The blouse she wore dipped past her cleavage. Lofton knew exactly her game now after the incident at Churchill's. He wouldn't underestimate her again. "Yes, sir?"

"Close the door and get ready to take some notes. I want a witness for this."

Lofton immediately realized the danger. He brought Amanda in to embarrass him. Sikes liked an audience. He'd done it the previous night at Churchill's with him and the chief. Now, the mayor was turning the tables on him and was going to use Amanda. She'd risen up to a level of confidant, or who knows what else after last night. Lofton had been in this role many times before, but this was different. He'd never heard the mayor verbalize his intentions before.

The mayor shook his head, his anger building.

Lofton flicked his eyes to his phone, hoping for some intel from Dan Flowers. Nothing had arrived.

The mayor pointed his finger directly at him. "You told me to cozy up to Ty Garrett because he was Clara Garrett's son."

Lofton watched his boss, understanding the game now. Whatever Garrett had done was going to affect the city. The mayor was laying it at his feet.

"You remember that advice, hot shot?"

Lofton glanced to Amanda, who didn't seem to be enjoying this display. She had her head down and was writing on her notepad.

"Do you remember that?" The mayor's voice raised, demanding an answer.

Lofton turned his attention to the mayor. If he was going to take a beating, he wanted to know why. "What happened, sir?"

"Answer my damn question!" the mayor yelled.

Lofton felt a calm inside now. If he remained still while the mayor was volatile, he would win this battle. "Yes, I remember that. Clara Garrett is a legend in Spokane political history. Her husband was well-respected and had a promising career before he passed away suddenly. In his absence, she went on to one of the finest careers on the city council and is still regarded today as the standard for a council president. Aligning ourselves with her and her son was a good idea for many reasons."

"Until he shot a man in the back," the mayor said, his right hand mimicking a gun. "You told me to back a loser."

"The shooting is still under investigation. I'm given to understand that there are legitimate explanations for the location of the suspect's wounds. Experts who will testify about it."

"Will they testify about the missing gun, too? What are you going to do about that, Cody? Create one out of perception and innuendo? You can't always sway people to think what you want."

"You'd be surprised," Lofton said.

The mayor grabbed a pad of Post-It Notes and threw it at him. Lofton stood his ground without flinching and the pad flew harmlessly past him. Amanda ducked even though the pad was nowhere near her.

"You stupid son-of-a-bitch," the mayor yelled. "Do you know what happened today?"

Lofton tucked his phone in the inside of his jacket pocket. He no longer cared what Lieutenant Flowers might tell him. He was now completely in control of this meeting.

"I have no idea."

"Garrett beat up two men. He put both of them in the hospital."

Lofton shoved his hands into his pants pockets. "That's impressive, don't you think?"

"Impressive? What the—"

The mayor grabbed a handful of papers and threw them at Lofton. They scattered before getting anywhere close to him.

"I don't know if I could beat up one man, let alone two," Lofton said. "Could you?" He glanced at Amanda, who was now watching him with a look of astonishment.

"Do you think this is funny, Cody?"

"No, sir. Not in the least. Two men versus one doesn't sound fair, does it? I'd like to know the rest of the story. I can't handle what I don't know and there's no reason getting upset until I do. These two men are in the hospital?"

"Yeah. One of them has a broken leg and the other has a concussion and a broken nose."

"Who knew? Ty Garrett is Bruce Lee," Lofton said with a smile.

The mayor picked up the stapler to throw, looked at it, and put it back down on the desk.

"Is that all that happened today?" Lofton asked.

The mayor dropped into his chair. "No. They also found drugs at his house."

"Drugs?"

"Am I stuttering?"

"I don't think so."

Amanda shook her head, appalled at what she was witnessing.

The mayor ran his hand over his mussed hair. Lofton realized that the affectation was meant to take after the one

Jack and Bobby Kennedy used to do. Problem was, it wasn't even close. "You're mouthy tonight, Cody. I don't like it."

"I understand."

"What are we going to do about this?" His voice was more subdued now, almost petulant.

Cody took a deep breath and let it out slowly. "Employees are a renewable resource."

"What's that mean?"

"It means maybe we should sacrifice Garrett now," Lofton said, being careful to plant the seed, but not make the final call. "We tried to use him for a higher calling, but it never panned out. Maybe we should find a new purpose for him."

"Which is?"

"Food for the wolves."

"How does that help us?"

"I'll figure that out. Now, we just have to show that he was a man out-of-control in his life before he ever got to the shooting."

"He's still a city employee. How much will the lawsuit cost us?"

Lofton shrugged. "That's a worry for another day and didn't you figure the city would have to pay something?"

"I did, but then there's the fact that Garrett's a man of color. That makes this more delicate."

"It does," Lofton admitted, "although, let's not get caught up in that. I mean, the man shot a guy in the back. Even if it was good, it still looks bad. I tried to spin it as much as I could, but it's clear Garrett wasn't willing to work with our agenda."

"Didn't you just give the *Spokesman* information to help change his story?"

"Yes, but by the time it comes out it will be yesterday's news. We'll have moved on. Tomorrow's news will be something different."

Sikes watched him briefly before asking. "Doesn't this get to you?

"What?"

"This. Always looking for new angles."

"No. It's what I do. It's how you got that chair."

Sikes sat up straight and pounded his finger on the desk. "I got this because of me. Because of my message."

"Yes, sir."

The two men stared at each other. Lofton knew the time would arrive at some point in his career where he would stand toe-to-toe with Sikes. He figured it would be over some political benefactor, or maybe when he decided to run for political office, but never over an officer-involved shooting.

Sikes leaned forward and rested his elbows on his desk. "We're done, Cody. You can go."

Cody looked up at the clock. It was almost 5 p.m.

"Are you working late tonight, sir? I can stay if you need me."

"No need. I asked Amanda and she volunteered."

Amanda looked up at Lofton and there was a moment of embarrassment in her eyes.

The phone on the mayor's desk buzzed. He pressed a button and said, "Yes?"

"Sir, your wife is here to see you."

"What?"

"Your wife," the receptionist repeated. "She said she's here to see you."

Sikes made a face at the phone. "Tell her to wait."

A couple seconds later the door to the mayor's office opened and Emily Sikes walked in with three small children. She wore a perfectly coordinated ensemble of shorts, T-shirt, and Converse tennis shoes. She had on a Spokane Indians baseball hat. The kids were dressed just as impeccably. "Drew," she said, "Why were you keeping us waiting at the receptionist's desk?"

She didn't wait for the mayor to answer before stepping inside. The three children ran to their father and hugged him.

Emily walked over to Lofton and kissed him on the check. "Cody, thank you for the tickets."

"Anytime," Lofton said.

When they broke their embrace, Emily faced Amanda. It took less than a second for her to give the new assistant a head-to-toe assessment. Lofton saw it coming, but the sheer coldness that the mayor's wife exuded toward Amanda made him feel suddenly uncomfortable. She was a woman not to be crossed. Emily smiled and held out her hand.

Amanda's eyes flicked to Cody before resting back on Emily. She stood and walked over to the mayor's wife, extending her hand. She winced from the firmness of the handshake.

"I'm Emily Sikes, Drew's *wife*. Cody's told me all about you."

"Yes, ma'am," Amanda said. "It's nice to meet you." Emily held on to Amanda slightly longer than polite company would dictate. When they released hands, Amanda quickly returned to her chair. She didn't look up from her notebook.

Emily then turned back to Mayor Sikes. "Grab your jacket, dear. You're taking us to the ballpark. Cody got us box seats. I have a change of clothes for you in the car."

The mayor's eyes slanted at Cody. "I can't," he said. "I've got work."

"Nonsense. Cody told me how much stress you've been under and this was a surprise as much for the kids as for you. Besides, you know what will happen if you don't do what I want." The playfulness in her voice failed to hide a slight hint of maliciousness.

Mayor Andrew Sikes watched his wife for a moment before nodding his head. He grabbed his suit jacket and followed her out of his own office without another word.

When the Sikes family was gone, Amanda looked to Lofton. "He'll get you back for that."

"He'll try."

Amanda's eyes ran up and down Lofton's frame. "Now that my night is free, would you like to have dinner?"

Lofton smiled. "I don't do seconds."

"Seconds?"

"I'm not going where the mayor has been."

Amanda smiled. "He wants to be with me, but I'll never be with him. He's kind of gross, actually."

"Then why lead him on?"

"I don't lead him on," Amanda said, watching Lofton intently.

"Yeah, you do. You're doing it to me now."

"Doing what?"

"You watch me with those doe eyes like I'm the most important man in the world. You listen with your mouth slightly open, like my thoughts are leaving your breathless."

She closed her mouth and slanted her eyes.

"That was the game you played with Baumgartner last night at the restaurant. Seeing you do it to someone else nearly sent the mayor over the edge. Maybe you don't want to get into bed with him, but you're definitely getting *to* him. I'm sure Baumgartner was feeling something, too. I've seen you pull the same stunt with some of the council members."

"I don't know what you're talking about," she said.

"We all play games, Amanda. I'm on to yours."

She searched his eyes before standing and leaving without a word.

TUESDAY

*Men are only clever at shifting blame from their own
shoulders to those of others.*
—Livy (Titus Livius), Roman historian

Chapter 25

It was shortly after seven when he arrived at the department. Captain Tom Farrell was an early riser, preferring to get a morning bike ride along some of the back trails when the weather was warm. Unfortunately, he had to forego that activity this morning due to an early meeting scheduled with the chief.

Farrell knew what had occurred with Ty Garrett, but he didn't expect so much heat from city hall.

He kept a watchful eye on the news, both local and national, up until he went to bed. It seemed as if the story was calming on the national level. There were bigger, more pressing things to worry about. Presidential squabbles with Congress had turned ugly, the stock market was wobbly, and pressure in the Middle East continued to build. A terrorist attack in a small European city Farrell couldn't pronounce got the most attention last night, even more than the candlelight vigil in Philadelphia for the man shot by police the previous week. Spokane and Officer Ty Garrett seemed to get a reprieve.

The local news was something different. They continued to poke at the story. Short pieces on several of the local news broadcasts were designed just to keep viewers engaged. Like a storyline in a soap opera, Farrell thought.

Then there was the article in this morning's *Spokesman-Review*. Normally, he read the paper in his office. However, this morning he scanned the front-page article while sitting in traffic and then finally pulled into a parking lot to read the entire thing.

Reporter Kelly Davis wrote an article filled with rumor and undisclosed sources. It was filed as an opinion piece allowing her to fill it with all sorts of conjecture disguised as journalistic queries. It suggested that there was strife between city hall and the police department on how they were protecting Ty Garrett. The article didn't fully state it, but it intimated that the PD was dangling Garrett out in front of the media as a distraction while they pursued another investigation. *Is this the age-old magician's trick of misdirection,* she finished the article, *getting the population to watch Garrett's supposed downfall while SPD does what it wants? When they're done, will they clear Garrett's good name and expect us to all go about our business, none the wiser?*

Farrell thought about the article while he walked into the department. She also had some interesting information on Todd Trotter's juvenile arrest record. That information wasn't released to the press. Legally, it couldn't be, so how did she come across it?

The only good part about reading the hard copy of the article instead of the online version was that he didn't have to see any of former police sergeant Sam Gallico's snide observations in the comments section. Gallico was pretty worthless on the job, so Farrell wasn't surprised that trend continued after he retired. How that guy had any credibility was beyond him.

The chief had scheduled the meeting at 7:15 a.m. in the briefing room. Baumgartner was notorious for quarter hour start times to meetings and Farrell had grown to accept it over the years. He walked in and the chief was sitting in one of the big, soft leather chairs watching the television hanging on the wall.

"Morning, boss," Farrell said as he entered the room.

Baumgartner lifted his chin toward the television. Farrell turned his attention to it as he sat down. The banner on the bottom of the screen read *Six Seconds of Brutality.*

The commentator, Carolyn Saunders, was an attractive woman with long brown hair. She stared at the camera and said, "For our viewers seeing this for the first time, please be prepared. It is extremely violent. This is amateur video taken yesterday of Spokane Police Officer Tyler Garrett assaulting two men."

The screen changed to footage that appeared to be from a cell phone, but the quality was very clear. Someone had taken it from their front porch as a lawn was seen in the foreground.

Garrett wore red running shorts and a gray tank top. Two white men stood opposite Garrett. The big one wore a British flag shirt with its arms cut off while the shorter man wore a camouflaged shirt and carried a club.

The video started just as Garrett stepped between the two men and punched the shorter man twice. He then kicked backwards into the big man's groin. Garrett grabbed the shorter man's head and brought his knee up to it with such force that Farrell cringed. As the small man crumpled to the ground, Garrett stepped to the side as the big man stood there, his hands still cupping his groin. Garrett side-kicked him in the knee, folding it at an unnatural angle. When the big man hit the ground, Garrett leapt on his chest, and punched him twice in the face.

When he stood, he leaned over the big man and screamed partially censored profanities down at him.

Despite the bleeps, Farrell knew exactly what he had said.

CNN switched back to the reporter who said, "I'm now joined by former Los Angeles Detective Jason Eckhart. Jason, what can you tell us about what you've seen here?"

Eckhart, a well-dressed white man in his early fifties, smiled and said, "First, Carolyn, we don't know the story leading up this confrontation. Was this a provoked response or an unprovoked action?"

Saunders said, "But, Jason, we now know that Garrett was arrested yesterday afternoon for both this assault and possession of drugs. Doesn't that lead you to believe this was an unprovoked action?"

Eckhart's smile didn't fade. "No, Carolyn. It doesn't. His response still might have been provoked and that really does change how certain elements of this should be viewed."

"By what you've seen, do you think he responded appropriately?"

"That's a different question. It appears to me that he may have responded with too much force. It's clear by his tactics that Officer Garrett was well trained. He dispatched those two men very quickly, but his level of aggression was off the charts. I believe he could have easily walked away without the final kick to the leg and he definitely didn't need to jump on the man to punch him twice more after he was incapacitated. At that point, his level of response was no longer warranted."

The video of the assault came back on the screen in slow motion with the banner and warning. Saunders and Eckhardt continued to talk, but Baumgartner reached for the remote and switched it off.

"What do you think, Tom?"

"That looks horrible."

"As the guy said, it doesn't tell the whole story."

"It tells enough. He coldly kicked that big man in the leg and then jumped on him. None of that is acceptable."

"He went too far," Baumgartner said, "but what took him there? What happened right before?"

"I don't know. Hopefully Talbott and Pomeroy can find out."

Baumgartner rubbed his chin, thinking. "Do you remember Rodney King?"

"How could I forget? I was in college at the time."

"What did he do to get that beating?"

"Wasn't it a traffic stop? He didn't follow commands or something?" Farrell said, embarrassed that he didn't fully know the answer.

"King was driving intoxicated," Baumgartner explained. "He failed to stop and then led the officers on a high-speed pursuit. When he finally pulled over he didn't obey commands. He threw off several officers who tried to control him, and a sergeant even Tasered him, but it didn't work. Finally, he charged one officer who struck him with his baton. That's when things went too far and really *looked* bad."

"It was bad," Farrell remembered. "No one deserved the beating I saw on TV."

"You're right. My point is this: the press had the entire video and could have shown the full story of the conflict, not just the end. However, they didn't because it wasn't good for drama, which isn't good for ratings. The complete video came out in court later, but by then, the damage was done. No one remembers the whole truth; they just remember what they saw on TV."

Farrell thumbed toward the blank TV screen. "Do you think there is more to Garrett's video?"

The chief shrugged. "If there is, we'll find out soon enough. Task your guys with getting a copy of the full video."

Farrell nodded.

"Can you imagine how bad this would be if Garrett picked up that club and hit one of those guys?" Baumgartner said, shaking his head.

"How do you think city hall is going to respond?"

Baumgartner smiled, wryly. "Worse than yesterday. Sikes is already distancing himself from me."

"They're going to blame you for Garrett." Farrell didn't say it, but he wondered if the mayor would ask for the chief's resignation. He didn't like the idea, as Baumgartner had been a strong chief. Besides that, Farrell didn't see anyone in the line of succession who could do a better job. He *definitely* didn't want the mayor going outside the department for a new chief.

The chief pointed at the newspaper. "You read the article?"

"Yes."

"Their plan is in there. They're mapping it out for us."

"Do you think the mayor is behind this?"

Baumgartner shook his head. "Not anymore. It's that sneaky bastard, Lofton."

"Huh."

"What else did you see in that article?"

"A leak," Farrell said.

"That's right. We've seen this problem even before the Garrett situation. Find it and plug it."

"What are we going to do about Garrett?"

"Has county interviewed him on the shooting yet?"

"No," Winter said. "Still on his seventy-two."

"This is has gotten out of hand really fast. Got any suggestions?"

Farrell nodded. "The way I see it, there's two choices: we either stand with our guy or we take a step back until the dust settles."

"I never thought you to be a man of political expediency, Tom."

"I hate the idea of political motivations affecting the career of any officer, but this is different. Garrett might not have gotten himself into this mess intentionally, but he sure as hell is making it worse."

"You think the fight was his fault?"

"I don't know, but he went too far. We can agree on that."

The chief nodded. "At the end, yeah."

"And who knows about the drugs, right?"

Again, another nod from the chief, this one more reluctant.

"Add them all together and it's too much."

"Isn't there a benefit to sticking by our man?"

"It may look good to the line level officers, but the rest of the world is going to be screaming *thin blue line*. I don't see any positive outcome at this point."

"There's another piece," the chief said, giving him a meaningful look.

"That he's black," Farrell said.

"Exactly."

"You can't let that be a factor," Farrell said.

"Have you been paying attention to the outside world, Tom? Race matters."

"Not here. What matters here is behavior. That's what we need to focus on. Behavior, and facts."

The chief leaned back in his chair and folded his hands over his belly, settling deep into thought.

Farrell waited patiently.

Finally, the chief let out a long sigh. "I don't want to abandon one of my men, Tom. It just doesn't sit right. This is a good department, full of solid men and women. What kind of message does it send to them if we just sacrifice Garrett to the wolves? If he isn't guilty—"

"Guilty of what, sir?"

"What do you mean?"

Farrell ticked off his fingers, one at a time. "Was it a bad shoot? Was he the aggressor in the attack? Is he into drugs?"

"I have a hard time believing it."

"I do, too. Garrett has always seemed like a solid officer. If any one of these things came along in isolation, I'd be right there with you, calling BS. But all three, one right after another?" Farrell gave him a knowing look.

"I see your point."

"I get no joy in making it," Farrell said. "At this point, he's going to have to weather these three storms, and so are we. It might be that what's in his best interest and what's in the best interest of the department are no longer the same thing. Where does your greater loyalty lie?"

"My loyalty?" the chief asked. "Or my duty?"

Farrell shrugged. "Either way, we have a responsibility to those other three hundred cops that wear this badge, don't we?"

"So, we suspend him?"

"That's my recommendation. Let's suspend him with pay pending the outcome of the criminal investigations."

"I'll advise the mayor."

"There's one final issue, boss."

"What's that?"

"Garrett's lifesaving award. We were supposed to present it to him tomorrow."

The chief shook his head. "Well, cancel the damn ceremony, Tom. We're not doing it from jail."

Chapter 26

Detective Clint was waiting at Harris's desk when she arrived.

"Good morning, Detective," he said, his tone cordial but reserved.

"You're in my chair," Harris told him.

Clint rose slowly and pulled out McNutt's desk chair.

"That's Shaun's desk," Harris sad.

Clint ignored her, settling into McNutt's chair. He planted both feet on the floor and leaned forward, raising his eyebrows. "We segregating chairs now?"

She scowled. "You know that's not it. It's about respect."

Clint gave her a doubtful look. "Respect, huh?"

"Yes." She opened her desk drawer and put her purse inside. It would sit there until the end of the day. "You know, like respecting the boundaries of an investigation."

"Or talking to your partner about something first, instead of running to daddy to whine and tattle?"

Harris felt her cheeks flush. "I did *not* whine."

"You did. You are now."

"No, I *didn't!*" she snapped. "You're not my partner. Shaun is my partner. You're the shadow."

Clint watched her with a clinical eye. "You've got a little bit of a potty mouth there, Detective."

"Screw you, Clint."

"Whoa!" McNutt said as he entered the bullpen. He strode over to the two of them. "What's going on? Get out of my chair!"

Clint rose with exaggerated slowness. "You people are touchy in the morning."

Harris said, "*You people?*"

"You know what I mean," Clint said.

"Sure I do," she said. "Different rules for you than us. Your indignation is righteous. Ours is contemptuous."

McNutt looked from Clint to Harris, not following the exchange. "What's the problem?"

"No problem here," Clint said.

Harris forced her emotions under control. She didn't like how easily Clint made her angry. Normally, she prided herself on her logic and emotional balance, but something about him got under her skin.

"It's fine," she said through gritted teeth. "As long as you remember your place."

"Excuse me?" Clint said. "My *place*?"

Frustrated, Harris threw her hands in the air. "As the shadow."

"Uh huh."

"I'm lead investigator," Harris said. "If you keep stepping outside the foul lines, I'll get you tossed off this case."

"Hunh," Clint grunted. "Seems to me you already tried. How'd that work out for you?"

Harris shook her head. "All I did is ask your bosses to yank your chain a little—"

"*Yank my chain*?" Clint interrupted, his hand mimed grabbing a leash and pulling it from his neck.

Harris ignored him and continued, "—to remind you whose investigation this is. That's it."

"Well, consider me reminded. Can we get to work now?"

"Fine." Harris bit off the word.

The three of them stood next to the desks, looking at one another awkwardly, and waiting. McNutt glared at Clint, but the SPD detective didn't seem to care. He finally broke the silence. "A briefing maybe?"

McNutt started to answer, but Harris interrupted him. She picked up her case file and flipped it open, all business. "All right. Here's where we're at. The canvass of the immediate area yielded no witnesses who saw anything of substance."

"No one saw anything, huh?"

"Not exactly, but our best witnesses didn't see anything prior to Officer Zielinski's arrival."

"One of the idiots even thought he was the shooter," McNutt interjected, but Clint continued to ignore him.

"We've run down several of Trotter's known associates and interviewed them," Harris continued. "So far, no real useful information there, either."

"Not surprising," Clint said.

"No, but we had to do it."

"True, true. What about the house?"

"We pulled the property records. The owners are Mark and Stephanie Seaver. Shaun did a background on them and it came back clean, so we are going to interview them later today."

Clint didn't seem impressed. "Forensics?"

"Not much is back yet. The shell casings had no prints, partial or otherwise. Whoever fired those rounds was careful."

Clint pressed his lips together in thought. "Not even partials, you say?"

Harris shook her head. "Why?"

"Just putting it through the grinder." He smiled absently. "What's that mean to you? The missing prints."

"It's like I said. The guy—"

"Or guys," Clint said.

She shrugged. "Either way...careful. Why?"

"I see a couple of possibilities. One, you've got an individual or pair of individuals who are cautious enough to wipe down ammo as standard practice before loading."

"Which is some paranoid shit, you ask me," McNutt said.

Clint shrugged. "You say paranoid, I say cautious. If wiping down ammo is a habit, then you're dealing with a certain kind of person. If it wasn't a matter of habit, but something done specifically for this event, then this shooting was definitely premeditated."

"If it was premeditated, then it wasn't a crime of opportunity," Harris said.

"That logic follows," Clint admitted.

"Didn't you say earlier that this was a crime of opportunity?"

"No. I said it *could* be. It could also have been an intentional ambush. There could have been one shooter or two. The evidence doesn't rule anything out yet."

Harris hesitated, mildly surprised. She expected Clint to dig in his heels on the issue of whether this was an ambush or not. His willingness to accept new facts so easily didn't fit his reputation, or her perception of him.

"Is that all you've got going?" he asked her. "The homeowners?"

"There's still forensics to come back, and the autopsy is today. Are you going?"

Clint shook his head. "The M.E. knows her job. She doesn't miss a thing. And you'll be there, right?"

"Yes." Autopsies were her least favorite part of the job, second only to crime scenes with ripe, decaying dead bodies. Yet she was the lead investigator and attending the autopsy was her duty.

"What else?" Clint asked.

"We still have a couple of Trotter's associates to locate. We're hoping for some kind of connection there."

"Hope isn't a plan."

"Oh, Christ," McNutt muttered loudly. "Such wisdom."

"Our *plan* is to locate these last two known associates of Trotter," Harris clarified, "and find out if there's a connection."

"It's a dead end."

"How do you know?"

"It's a dead end," Clint repeated. "You know it, too."

"It's a loose end, not a dead end," Harris said. "One we have to sew up."

"You should interview Garrett now," Clint told her. "Before this other stuff gets out of control."

"Interviewing the shooter is the last step in the process."

"Interviewing him now is the best step."

"We'll interview him after his seventy-two is up, and when we've got everything else handled."

"Is that what it says to do in your little green investigator's book?"

"Listen—" Harris began, but McNutt stepped forward and interrupted her.

"I've had just about enough of your crap, Clint," he growled, puffing out his chest. "Cass is lead, you're the shadow. What is so hard about that?"

Clint ignored him, leaning slightly to the side to look past him and meet Harris's gaze. "Interview him now. It's the best move. He can clear some things up. If you wait until—"

McNutt thrust both arms outward toward Clint's chest, startling Harris.

Except Clint was no longer there.

Clint leaned and turned, his movement flowing. He caught McNutt's right wrist as it went past him and twisted it while he grasped the detective's fingers with his other hand and stepped slightly forward. A seemingly small downward motion brought McNutt's hand toward his own chest, bent around at an uncomfortable angle. He let out a surprised, painful grunt and dropped to his knees.

Harris recovered from her surprise. "Let him go!"

"I will," Clint said.

"Now!"

Clint leaned forward slightly, applying more pressure. McNutt let out a small cry and dropped further, his buttocks slamming into his heels. Clint put his face near McNutt's. "A pound or two more and your wrist shatters, Detective."

Harris took a half step toward Clint but he shot her a dangerous look, so she stopped. Then she dropped her hand onto the butt of her gun. "Let him *go*."

Clint turned away from her, back to McNutt. "How about I let you go, like she asks? You be cool, and we just pretend this didn't happen?"

McNutt didn't reply for a second, but then bobbed his head twice.

Clint released him and stepped away.

Harris braced herself, unsure if McNutt would charge at Clint or even go for his own gun. The muscled detective just glared at Clint while rubbing his wrist. Clint stared back cautiously.

"This can't happen," she said.

"It didn't," Clint said. He turned to her. "Now, are you going to interview Garrett or what?"

Harris looked at him in partial disbelief. She had difficulty processing what had just occurred. Cops argued, but fighting in the detectives' office? She never even heard of that, much less seen it before. Clint's otherworldly calm and his ability to return to their prior conversation unnerved her.

"When the time is right," she told him. "Not before."

"The time is right."

"Says you," McNutt said.

Clint pressed his lips together and shook his head. "Who exactly is pressuring you to tank this case?"

"No one!" Harris's cheeks flushed again.

"Then why are you being so by-the-book? Garrett's ready to talk."

"I'm going by the book because that is how professionals conduct investigations. That's the reason there is a book, Clint. I follow procedure. I don't cowboy my way through things. Maybe that's how you run your cases but not me."

"What's your closure rate?"

"Go to hell."

"Mine's high. If it was a batting average, I'd be Ted Williams. You know how I get there?"

"I'm sure you're going to tell me."

"By the book."

She looked at him, confused. "That's what I just—"

"*Until* the evidence or the situation makes it clear that I need to deviate from the book. Then I do that. Which is what you should do now."

She sat in her chair, exasperated. "I don't even know if I can interview Garrett now, after you contacted him. The whole process might be tainted."

"Not an issue. We didn't discuss any specifics on the shooting. I'll cut you an additional report to that effect. Now will you go see him?"

Harris stared at him for a long while. Then she said, very deliberately, "I will interview Officer Garrett when his seventy-two hours is up, and he has his attorney present, after I've cleared these other matters and attended the autopsy. All as per protocol."

Clint frowned. "Typical county." He glanced at McNutt and then back at her. "Bush league."

Before either of them could reply, Clint turned and strode away.

McNutt twirled around in his chair and sank into it, still rubbing his wrist. She could sense his embarrassment but didn't care. She had bigger concerns than his damaged ego.

"Stupid Honey Badger," McNutt muttered. "I should file a complaint against him."

She didn't bother looking at him. "You tried to push him first, Shaun."

McNutt didn't reply right away. Finally, he said, "I said *should*, not *would*. Still, he's a menace. The guy's a loose cannon."

He seemed to be waiting for her to reply. She said nothing, gathering together her notebook and a pair of pens for the autopsy.

McNutt let out a small, forced chuckle. "He's a loose cannon with a screw loose."

She didn't laugh at his joke. Instead, she picked up the case file and her notes.

"You want to get coffee, Cass?"

"No. I've got the autopsy, you've got the possible Trotter associates."

"Okay." He sounded dejected. "We've got the Seavers later. Both of us."

"Yes," she conceded.

What a joy *that* will be, she thought.

Chapter 27

Cody Lofton stopped at Amanda Donahue's desk, which was located just outside Mayor Sikes' office.

"Good luck," she said, her eyes indifferent and her mouth closed. "They're waiting."

Lofton shrugged and then readjusted the lines on his suit. He looked good and he knew it, but of all days it was necessary. Today would be a bloodbath and he needed his best armor for the fight.

He'd seen the Garrett video early in the morning and had gotten a text warning from Lieutenant Dan Flowers. The department was on the hunt for the information leak. Beyond his normal duties, Lofton knew he had to defend against four different angles of attack coming at him: the Garrett video, the leak of information, Mayor Sikes' anger over Lofton's involving his wife, and Amanda Donahue. He'd planned his day before leaving his apartment. He would at least plant a seed with Amanda to begin building some sort of strategic relationship.

"I'm sorry," he said.

"What?"

"I'm sorry how I spoke to you yesterday," Lofton said. "It wasn't called for."

Amanda's look softened. "They're waiting for you."

"I thought about it last night and regretted not taking you up on your dinner offer."

Lofton imagined a switch flicking on as the old Amanda returned. Her eyes widened, and her mouth opened slightly. She immediately gave Lofton the impression that he was the most important man in the world. If he hadn't expected the move, it could have been intoxicating.

"You're taking a long time getting in there." She leaned forward and whispered. "Aren't you worried?"

"They can wait. It's more important to make amends with you."

Her smile seemed genuine to Lofton, but he couldn't tell for sure. He decided to accept nothing as true around Amanda but pretend everything was as she wanted.

"Does he want you to come in and watch?" Lofton asked.

"Not today."

"Too bad," Lofton said, "I would have liked you in there."

That brought a bigger smile and softer eyes. He left her and headed into the mayor's office. When he stepped inside, he closed the door.

"You're late," Mayor Sikes said, anger in his eyes.

Lofton nodded, choosing to ignore any type of response and sat on the couch next to Chief Baumgartner. On the wall, FOX News was on with the sound muted. The Ty Garrett video was playing in a smaller box while a panel discussed what they were watching.

"The chief was telling us what he knows about this video."

Baumgartner sat on the edge of the couch, his back straight. He looked directly at the mayor, not answering.

"Well?"

"I already told you we don't know anything about this video. We're tracking it down."

Red blotches on the mayor's checks formed. "How did this video get by your guys, Chief? Aren't you supposed to be Spokane's Finest?"

Lofton remained impassive, but he winced at that. Sikes was throwing verbal jabs today without thinking. It started last night when he yelled at Lofton. He'd never seen the mayor come unglued like that. However, the mayor had never been through anything like the Garrett situation. No one in this city had. Other, lesser controversies had happened on the previous mayor's watch, and while Sikes rode the wave of dissatisfaction they caused, in truth, they were minor league compared to what was happening now.

"Not everyone talks with us," the chief said. "Some people are looking for their own fifteen minutes of fame or to make a quick buck. We'll get the video and when we do, we'll know if there is more to the story."

Sikes looked to Lofton. "I hope you had plenty of time to think about this last night while I was at that ridiculous ballpark."

"Was it a good game?" Lofton asked, purposefully testing the waters.

Sikes stiffened, a reaction that Chief Baumgartner caught and watched with curiosity.

"The game was fine."

"The kids had a nice time? Did they like the surprise?"

"Yes," the mayor said, curtly. "It was nice for them."

Baumgartner glanced at Lofton who said, "The mayor took his family to an Indians game last night," Lofton told him. "I arranged for Otto, the mascot, to visit them and bring autographed baseballs from the team."

The chief smiled, bemused. It was becoming well-known that the mayor wasn't a fan of sports or family outings. He must have hated the evening.

"I blame you," Sikes said, his lip curling.

Lofton nodded. "Yes, sir."

"If you had stayed out of it, we wouldn't be involved."

"Okay, sir," Lofton said, realizing he wasn't talking about the ballgame.

The red blotches had fully formed and flushed his face. The mayor raised his voice, "I could have controlled this situation if it wasn't for you."

"I understand." Lofton's calm voice was having the opposite effect on the mayor.

"You should have seen it coming!"

Baumgartner glanced at Lofton with the same look of surprise Amanda had given him yesterday.

"This is your fault, Cody."

Lofton remained quiet. Baumgartner lowered his eyes then, not wanting to attract the mayor's attention.

Sikes looked between the two of them, his breathing ragged. He focused back on Lofton. "What should we do?" he asked finally.

"I don't know," Lofton said.

"What?"

"You've told me this is my mess, sir. Maybe my suggestions are wrong."

Sikes leaned back, watching Lofton with suspicion. "Yesterday, you said we need to sacrifice Garrett. Do you still think that?"

Lofton shrugged. "You know, I'm not really sure anymore."

Sikes looked to Chief Baumgartner, who said quickly, "We're suspending Garrett pending the criminal investigations into his assault and the drugs."

"Will the union let you do that?" the mayor asked. "He hasn't been found guilty of anything yet."

Lofton winced internally at the question. The mayor never was a detail guy.

"It's not punishment. It's an administrative suspension," Baumgartner explained. "He's off but with pay. The union has no say in the matter as long as we're actively investigating his conduct."

The mayor turned back to Lofton. "How will that play?"

Lofton squinted and looked to the ceiling, as if he was struggling to contemplate a thought. "Okay, I think?"

Sikes slapped the arm of his chair with all of his force. "Damn it, Cody!" he yelled. "Quit screwing around. I need your help!"

Lofton stared at him and let his last four words hang in the air.

Sikes realized what he had said, and he repeated them more calmly. "I need your help."

Lofton nodded and pretended to think, but it was only for show. He already knew the plan the moment he saw the video of Ty Garrett assaulting the two men on national television. Once he heard the outcry and saw the way the winds were blowing on social media, there was only one thing to do. "Embrace the video," he said finally.

"What the hell?" Baumgartner blurted.

Sikes held his hand up to the chief. "Explain, Cody."

"Everyone is going to expect you to distance yourself from this video," Lofton said. "Don't. Call a press conference immediately. Announce the suspension as the chief has suggested and then publicly thank the maker of the video."

"We don't want to encourage more people making videos," Baumgartner said.

"Why not?" Lofton challenged.

"Yeah, Chief, why not?" Sikes said, turning on the chief. "I want *my* officers out there with honor and integrity. Hopefully, more videos will show that."

Baumgartner smirked. "They won't."

"Why? Do you only employ crooked cops? Are ethics something lacking on this department? Should I contemplate a leadership change?"

"That's not what I meant," Baumgartner bristled. "My cops are good, dedicated cops. I meant that people will only take videos of officers when they think they're doing something wrong."

"Great," Lofton said. "Let them. That's part of the message you should deliver, sir. The other part is to take videos of the other two hundred plus good officers out there doing good things. Let's heal this community by showing good works."

"Let's plant a rose in a pile of dung, so to speak," Sikes said.

"Exactly," Lofton said, nodding.

"And Garrett?"

"He's on his own. Let's see how this plays."

Baumgartner shook his head in disgust.

"You don't approve, Chief?" Lofton asked.

"No, I think that—"

"I don't give a damn what you think right now," the mayor said. He turned his attention to Lofton. "Cody, how do we proceed?"

Lofton experienced a sense of satisfaction. He tried to keep the sound of it from his voice. "Chief, can your people find the maker of this video by this afternoon? It shouldn't be hard by watching it again. Should only be a few houses. Let's get that person in here as part of the press conference and publicly thank them for helping keep a watch on our city. Let's make this an issue bigger than Ty Garrett. Let's make this about watching out for each other."

Baumgartner lowered his head, but Sikes was nodding. He saw the possibilities. "We can spin this into an uplifting message then. Something like *I am my brother's keeper.*"

Lofton nodded. "Exactly, but maybe we should work on a better slogan."

Chapter 28

"Are you okay?" she asked, her voice full of concern.

"I'm holding up," Ty Garrett said, pressing the telephone receiver into his ear. He was in the holding area of the county jail. The jailers had cleared the area to allow him to use the telephone. The staff had been more than accommodating to Garrett, a professional courtesy as they'd worked together for many years. No one could believe he was on this side of the line, including Garrett.

"How did this happen?" Angie said.

Garrett leaned against the wall. "I'm still trying to figure that out. I was attacked by two men—"

"I saw the video."

"There's a video?" Garrett said. "What video?"

"Someone recorded your fight with a cell phone."

"That's good," he said, tapping the wall, excitedly. "It'll prove I'm innocent then."

"It doesn't look so good, baby."

"What do you mean?"

"Well…"

"Just tell me, Ang. They've got me in solitary. I've got no access to television or the internet, right now."

"The video starts in the middle of the fight. Then…" Her voice trailed off.

Garrett replayed the fight in his head. "Damn," he muttered.

"You looked wild in that video. I was scared of what I saw."

"Why would you be scared?"

"I've never seen you like that before."

"I've never been attacked like that before. I was fighting for my life and my family," Garrett said.

"They said you've been arrested for drugs."

"Yeah."

"Where did the drugs come from?"

"I don't know. They were under the bathroom sink."

"Under our sink?" Anger burst through her voice. "How did they get there?"

Garrett shrugged. "Someone must have gotten in somehow."

"Someone was inside our house?" Angie yelled. "A stranger was inside my home?"

"It's the only thing that makes sense."

"You don't sound so sure. They weren't your drugs, were they?"

"No! Are you kidding me?" Garrett gripped the phone tighter.

"Don't you raise your voice at me, Tyler Garrett. I didn't do anything wrong." Angie was hysterical now. "I'm two hours away from our home and you tell me that someone planted drugs inside *my* bathroom. The bathroom where I bathe *our* children. I want to know what the hell is going on up there. What kind of trouble have you gotten yourself into?"

"I'm not into anything, baby."

"Then why in the world would someone plant drugs in our house? It doesn't make any sense. You see that, right?"

Garrett took a deep breath before answering. "Angie, I've been thinking about it non-stop. Nothing makes sense anymore. The only thing that I can even point to is the guy I shot, Trotter. He must have been connected. I must have crossed the wrong person by shooting him. If that's not it, then I don't know what I did to deserve what's happening. Everything is crashing down on me now."

The phone was silent for a few seconds before Angie softly asked, "How long are you going to be in there?"

"No idea. Please stay with your folks until we get this figured out, okay? I don't want you coming home until I'm there. Not after those two guys."

"Okay," she said, her voice returning to normal.

"Hey, baby, the guard is giving me the signal to wrap this up. I've got to go. I love you. Tell the kids I love them."

"I love you," Angie said.

Garrett hung up and turned around.

The jailer, a big country boy who went by the nickname Tater, waited for him to gather himself. After a minute, Garrett rubbed his eyes with the palms of his hands and walked over. "I appreciate you clearing the area for me to make a call, Tater."

"You're good people, Ty. We don't know what's going on out there, but you've always been straight with us. We'll take care of you in here."

Garrett patted Tater's arm in appreciation.

"Let's go," Tater said, softly.

Due to Garrett's law enforcement status, he was being kept in isolation. Everyone knew the potential danger because of his employment history. As they walked down the hall, a lone inmate with a large dust mop was sweeping the floor. "Against the wall," Tater commanded, his voice leaving no room for doubt that if it wasn't obeyed there would be ramifications.

The inmate, a large Hispanic, immediately did as commanded. Spider-web tattoos ran around his neck and his dark hair was slicked back. He watched Garrett closely. Tater focused on the inmate and Garrett sensed the jailer's tension. As they approached, the inmate slowly stuck out a balled-up fist and nodded. It was not a sign of aggression, so Tater didn't reprimand him.

As they passed, Garrett fist-bumped the inmate and nodded back.

Tater looked over his shoulder a couple times as they continued down the hall. He finally looked at Garrett and asked, "What the hell was that about?"

"No idea," Garrett said with a shrug, "but if a guy wants to be my friend in here, I'll let him."

Chapter 29

Detective Clint pulled to a stop, positioning his Crown Victoria as close as he could to the location of Ty Garrett's patrol vehicle the night of the shooting. He got out and stood in the open doorway of his car, surveying the scene. As he did, he drew on his memory of the night of the initial investigation, then glanced down at his own diagram for verification.

This was it.

He swept the field of vision, noting how different it looked in the daylight. The backdrop Ty Garrett had when he fired at Trotter consisted of houses. Clint felt some relief that Garrett had only fired twice in that direction, at least according to his tactical debrief with Lieutenant Flowers. Harris had accounted for both rounds. One was in Trotter's body and the other one shattered into the dashboard of the Chrysler.

Turning slowly to the right, he surveyed the scene until his eyes came to rest on the house from which Garrett said shots had emanated. Clint believed two shooters was most likely. Contrary to what he'd told Harris, Garrett had given him a brief, unofficial account of the shooting before the corrections officer had returned to take him back to his cell. The cavalcade of shots Garrett described sounded more like one burst from two shooters than two separate bursts from one shooter.

Two people, by definition, meant a conspiracy.

Even more so if Trotter was involved. Shaking down his known associates wasn't likely to accomplish anything. Even if someone knew Trotter was involved, no one was going to admit it. There was no incentive. Trotter was dead. He couldn't talk, and everybody knew it. Keeping your mouth shut is the golden rule in the criminal world. If a detective is going to convince someone to violate that code, it would take considerable evidence. With no chance that Trotter was talking, Clint didn't see where Harris had any kind of leverage to use.

Still, Clint knew Harris was right to run down those loose ends. He also meant what he'd said about being nimble when it came to an investigation. Going by the book just because it was the book was being a slave to the system instead of a free thinker. With things heating up around Garrett, Clint was worried they might not be able to get a clean interview if they didn't do it soon. He knew that if he was Garrett, he'd be thinking seriously about not talking to anyone about anything. It was clear that something was going on and forces were aligning against Garrett. Harris and her strict adherence to policy wasn't helping. His own police department had just arrested him. Clint fully expected the next step would be the admin and city hall would hang Garrett out to dry as a political, sacrificial lamb.

Why attack Ty Garrett? Clint wondered. Or, was he onto something when he first thought it was a crime of opportunity? Maybe the location was planned, the shooting was planned, but Garrett was just the unlucky patrol car that Trotter came across first and then led to the ambush. Was this part of the war on police that had been building for years? Or did they target Garrett specifically?

He thought about that, right back to his first question. If Garrett was the specific target, then why? Because of something he'd done on the job? Clint thought of the many men and a few women that he'd arrested over the years, and the ones he'd sent to prison. Revenge was a very prevalent motivator in people, at least based upon what he'd seen in his years on the job.

He knew he couldn't rule out straight up racism, either. Spokane wasn't the Deep South, full of institutional, overt racism but there was a different kind of hate that lived here. Clint called it ninja racism, because it blended in most of the time. But when there was a chance for it to come out, the impact was just as powerful as the more open kind. In his mind, it was entirely probable that the men who attacked Garrett while he was on his run were motivated by their racial hatred. For years, North Idaho had been a beacon for groups urging racial purity. They set up camp in Hayden, less than an hour northeast of Spokane. That was the connection he thought Harris and McNutt ought to be looking at more closely. Who were those two? Maybe they were the shooters and decided to finish the job with a club instead of a gun. Yeah, it was pretty stupid, but it made a sort of sense, didn't it?

Clint wondered if those two had any connection to Trotter. That would be worth exploring.

He stopped halfway up the walk to the house. The door would be locked again, and he didn't feel like breaking in just to look around. Maybe he'd ask Harris to meet him here, so they could walk through it together, sometime after she finally interviewed Garrett. If she and her Wonder Twin could break away from interviewing John and Mary Homeowner, who he doubted more and more had any involvement at all.

His gaze drifted to the small realty sign standing off to the side of the walkway. *Kayla Trent Sells Homes!* it read. He smiled.

Tri-Mark Realty took up the first floor of a downtown building. A swarm of real estate agents bustled around the office. A couple of them looked his way with a predatory anticipation when he walked in. Clint felt their appraisal as they seemed to be considering whether he was a fish to land or not. When he badged the receptionist, they immediately lost interest.

"Detective Clint," he said to her. "I'm looking for one of your realtors."

"Certainly. Who are you looking for?"

"Kayla Trent."

The young woman behind the desk smiled at him. "Of course, but I think she's at lunch with her boyfriend already. Were you supposed to meet them or something?"

Clint gave her a blank look. "Why do you say that?"

"Oh," she said, slightly taken aback. "I guess I just thought that since you were…never mind."

"No, it's all right. What did you think?"

"Well, you're a police officer and so is her boyfriend. I thought you might know him."

"Who's her boyfriend?"

"Justin something."

Clint thought for a moment. "Pomeroy?"

"Yes, that's it. You know him?"

Clint gave her a wide smile. "I do. Do me a favor, okay?"

"Of course."

"Don't say anything to either of them. I'll catch up to them later and surprise them. Can you do that for me?"

"Sure."

Clint thanked her and left.

In his car, he mulled it over.

The house where the shooters ambushed Garrett from was for sale. The realtor for the house was the girlfriend of Detective Justin Pomeroy. Pomeroy and his partner, Butch Talbott, were the detectives who arrested Garrett for possession of drugs and assault.

Coincidence existed in this world, but in Clint's experience, the more nefarious the coincidence, the less likely it was actually a coincidence and the more likely it was intentional.

The assault on Garrett still bothered him. Was it part of whatever was going on against the officer? If so, who was behind it? Or was it just hick-fueled racism?

An even bigger problem than the assault was the drugs. If they indeed belonged to Garrett, then he was dirty. That certainly seemed to be how the media (and, he guessed, the admin) saw him. Clint wasn't so sure. Perhaps, Garrett arranged the attack on himself? The very idea was ludicrous. Clint supposed that the attack could be drug-related, but he seriously doubted it, just like he doubted the man was involved in drugs at all.

That meant someone planted the drugs. Talbott was the best candidate. Why would he do that?

Clint's mind clicked through the Byzantine maze of potential storylines. The possibilities rang in his ears. There were so many variables that he had a difficult time forming a solid theory. He needed more information, even if it only helped him with the process of elimination.

He found Kelly Davis at Atticus Coffee, the one habit that he knew she rarely broke. She had her face up to take in the sun with her eyes closed. A half-empty cup of iced coffee sat on the table in front of her. When he blocked her sun and his shadow fell over her face, she opened her eyes and regarded him calmly.

"Detective," she said. "Haven't seen you in a while."

Clint smiled, but there was no humor in it. The last time they'd crossed paths, she'd been hounding him for information on a dead prostitute that was rumored to have been routinely servicing a state senator whenever he was in town. The fact that it was a male prostitute made it even more salacious for the Spokane crowd, so Davis was eager to get confirmation. Clint wouldn't give it. He'd determined that the rumors about the senator were true, but he'd also confirmed he was in Olympia when the murder occurred. That made the assignation irrelevant to the murder investigation, and Clint wasn't about to share it with the media. He barely even shared relevant facts unless he was forced by his bosses, much less the irrelevant ones.

"I read your article this morning," he said.

"I'm honored."

Clint pulled out the chair next to her and sat down. "Very informative."

"It was an opinion piece, but I'm glad it still informed," Davis said.

"Who's your source?"

Davis looked at him innocently. "Aren't you just direct?"

"I don't have time to play patty cake. You're getting your intel from somewhere."

"Says you."

"It's obvious. Is your man inside the department or city hall?"

"Maybe it's a she."

"I don't care if it's a talking parrot. I just want to know who."

"You know I won't divulge my sources."

"I need to know."

She gave him a sardonic smile. "Kind of like I needed to know about a certain senator last time we talked? I seem to recall you saying something about a confidential informant during that discussion."

"This is different."

"Yeah. This time I have the information and you need it."

"No. All you wanted was dirt on a politician to write something sensational."

"It's true, then?"

"It doesn't matter."

"Funny, I didn't have you pegged for a Republican, Ward."

Clint scowled. "It's Wardell and I'm not. I just don't see why you are so eager to wreck a man's life just for entertainment value. You're doing it with Garrett, too. Your article is building a case against him in the public eye."

"His actions are doing that."

"His actions are still being investigated."

"Which actions do you mean? The shooting, the beating, or the drugs?"

"All of it, yet it won't matter what the investigation shows. He's not going to get a fair shake if you and your pals keep playing this for ratings."

Clint had sought out Davis because her opinion piece had tickled the back of his brain, especially the more he thought about the new information concerning Pomeroy's connection to the ambush house. He wanted to know who was feeding information to the newspaper about the case.

Davis reached for her iced coffee and took a long sip, eyeing Clint over the top of the cup. When she put it down, she said, "You think he's clean? In all of this?"

"I'm not here to be another source for you, Kelly."

"Off the record, then."

Clint considered. He believed most, if not all, journalist were snakes. He avoided talking to them unless he had to. He'd been misquoted before and seen facts twisted to suit the story the reporter wanted to tell, but he knew that everyone had a set of values and a code and honoring the phrase "off the record" was one thing that seemed to be sacrosanct with all of them.

"Off the record," he repeated.

"Yes."

"I don't see anything wrong with the shoot."

Davis' eyes bugged out at him. "He shot an unarmed guy in the back!"

"It was an ambush. I think the rest will be cleared up."

Davis shook her head in disbelief. "What about the beating? They're calling it 'six seconds of brutality' on TV."

"It's six seconds of TV bullshit."

"Hey, I'm a newspaper writer, you won't get any argument from me. Still, the video looks vicious."

"I have it on good authority that the video doesn't show the entire story."

"He's clean there, too?"

"Might be."

"And the drugs?"

"I thinks so, but I don't know for sure. That's why I need to know your source."

She shook her head again. "I can't do that."

"It's important."

"Why?"

"I need to know if your information is accurate."

Davis considered. "How about if I tell you I believe it is? Is that good enough?"

"No."

"I wouldn't have printed it if I didn't think it was reliable."

"That's not entirely true. If you can cite a source, you can run with it. Especially if it sells papers."

She leaned back. "We're back to not playing nice again, huh? If that's the case, how about we go back on the record?"

It was Clint's turn to give her a long look. Then he said, "You really don't care what happens to this man, do you?"

"Why do you care so much?" she asked, turning it around on him. "You seem hell-bent on proving him innocent."

"It's not about that. What's happening to him is the same thing I've seen happen to good men too often. The bosses conspire, they use them, and they destroy a career or an entire life. Then they just move right along, as if nothing happened. Sometimes it's about power, sometimes politics, sometimes hate. I don't know which it is here. Maybe all three. A good man is getting caught up in all that, and I can't let that happen." He looked at her meaningfully. "You should care about that, too."

"It's not my job to care about him. It's my job to write the truth."

"No, it's your job to sell newspapers."

"That, too. I need people to read my words. I don't have a cushy union job like you."

Clint stood then. It was one thing to listen to a reporter's self-righteous justification for being one step removed from writing for *The National Enquirer*, but when she called the job he did cushy, that was too much.

"I feel stupid," he said as he left. "When you said you wanted the truth, I thought for a second we were on the same side."

Chapter 30

End of day press conferences typically held little appeal for Cody Lofton. They were often poorly attended by the press, council members or the caring public. This one was different, however. Networks like CNN, FOX News, and MSNBC had reporters and camera teams on scene. They were begging for exclusive one-on-one interviews with the mayor and Chief Baumgartner. All had been refused.

That didn't stop others, though, from accepting invitations to be interviewed. Several city council members had jumped at the chance to be in the spotlight of national television.

Sikes was beside himself with the unwanted attention. He loved being the big fish in a little pond but did not like being a little fish in a big frying pan. The mayor had spent most of the day in front of the television watching various takes on the Garrett video. Whenever the city was brought into the discussion he would go into hysterics.

"Why are they saying we are responsible for Garrett? We didn't make him."

Lofton had repeatedly tried to calm him, but to no avail.

"It feels like they're coming after *me*," Sikes whined.

He had asked Lofton if there were ways to immediately stop the storm by terminating Baumgartner. Lofton assured him that would only make the story bigger and uglier.

Truth be told, Lofton was now worried about the press conference.

Much had occurred regarding Garrett in such a short amount of time and the mayor was not handling the overload as he should. He looked tired and wasn't carrying the weight of responsibility well.

Sikes had spiraled into a myopic conspiracy and Lofton couldn't understand why. Sikes was normally smarter than what he displayed. The only reason Lofton could find was the amount of television coverage they were experiencing. Never had anything Sikes and Lofton been involved with received this much coverage. Lofton found it unsettling, but he resolved it by turning off the coverage and focusing on the various tasks at hand. Sikes did the opposite and developed tunnel vision on the problem.

Lofton hadn't seen the man in this light before. He always knew that Sikes had his stress points, but to see him crack so easily was disappointing.

The late afternoon sun had moved into a position behind city hall, so it made using it to his advantage with the press conference impossible. Scheduling a press conference in Huntington Park behind city hall would have been an option for a normal, smaller conference, but that wasn't a possibility for today.

The crowd in front of city hall was at least a couple hundred people now. They were roped off behind the news crews. Many of the onlookers had homemade signs. Some of the signs read *All Lives Matter*, *Impeach Sikes,* and *Free Garrett.* One had blood splattered lettering on a blue background that simply bore the acronym *FTP!* The meaning was clear enough, but the rest of the message was scrawled beneath each bolded letter.

Due to the attendance, a contingent of police officers was required to block off a portion of the street and redirect traffic away from city hall. The officers maintained a professional demeanor, ignoring the inflammatory signs and the occasional taunts, but their presence only served to heighten the tension.

Cody Lofton exited the building behind Mayor Sikes, Chief Baumgartner, and Captain Farrell. Amanda Donahue was beside him. The crowd noise jumped several levels as those in attendance soon started with catcalls.

It's a circus, Lofton thought, and immediately smiled.

"What's so funny?" Amanda asked.

"This. It's amazing."

Mayor Sikes stepped up to the lectern and reached into his jacket for his notes. When he couldn't find them, he glanced over to Lofton, who shook his head. Sikes looked at the crowd and his hands gripped the edges of the lectern. He was already sweating profusely, and red blotches had formed on his cheeks. "Thank you for coming this afternoon."

"Said your girlfriend," someone yelled from the crowd.

Sikes scowled, scanning the crowd, then continued, "I'd like to recognize Chief Farrell and Captain Baumgartner."

Lofton made eye contact with Baumgartner and apologetically shrugged for the mayor's error.

"I'd also like to recognize my chief of staff Cody Lofton and my assistant, Amanda."

The mayor smiled too long at Amanda and she knew it. The crowd knew it as well. She glanced at Lofton who shook his head.

Someone in the crowd wolf-whistled and several people laughed.

The mayor recovered and said, "We're here today to talk about Officer Tyler Garrett. A great officer, one of Spokane's finest—"

"Murderer!" a voice yelled.

"We don't know that," the mayor responded.

Lofton cringed. He was engaging with the audience and hadn't even started to get his message across.

The mayor rocked the lectern forward as he spoke. "As you know, Officer Garrett was involved in a shooting—"

"Sir, what do you know about the video recording of Officer Garrett's assault?" Kelly Davis from the *Spokesman-Review* yelled.

"We have the person who made the video here with us," Sikes said, pointing at a mid-fifties Hispanic woman in a floral dress. "I'm sorry I forgot your name."

Lofton shook his head in disbelief. They had scripted this presentation perfectly. It would have played beautifully, but now it was train off the tracks and running downhill.

"Rena Alvarado," the woman shouted.

"Rene Alzado," the mayor said, "is a citizen—"

"Rena Alvarado!" the woman shouted and then shook her head in disgust.

The crowd laughed at the mayor's mistake and it took him a moment to realize what had occurred. His face flushed with embarrassment and he was now completely flustered.

Lofton lowered his head and closed his eyes. He no longer wanted to witness this train wreck.

"Rene," the mayor said, still getting the woman's name wrong, "is a citizen we are deeply proud of for coming forward with this video."

Lofton felt a hand slide into his. He opened his eyes and saw Amanda looking at him.

"It will be okay," she said. Her look was one of genuine care. Maybe this was the true Amanda, Lofton thought.

Lofton knew better than to believe that for long, though. He smiled and squeezed her hand, responding the way she wanted. This was still a game with rules he knew by heart.

He returned his gaze to the lectern and watched the mayor butcher the rest of their message.

Chapter 31

Detective Cassidy Harris stared out the passenger window of the plain marked Chevy Caprice detective's vehicle. Beside her, McNutt drove, tapping his fingers on the steering wheel to the heavy metal song on the radio.

Harris ignored him, and the thrashing guitars, and kept to her own thoughts. It used to be that when she made good time on a case, she felt positive about it. Tasks checked off the list seemed like progress to her. Such things made sense in her world. As she gained experience as an investigator, she started to differentiate between completing tasks and making progress. She learned that you could do a whole lot of work, finish a slew of tasks, all without accomplishing much of anything.

When she talked to her lieutenant, he never started the conversation by asking what tasks she'd managed to cross off her to-do list. He asked about progress. What did they know? How close were they? It was only if they had been stymied on the progress front that he turned to asking what they'd actually done. She imagined that there was a chapter in some management book somewhere about always having some kind of beans to count, some kind of sacrifice to offer to the white shirt gods on Brass Row.

So far, if she measured this case by task completion, they were buzzing along like a pair of fighter jets. But progress? The best Harris could offer up is that they had done some elimination work.

The autopsy revealed nothing that surprised her. The hole in Trotter's back was confirmed as an entry wound, and the M.E. found the badly damaged bullet inside the body. She doubted that it was intact enough for a match to Garrett's service weapon, which kept things from being as clean as she'd like. It appeared to be .40 caliber rather than .45, so that was probably enough to seal it. Plus, Garrett said in his tactical interview that he fired at Trotter, and she assumed he'd confirm this in her interview with him.

The biggest downside to the bullet being fragmented is that McNutt would likely seize on the no-match as vindication for his "impossible to match Glocks" position, and lord it over her.

Trotter's blood came back with some alcohol and cocaine in his system, but only in amounts that would cause minor impairment, especially in a habitual user. He wasn't drunk or stoned, just buzzed.

There was no gunshot residue on either of his hands, leading Harris to the conclusion that he hadn't even fired a gun recently, much less shot one at Garrett that night. That didn't mean Garrett didn't perceive a threat, but it did mean that the threat wasn't real. This was another point she'd have to cover in her interview with him. If he was threatened by some action Trotter took and depending on the timing of the shots from the house, she didn't believe the prosecutor would rule the shooting as criminal.

Harris didn't worry about that. Usually, her recommendation mattered in a homicide case. Though according to the OIS protocol, the investigating agency sent the case to the prosecutor without recommending charges or offering conclusions. Hers was a straightforward, fact-gathering role.

So was the M.E.'s, for that matter. Unfortunately, all of the other facts that the M.E. recorded did nothing whatsoever to help her case. Like Harris, it seemed like the M.E. was sometimes caught in the same vortex of completing tasks versus making progress.

McNutt had made no progress finding Trotter's associates, she quickly discovered. When she'd cleared the autopsy, she'd thought about sneaking in a quick lunch with her friend, Amy.

She had little contact with her friends outside of law enforcement, much less any opportunity to date. There was a danger to surrounding yourself with nothing but cops. Intellectually, Harris knew this, and emotionally, she didn't want it. Time demands boxed her into that behavior, and when she had some free time lately, she discovered that there were fewer and fewer people without a badge that she could call. Or wanted to.

It didn't matter anyway, because McNutt checked in with her before she could even dial up Amy to suggest lunch. He was eager to interview the Seavers, or so he said. Then *he* suggested lunch and saying yes seemed the easiest route. She was hungry, after all. She briefly considered the fact that she could go eat a sub sandwich less than an hour after watching a human body being dissected on a stainless-steel bed but wasn't sure she really wanted to examine that thought any further.

McNutt bought her lunch. When she protested, he waved her off. "You get the next one," he said, which, of course, ensured there'd be a next one. Or gave him a chance to rack up a few "next ones" and then suggest a single dinner date to wipe the slate clean. Probably to celebrate success on some case, she imagined.

Harris knew she'd say no to that, but she wondered how many more years it would take before the easiest thing to do would be to just say to hell with it and go to bed with McNutt or someone like him. To hell with respect and being seen as a professional. How did screwing another cop change that? It didn't for the men on the job. Maybe it wouldn't for her.

She doubted it, though. Double standards died hard. That wasn't really the point, anyway. The point was, how long before she didn't *care* anymore?

This is why I need friends who aren't cops, she thought to herself.

The Seaver interview was a dead end, just as the self-righteous Ward Clint had predicted. The couple was barely thirty, and the house where the shooter had been was their starter home. They bought it five years ago, renovated, and once both of them finished college and started climbing the corporate ladder, they quickly upgraded to a nicer home in a nicer neighborhood. Neither one had a criminal record, and only the husband had so much as a speeding ticket.

They were now back to running down Trotter's known associates, something McNutt seemed capable of doing only if she held his hand while he did it.

Harris glanced over at him. His muscled forearm flexed and twitched as he tapped the top of the steering wheel rapidly in time with The Scorpions. He was so sure of himself, and she both admired and pitied his confidence.

McNutt caught her looking and flashed her a rakish grin. "*There's no one like you!*" he sang, badly out of tune.

"Who sings this?" she asked.

"The Scorpions."

"How about we keep it that way?"

His smile faltered slightly, but he took it in stride. Harris was pretty sure his brain had already processed the jibe as flirting. Hell, maybe it was. She pointed to Central Avenue as they approached. "Here's our turn."

McNutt swung the Caprice to the right and slowed for the residential street. As they approached the address, Harris flipped open her case file, peering down at a mug shot of a wiry Hispanic man.

"Ernesto Ocampo," she read aloud. "Two arrests for possession with intent to deliver, one for assault. No felony convictions, though he pled out to the assault as a misdemeanor. Do you have any idea what happened on the drug charges? There's no resolution in here."

"Both dropped," McNutt replied. "I called the narco prosecutor. She said there was enough probable cause to charge but no way could she prove it in court beyond a reasonable doubt. Whatever that means."

"Well, he and Trotter were never linked on any criminal case, but SPD patrol filed a field interview that had the two of them parked in the same empty parking lot at two in the morning, smoking cigarettes and talking."

"What a crime spree."

Harris shrugged. She admired the patrol officer investigating what amounted to mildly suspicious circumstances, and then taking the time to record the event. It would have been just as easy for him to let the whole thing go once he figured out he had nothing criminal. Or even easier to have just driven right on by without stopping at all.

"We are truly scraping the bottom of the barrel now, as far as leads go," McNutt said. "I can't wait to interview Garrett and put this thing to bed."

Harris didn't reply. With no leads on who the shooter was, she didn't think they'd be putting this case to bed, even after interviewing Zielinski and Garrett. Or at least, if they did, it wouldn't be a restful sleep.

As they approached Ocampo's rental house, she spotted a pristine purple car. The square frame sat low and the impeccable body shone. It stood out in a neighborhood full of mostly working-class cars and beaters.

"Waste of a work of art," McNutt said. "1962 Chevy Impala, built in Detroit, destroyed by Mexico."

Harris ignored his comment, jotting down the plate and calling it in. The dispatcher returned almost immediately, confirming the car was registered to Ocampo.

"At least he's home," McNutt said. "That's something."

It was another check mark on the list, Harris agreed. Whether or not it was progress, they'd have to wait and see.

At the door, McNutt gave a solid rap. It wasn't quite as thunderous as a graveyard knock, but it was something more than a polite one. Harris preferred to come in a little softer at first. It was easier to ramp up than to ease down, but she didn't think McNutt entirely agreed with that philosophy.

The door swung open. A heavyset Hispanic man appeared in the entryway, scowling. Harris could see he made them as cops immediately.

"The hell do you want?" he said, his words heavily accented.

Harris showed him her badge, though she knew it was unnecessary. "Detectives Harris and McNutt."

"Mc*Nutt*?" He grinned maliciously. "Which one of you is Mc*Nutt*?"

"I am," McNutt said. "You got a problem with that?"

"No, man. It's hilarious either way, *ese*."

"I ain't your *ese*," McNutt growled.

"No kidding, *pendejo*."

"We're looking for Ernesto Ocampo," Harris interjected, breaking up the pissing match before it went too far. "We just want to talk to him. Have him come to the door."

The man spread his hands. "He's not home, *chica*."

Harris pointed toward his car.

The man followed her finger, then shrugged. "His girlfriend picked him up, like two hours ago. I think they were going to Yakima, to see his sister. She's sick or something."

"They took her car, not his?"

He nodded. "Better gas mileage, you know? Those semis, they throw up rocks and other crap. 'Nesto doesn't want his baby getting chipped."

"So, he leaves it on the street in this neighborhood?" McNutt asked sarcastically.

The man scowled, the first genuine reaction Harris had seen since he opened the door. "I watch over it. No one on this block would touch it, anyway."

"When will he be back?" Harris asked.

"Coupla days. She's not dying or nothing."

"What's your name?"

"Am I under arrest?"

"No."

"Then you don't need to know my name."

"Fine," Harris conceded. "How about you let us come inside and take a quick look around to confirm Ernesto isn't here, and we'll be on our way."

"I told you, he went to Yakima."

"I know. I just need to confirm he isn't here."

"You calling me a liar?"

"Not at all. My boss is kind of a hard ass. If I tell him you said Ernesto wasn't here but we didn't check to confirm, he's going give me a hard time."

The man looked her up and down. Then he said, "Well, maybe you ought to change jobs or something. Get a new boss who treats you right. Because I don't let no police in my house without a warrant, *entiendes*?"

He closed the door.

They walked away, McNutt muttering insults. Harris waited until they were back at the sidewalk, then asked him, "You think he's there?"

"Probably. They all lie."

Harris hoped "they" meant criminals. "Could be, but the story made sense, too."

McNutt shrugged. "It's the bottom of the barrel, anyway. Let's check back in two days. By then, we'll have our interview with Garrett. We can even ask him if he ever heard of this jack wagon."

Harris agreed. "All right. Let's try the other guy."

They had more luck with Peter Yates, finding him at the second address they tried, which was the age-old standby for male criminals—his mother's house. Mom didn't even bother lying for him. She just swung open the door, pointed through the kitchen to another door that they quickly discovered led to the basement.

Yates was a skinny white man with long hair and a scraggly beard. He sat on a futon and was playing a video game on a small TV when they entered. From the cursing, Harris imagined it wasn't going well for him.

"Peter Yates?" she asked, causing him to jump. When he saw her badge, he paused the game and set aside his controller. His expression became sullen.

"What do you want to hassle me about now?"

"We just want to talk."

"About what?"

"You knew Todd Trotter, right?"

Yates snorted. "That douche bag? Yeah, I knew him. You guys killed him, and he still owes me forty dollars."

"Why'd he owe you money?"

"He lost a bet. Why do you care?"

"We're investigating his death. We're trying to fill in some missing pieces about him."

"Isn't that convenient?" Yates said. "First you shoot him in the back for no reason, and now you get to investigate it yourself? Gee, I wonder how *that* will turn out?"

"We're with the Sheriff's Office, not SPD."

"Like that makes a difference. A cop's a cop."

Harris moved closer to him, ignoring the stench of body odor and other smells she'd prefer not to classify. "Look, Pete, it's our job to find out what happened in this shooting. If it was a bad shoot, we need to figure that out. You might know something that can help us."

"I don't help cops."

"You'd be helping Todd."

"The news is saying that he didn't have no gun and that moolie cop shot him in the back, anyway. If a white cop did that to a black guy, there'd be riots already."

Harris cringed at the epithet but hid her reaction as best she could. She kept her voice neutral. "I don't know about any of that. I do know that we are trying to get to the bottom of this. The real bottom."

Yates eyed them suspiciously. "Are you saying that they might actually nail that cop for this?"

"We want the truth. Even if it is painful."

Yates nodded slowly, as if processing her words. "All right," he said reluctantly. "Ask your questions."

"How did you know Todd?"

"We run in some of the same circles, that's all."

"He dealt drugs." Harris looked at him impassively.

Yates squirmed slightly in his seat. "Yeah, so? I like to party, and news flash, some parties have drugs. Sometimes I'd see Todd at parties. He had good stuff."

"Parties where?"

"Wherever, man. Parties, they just…happen."

"Here?"

Yates shook his head. "No, my ma would never allow it, but there's always something doing somewhere, if you know people."

"You ever party with Ernesto?"

Yates shook his head. Harris didn't see any sign of deception in his reaction when she spoke the name.

"You know Ernesto? Drives a purple Impala?"

A flicker of recognition showed in his eyes. "Yeah, man, I seen that car running up and down Division Street some nights. Maybe parked in the lot at the auto parts store with all the other cool drives."

"You don't know Ernesto?"

"No. Nice car, though."

"How about Ty Garrett?" McNutt interjected. "You know him?"

Yates narrowed his eyes. "I know the name. Wait, isn't that the cop on TV? The one who killed Todd?"

"It is."

"Why would I know him, other than to get hassled by him?"

"We're just asking."

"Man, you got some stupid ass questions going on here."

"How about this?" Harris asked. "When was the last time you saw Todd Trotter?"

Yates thought about it. "A week and a half ago. Maybe two."

"Where?"

"Some house on the west side. Backyard barbecue party."

"Whose house?"

"I didn't know the guy. I don't even remember how I ended up there. I think my boy Todd told me about it."

"Now he's your boy?" McNutt asked. "Two minutes ago, he was a douche bag."

"Man, you need to step back." Yates shook his head in disbelief. "He can be both, a'ight?"

"Did he talk with anyone else at this party?" Harris asked.

"Lots of people. So, what?"

She glanced at McNutt, who gave her a nearly imperceptible head shake. This was going nowhere. She decided to take a shot.

"Do you own a gun, Peter? A .45?"

Yates looked at them both, and then broke out laughing. "A .45? Yeah, I own two." He pointed at the video game. A first-person view showed a pair of hands in the foreground, each hand clutching a 1911 Colt .45. "They lay out zombies like a bazooka."

Back in the car, Harris checked another task off her list.

Beside her, McNutt shook his head in disgust. "The guy's thirty-two years old and living in his mother's basement. I'm sure he's sucking up food stamps and welfare while he's at it."

Harris wasn't in the mood to rehash a frequent discussion amongst cops. Instead, she steered things back to the case.

"We got nothing from forensics that helps," she summarized. "Autopsy is what we'd expect. The homeowners are clean as a whistle. Did any of Trotter's associates ping on your radar?"

"They all did. They're dirt bags."

"You know what I mean."

McNutt shrugged. "No, not really. Most of them had something dirty going on, you could tell, but I didn't get the feeling any were involved in our shoot."

Neither did Harris. She couldn't recall any tells that showed through in her interviews or mistakes in any statements that made her suspicious. It was looking more and more like the shooter wasn't one of Trotter's associates. Or at least one they'd interviewed.

"What do we have? A follow up interview with Ocampo in a couple of days, Zielinski's interview and then Ty Garrett's interview. What else?"

"We could go back and re-canvass. Expand the boundaries. But that's pretty much it. Unless you want to check in with the Honey Badger for advice."

Harris scowled. She would have to give Clint an update but preferred to limit it to that. "Let's head back to the station. I want to set up a time to interview Zielinski and to start prepping my questions for Garrett's interview. Would you call Dale Thomas, the union president for SPD? Tell him I want to interview Garrett as soon as possible once his seventy-two is up."

"You bet."

Cassidy stared out the passenger window as the homes of northern Spokane flitted by, wondering if she was actually going to get to the bottom of this incident, or if the whole thing was bottomless.

WEDNESDAY

Three can keep a secret, if two of them are dead.
—Benjamin Franklin, a United States Founding Father

Chapter 32

Ty Garrett stood in front of the out-processing deputy, Rob Utley, who handed him a brown paper bag that had been sealed and taped. When he'd been in-processed, Garrett had to remove all of his personal items and put them into that bag.

Utley's bald head shone under the fluorescent lights. He was a fat man whose girth and poor attitude had led him to a position with the least amount of activity and minimal contact with normal citizenry.

The deputy read from the list on his clipboard, "Khaki shorts, blue T-shirt, white shoes, socks..."

Utley droned on while Garrett opened the bag and removed his clothing. Inside the bag was another envelope with his smaller contents: wallet, watch, and house keys. The wallet contained fifty-three dollars in cash, a couple credit cards, and his driver's license. He'd left his phone at home on purpose when he was arrested.

Utley eyed Garrett with suspicion and a slightly curled lip as he verified the contents of the paper bag.

"Got something to say?" Garrett asked.

"Not to you." Utley sneered and dropped the clipboard on the counter. "Sign there for your stuff. When you're done, there's a restroom over there where you can change. Leave the jail issued clothing on the shelf."

Garrett looked to where Utley was pointing then nodded. There was no sense in arguing with the fat man, so he signed his name, took his clothing and left.

When he stepped outside the jail, Garrett faced the Public Safety Building, which had felt like his second home for a decade and where his brothers and sisters were still working. He knew some of them might see him if they were sitting near the windows of the detectives' office. He considered walking out of the compound the back way, but that would walk him along the windows of Mahogany Row where the chief's and captains' offices were.

Instead he headed right through the general parking lot where officers arrived throughout the day with suspects to book into jail. Garrett kept his head down and didn't see anyone he knew. He walked into the nearby neighborhood, taking side streets until he ended up at a 7-11.

Garrett purchased a pre-paid cell phone and a Red Bull. After he paid with his credit card, he asked the kid behind the counter for the number of a taxi company.

Outside he made the phone call, confirmed they took credit cards and gave them his address. Ten minutes and a Red Bull later, a white SpoCab arrived and Garrett slid into the back seat.

The driver, an aging white man in a white shirt and bow tie, eyed Garrett with caution. "Where to?"

Garrett gave him his address on the Five Mile Prairie. Whether it was the address or the length of the fare, the driver smiled.

The drive took roughly ten minutes and Garrett let his mind wander to earlier events of the day.

He appeared in court at 9 a.m., the first case on the docket.

He had expected to be represented by a public defender, since it was only first appearance, but Pastor Al Norris had arranged an attorney for him. He had worked with a group in the local community to raise support for Garrett's defense. Regardless of the video of the assault, several affluent members of the black community had been willing to come to his aid after Norris' request. They hired Pamela Wei, a five-foot-two ball of indignation out of Seattle with both a courtroom and a media pedigree. Wei took her time getting into the courtroom to brief Garrett, instead spending time with several reporters in the hallway. She wore a dark blue pantsuit and high heels. Her black hair fell past her shoulders.

"There are only words four words I need to hear from you today," she told him without greeting, right before the bailiff called for all to rise. "Those words are 'thank you, Your Honor.' That's it. Got it?"

Garrett nodded.

When the proceedings started, the judge read off the charges Garrett was booked under. Wei immediately requested that Garrett be released on his own recognizance.

"Justification, Counselor?" the judge asked by rote.

"Your Honor, Mr. Garrett is a long-standing member of this community. He has deep family ties. His employment history is consistent throughout his adult life, even while he was attaining his college degree at a local university. His life has been one of service to the people of Spokane. We acknowledge that the charges against him are felonies but not even the most cynical of people can believe Mr. Garrett is a flight risk. In fact, Mr. Garrett is extraordinarily eager for the opportunity to publicly answer to these specious charges and to clear his good name." She sat down and glanced over at the prosecutor, waiting.

The prosecutor shuffled a couple of papers and cleared his throat. "Uh, Your Honor, the state recognizes defense counsel's argument. Mr. Garrett was booked into jail based on the probable cause of the arresting detective. However, as of this morning, no probable cause affidavit had been filed pursuant to this arrest."

Wei sat up straighter in her chair, as if poised to rise.

The judge looked down at the prosecutor with a trace of irritation. "Then am I to understand that you are dropping the charges, Counselor?"

Garrett's heart raced at those words, but the exhilaration lasted only a moment.

"No, Your Honor. Since we haven't received the paperwork from the police department, the state has no choice but to request that Mr. Garrett be held until my office can coordinate with investigators on this matter."

The judge cast a withering look at the prosecutor. "I will not deny a man his freedom so that you can get your paperwork in order, Counselor."

"Yes, Your Honor."

The judge turned back to Wei. "Anything further from the defense?"

Wisely, Wei said, "No, Your Honor."

"Then it is the ruling of this court that the defendant, Tyler John Garrett, is hereby released from custody. All charges in this matter remain unresolved, and the state may file said charges with the court at a later time in accordance with state law and court rules. This hearing is over."

Wei patted Garrett on the forearm.

"Thank you, Your Honor," Garrett said.

While Pamela Wei reveled in the media spotlight, Garrett was quietly ushered back to his cell to gather his things.

Garrett refocused as the taxi entered his neighborhood. Up ahead he saw an unmarked car sitting in front of his house.

"Keep driving," Garrett said.

"What?"

"Drive on by the address I gave you. I'll give you a new location in a minute."

Garrett slowly sunk down in the back seat until he was eye level with the car door. As the taxi passed the unmarked patrol car, he saw two detectives sitting inside.

Talbott and Pomeroy.

The taxi left the neighborhood and Garrett pushed upright in his seat.

"Are you in some kind of trouble?" the driver asked, looking at Garrett in the rearview mirror.

"No."

"Those were cops back there."

"I know. I'm a police officer, too."

The driver looked at him several times in the rearview mirror. "You're that guy on TV."

Garrett looked at met his gaze in the mirror. "Is that a problem?" he asked, his voice challenging.

"Not for me. I hate the police. No offense."

Garrett looked out the window. "None taken."

The taxi dropped him off at the corner of Fourth and Thor. Garrett put his back against a nearby building and dialed a number he'd called for years, hoping the friend would answer a call from this number.

He picked it up after the third ring. "Hello?"

"Hey, buddy, it's Ty."

Ray Zielinski inhaled audibly. "Oh, man. Uh, how are you?"

"I've been better."

"Yeah, I'll bet."

"Hey, can we meet? I need to talk."

"I can't," Zielinski said.

Garrett closed his eyes. "Why not?"

"I'm scheduled for an interview with the county detective on your shooting. It probably wouldn't look good if we were seen together right before that. People might think we were getting a story together or something."

"Yeah, I guess you're right." Garrett sighed, then asked. "At least tell me how things are going inside the department right now. I'm frozen out."

"It's bad, man. The whisper stream says you're untouchable. Detectives are talking to your friends and associates, right now. They called me in yesterday and interviewed me. Asked me if I knew that you were into drugs."

"Who's leading that charge?"

"Talbott."

Garrett opened his eyes, watching traffic as it passed.

"Some are saying it's a witch hunt, but it's got a lot of guys worried. When you get called in and a detective starts poking at your life, you never know, right?"

"Yeah, you never know."

Zielinski remained silent on the other end of the line. Garrett could sense something going on with the veteran officer. "What gives, Ray? Are you buying into Talbott's line of crap?"

"No."

"Then what is it?"

"It's just...a couple of things got me wondering, is all."

"Like what?"

Zielinski cleared his throat. "Like why didn't you call for back up, for starters?"

"For *starters?* There's more?"

"Yeah, I guess there is, if I'm being honest. I wonder what you saw that made you shoot at Trotter. Why you charged the shooters in the house and why didn't you turn on the dash cam?"

"You're kidding me, right?"

"No," Zielinski said, but his voice wavered slightly.

Garrett shook his head in disbelief and anger. "I thought you knew me better than that, Ray. Hell, I thought I knew *you* better. Someone's coming after me, I need help, and all you can do is doubt me."

"They're just questions. No big deal."

"Just questions, huh?" Garrett made no attempt to keep the sarcasm out of his voice.

"Yeah," Zielinski said. "Just things I was wondering about."

"You know what I wonder?" Garrett asked.

"What?"

A long moment of silence filled the airwaves between them. Garrett could hear Zielinksi's breathing on the other end.

"Never mind," Garrett said finally, and ended the call.

Garrett crossed the street and entered Oak's Barbershop. A young man was seated in one of the chairs while a barber cut his hair. James Brown's "The Payback" played on the old stereo located in the middle of the shop. The barber sang along tunelessly with Brown as he cut the young man's hair.

In the corner, an older gentleman sat reading *Sports Illustrated*. He looked up from his magazine and smiled automatically at Garrett. When he realized who he was smiling at, he tossed the magazine on the table to his side and stood.

Delmar Oakley, who was just months from seventy years old, hurriedly walked to the front of the store. He wrapped his arms around Garrett and held him tightly. Garrett hugged him back. When they broke the embrace, Oakley held the younger man by the arms and smiled. "Garrett, what are you doing here?"

Oakley refused to call Garrett by either his first or middle names. Garrett never understood why when he was younger, but as he grew older he assumed it was because the names were a little too pale for Oakley's liking.

"I had nowhere else to go," Garrett said. "I figured it was time to come home."

Oakley said, "Let's go into the back and talk."

They sat in the small kitchenette at the rear of the building. Oakley poured them both a glass of unsweetened tea.

"Why do you drink it this way?" Garrett asked.

"Sugar ruins the taste, son. It's better this way."

Garrett sipped the tea again and cringed. "Oak, you're ruining the experience."

Oakley pulled out a couple sugar packets from a drawer and tossed them on the small table. "Here you go, poison yourself. Now tell me what's going on."

Garrett laid out the events of his life, from the shooting to his release, including the recent news that there was now a witch-hunt within the department. As he told the story, Oakley listened attentively, exactly how he used to do whenever he told him stories about school. When he was finished, Garrett said, "Now, I've got to figure out what to do. I didn't do anything wrong."

"You know it isn't always about wrong and right. Sometimes it's about black and white."

Garrett nodded. "I feel boxed in and I don't know why these people have turned against me."

"It's clear you've only got one choice, son."

"What's that?"

"The other brother in this mess," Oakley said, tapping his finger on the table for emphasis. "He's the only one looking out for you, right?"

Garrett shook his head. "He's not looking out for me, Oak. He's doing his job."

"If he's doing his job the *right* way, the *honest* way, then he's looking out for you."

Garrett ran his finger around the rim of his glass, thinking about Oakley's words.

"You should call him, Garrett. He's the only one who will give you a fair shake."

The younger man sipped his tea and then nodded. "I'll call him because you said so, Oak. I've always appreciated your guidance."

Oakley patted his hand. "Good, good. Now, it's my turn. Can I ask you a question?"

"Sure."

"How's your mother?"

Garrett smiled. "You ol' dog. Why don't you just go and see her?"

Oakley waved his hand dismissively. "She'll never give me the time of day. She's never gotten over your father's passing. Even when you'd come and hang out in the shop with us, she never took to me. Probably because of all the bad lessons you kept picking up around here."

Garrett shrugged. "I was an impressionable child. You should have been more careful with the things you said around me."

"Remember that time you went home and asked her what 'popping a cherry' meant?"

Garrett laughed. "She lost her mind when I told her I heard it from you."

"She came down here, waggled her finger in my face, and told me that I was corrupting a future leader of this city. I swear I fell in love with that woman that very day."

"You never told her, though."

Oakley's look became pensive. "She's city council and I'm the council of chairs. It's different levels, son. She had no interest in me. It didn't fit in with her plans. It's okay, though. There were plenty of ladies along the way."

"The legend of Oak," Garrett said, playfully shaking his shoulders.

"It grows bigger every year."

They both laughed loudly.

When Oakley left him to attend to a customer, Garrett took a business card from his wallet and dialed the number on it. He left a message and hung up.

Less than two minutes later his phone rang.

"Hello?"

"Is this Ty Garrett?" the gravelly voice asked.

"Yeah. Wardell?"

"Yes."

Garrett hesitated before asking, "Are you available to talk?"

Chapter 33

For twenty-five minutes, Lieutenant Dan Flowers paced his office, fuming. He'd called Talbott and ordered him back to the station, but the detective seemed to be taking his sweet time. Every minute that went by, Flowers' anger increased, along with the queasy feeling in the pit of his stomach.

Texting Cody Lofton with a succinct update had done nothing to make him feel better. Neither did his short phone conversation with Captain Farrell.

"Find out what the hell happened!" Farrell had barked at him. "The chief is all over my ass about this and I don't have answers."

"Neither do I," Flowers told him.

"Get them!"

The line disconnected, but the image in his mind was one of Farrell slamming down the phone.

So, he called Talbott then he paced.

He was the commander of the Major Crimes Unit, so ultimately anything that happened on any robbery, rape, serious assault, or homicide case was his responsibility. Running the unit sometimes felt like herding feral cats. Cops were strong-willed, Type-A people for the most part already, and once they got a gold shield some detectives amped up the superiority factor. Add the prestige of MCU and they sometimes believed they were untouchable. Butch Talbott definitely fell into that category, and since they'd become partners, Justin Pomeroy was exhibiting some of the same behaviors.

As Flowers moved around his office, trying to bleed off his anger and anxiety, he sensed another emotion lurking underneath. Frustration. He was responsible for the results and actions of his detectives, but he didn't have absolute control over their actions or whether they achieved results. In a way, it seemed unfair. More than that, it seemed unduly difficult.

How hard is it to file a charging request? he raged silently. It was something that every detective did any time they had developed charges.

His cell phone buzzed, and he checked it. It was a text from Lofton.

How could this happen? Fix it.

Great, Flowers thought. Garrett shoots a guy in the back, gets into an ugly fight that is videoed, might be a drug dealer on the side, his own detectives dick up the charging paperwork, and somehow all of this was his fault.

By the time Talbott rapped on his door and strolled in with Pomeroy, Flowers was seething with anger.

"You rang, El Tee?"

"What are you doing here?" Flowers asked the junior detective.

Pomeroy looked from the lieutenant to his partner and back. "I thought you wanted us both."

"Poms and I were just pulling into the parking lot," Talbott said. "I told him you wanted to see us. Was I wrong?"

Flowers shook his head, anger building. "Get in here and close the door."

As soon as Pomeroy shut the office door behind him, Flowers launched into a tirade. He'd planned some of it in his head while he waited, but it didn't come out exactly as he hoped. His anger and frustration got in the way of structure and cogency. Still, it felt good to rail at them both, and some of the tension he was experiencing dissipated. By the end of it, he'd wanted the paint to be curling off the walls of his office. Instead, Talbott stood impassively, seemingly unaffected. Behind him, Pomeroy shifted nervously.

Flowers stared at Talbott, trying to add an exclamation point to his rant. Then he growled, "Explain yourself, Detective."

Talbott turned his hands up. "Is this a performance counseling, Lieutenant?"

"What the hell does that mean?"

"I'm just wondering if I need a union rep in here, that's all."

Flowers shook his head, his anger flaring. "Don't try to deflect. Garrett didn't get charged. He's out of jail. I'm getting questions about why, and I don't have answers. Give me the damn answer!"

Talbott pursed his lips. "All right, sir. I've got a few answers for you."

"Good."

"For starters, why do we need to write the charging affidavit in the first place? Everywhere else in the state, the prosecutor does that, but in this county—"

"We're not here to argue the process."

"Maybe we should. Poms and I are trying to investigate a case. We need to be out in the field doing that, not stuck at our desk doing a lawyer's job. They've got all the information they need in our preliminary report. Any lawyer can type out an affidavit as easily as we can. Hell, they're the ones who've been to law school."

"They need more complete information."

"Not to charge. The threshold for the prosecutor to formally charge is the same as it is for us to arrest—probable cause."

"No, it's not," Flowers snapped. "And you know it. The prosecutor has to believe that he can prove the case beyond a reasonable doubt."

"That's their own self-imposed ridiculous guideline," Talbott countered. "The law says probable cause, and they can charge on PC."

Flowers shook his head. He'd had long conversations about this with the prosecutor's office, and knew that while Talbott was technically right, he was wrong for all practical purposes.

"Their code of ethics is clear on this point. The lawyer must reasonably believe—"

"Code of ethics? From a lawyer? Are you kidding me, El Tee?"

Flowers waved away the entire subject. "Enough. The process is the process. Why didn't you get the charging request over to the prosecutor?"

Talbott exchanged a look with Pomeroy, then back to Flowers. He motioned to the chairs in front of the lieutenant's desk. "Mind if we sit down?"

Flowers shrugged. Anything to get an answer.

Both men sat. Talbott leaned forward in his chair, interlacing his fingers. "Listen, Lieutenant. You're right. We should've got the paperwork in, and we didn't."

"Why not?"

"Strategy."

Flowers hesitated, a little confused. He walked around his desk and settled into his own chair, his mind whirring. "What do you mean?"

"We think Garrett is dirty, but he's not using. He's trafficking. I'll bet my retirement that the tox screen on his blood from the night of the shooting comes back clean."

Flowers would normally have a hard time believing any of that, but he saw the drugs under the sink with his own eyes. "Charge him then. Your case is solid, right?"

"We think so. They'll appeal on Fourth Amendment issues, but we were in the house legally. I had permission to use the bathroom. Opening the cabinet to get a towel was a reasonable act, and so the discovery will hold up."

Flowers shook his head, still confused. "Then why not..."

"Here's the thing," Talbott said. "There are still going to be people who believe he didn't do it. I mean, it's his house, his bathroom, but certain people out there still won't believe it. They'll say I planted it there for who knows what whacked out reasons they come up with, or that some nefarious 'they' somehow managed to break into his house and put it there for me to find. It'll be straight out of a Ward Clint conspiracy theory. Hell, with the Ninth Circuit's track record, they might be able to win on appeal with that lame argument."

Flowers stared at him. This was the most elaborate excuse he'd ever heard for why a detective messed up his paperwork.

"So," Talbott said, "Poms and I decided we needed more. We weren't going to get that if Garrett was sitting in jail awaiting trial."

It took a second for Talbott's words to sink in. "Wait. You did this *on purpose*?"

Talbott nodded. "We needed Garrett out of jail. To see what he'd do."

"You're kidding me!"

"No."

"This...this is just..." Flowers searched for words to express what he was feeling.

"Think about it, El Tee. Garrett's under a lot of pressure. He'll make a mistake, and hopefully we'll be there when he does."

Flowers blinked, thinking it through. "You think all of this is connected somehow? The shooting, all of it?"

Talbott shrugged. "I can't say for sure. Maybe it's all coincidence. It makes a certain kind of sense, doesn't it?"

"It could," Flowers admitted, unsure.

"Either way, if he's out and about, and he's dirty, something's gotta give. We get a better picture, and we get evidence to shore up the case."

Flowers considered it. Then he asked, "Where were you when I called?"

"Sitting off Garrett's place, hoping to get an eye on him."

Flowers felt a surge of guilt. The last thing a good leader did was get in the way of the men and women who were doing the job. The guilt was immediately replaced with frustration and anger once again. "Why didn't you bring this to me?" he demanded. "You can't just make a plan like this and not involve management."

Talbott and Pomeroy exchanged another glance before Talbott answered. "A couple of reasons."

"I'd like to hear them."

"You read the paper?"

"Of course."

"Then you've seen the stories in there about this case and the shooting."

"Yes. So, what?"

"So, with the information they've got, it's obvious there's some kind of a leak around here."

Flowers said nothing. He hoped the warmth he felt on his face wasn't showing.

"I don't know if they're getting their info from city hall or the department," Talbott continued, "but it doesn't matter. The details originate with us, regardless of what point downstream they get shared."

"You don't trust me," Flowers said as convincingly as he could.

"It's not you," Talbott said, "but somewhere up the line, there's a security issue. We couldn't afford for this to get out. There's one more thing, too."

"What's that?"

"We're protecting you, El Tee."

Flowers gave him a surprised look. "Me? How?"

"Well, you and the admin. By tanking the paperwork, it's all on Poms and me. We screwed up. Garrett's out because of us. You can tell it that way all the way up the line, including city hall."

Flowers realized Talbott was right. It would work. He imagined there'd be a little bit of pain in it, but nothing insurmountable.

"While we're waiting for Garrett to slip up and show us who he really is, you and all the brass are insulated. It's on us, not you. You have plausible deniability. Later on, if things go right, we can say you knew all along, but if things don't..." He trailed off with a shrug. "A couple of dumb ass detectives dropped the ball. You write us a formal reprimand or something, and it's done."

Flowers looked to Pomeroy. "You support what he's saying?"

Pomeroy glanced at Talbott, then looked back to the lieutenant. "Yes, sir. Definitely. Just as he said."

Flowers studied them both. He felt a surge of pride that these two were willing to have their own reputations damaged for the good of the department and their superiors, all in the interests of solving a case. This was the kind of selflessness he wished he saw more often.

"Gentlemen," he said, "carry on."

Chapter 34

Garrett waited in the back of the barbershop for Clint. The detective told him it'd be an hour before he could make it to the location, and Garrett was content to sit and wait in the comfortable confines of what had once been a second home to him. He thumbed through a couple of outdated magazines. The newest issues were out front for paying customers.

A steady stream of old school music had played through the shop for the hour. Several songs from fifties blues to seventies funk. Oakley had several mix tapes that customers still brought him. He refused to jump to the digital era and his customers were more than happy to oblige.

Oakley pushed aside the curtain to the back area and poked his head in. "Somebody's here to see you, son."

Garrett was surprised. Clint had made good time.

But it wasn't Clint who brushed past Oakley into the back room. Instead, the large frame of Bo Sherman took up the space. "Hey, brother."

"Hey, man." Garrett rose to greet him. A slight uneasiness filled his gut, but he tried not to show it. The two clasped hands easily and engaged in a quick, manly half-embrace with their free arms. "How'd you know I was here?"

Sherman chuckled. "Doesn't take a rocket scientist, my man. You weren't at your house. You aren't going to bring this weight on your moms. Where else are you gonna go but the world-famous Oak's?"

Garrett spread his hands. "Here I am." He looked closer at Sherman, waiting for the bigger man to make the next move. "How about you?" he asked. "You on the job?"

"Nah, I mean, you and I both know we're always on the job, that's just how it is, but right now is just about Bo needing to talk to Ty."

"All right."

Sherman gave him a meaningful look. "I'm serious, man. You see me in a uniform? No. And I'm all by myself. I'm not even packing."

Garrett looked him up and down, not seeing a gun anywhere. "Uh-uh," he finally said. "No way you're not strapped. What is it, an ankle holster?"

Sherman laughed, holding up his hands. "All right, all right. You got me. But that don't mean anything, and you know it."

"I believe you, Bo. What do you want?"

Sherman settled into the chair across from Garrett's, so Garrett sat, too. "I'm just checking up on you," he said. "Things are getting crazy, you know?"

"Tell me about it."

"Anything I can do?"

"I don't know. What can you tell me?"

"Not much. The word is, number one, don't talk about this. Number two, you might be dirty."

"That's not true!"

"I hear you, brother, but it isn't playing well."

They were both quiet for a time. Then Sherman said, "You know, I never did get a chance to thank you."

"*Thank* me? For what?"

"Before you came on, I was pretty much the only black man the department had. Oh, they had Clint, but he ain't exactly the type you trot out at community meetings, is he? And there was Tammy Preston, but she was covering the female thing. That left me. Anytime they needed to show diversity, they'd call up Bo. Photo ops, block watch, school talks, the whole damn thing. You know what I mean?"

Garrett nodded. "I guess it comes with the territory."

"I guess, but once you hit the academy, they eased off me. Besides, you were a homegrown kid, which was perfect for them. Since I lateraled from Chicago I'm sure they were always a little bit nervous that it'd turn out I was dirty back there, or gangster, right?" He chuckled. "Folk Nation or some such."

Garrett didn't laugh.

"Anyway," Sherman continued, "you were what you were and so they started throwing a lot of that extra work your way. I was glad to be done with it, even though I will admit I missed the overtime pay. I got to focus on doing patrol work, and it gave me more family time, too. I gotta say thanks for that, man. Truly."

"I'm glad it worked out that way," Garrett said.

Sherman nodded slowly. "How things work out is a funny thing sometimes."

"Yeah, well, I'm not laughing right now."

"I hear you. Being a symbol for something is a heavy weight." He paused, then said, "You know, in a way, they were right."

"Who?"

"The brass. All the white shirts. About Chicago."

Garrett stared at Sherman. "Man, if you're about to confess something, I really don't want to hear it."

Sherman smiled slightly. "Nah, man, I'm not dirty and I sure as hell ain't gangster. But Chicago *is* a whole different world than Spokane. Different people, different city. Different crooks and different cops."

"Yeah?"

"For sure. Back there, it's not a question of whether or not there are some dirty cops. It's just a matter of figuring out which few they are. Here in Spokane, though?" Sherman shook his head. "Most everyone is a damn boy scout, and I like it that way."

"That's not how people are seeing me right now."

"True, but that's the media and civilians. What do they know? I mean, really? You and I do this job, and we know what's what. You ever seen another cop be dirty since you've been here? I'm not talking bending a rule here or cutting a corner. I mean, flat out *dirty*."

Garrett considered, then shrugged. "No, I guess not."

"Me neither. Chicago was different that way." He thought about it, then said, "The way business is done there is a lot different, too."

"Different how?"

"Darker," Sherman said. "Deeper. Everything is politics."

"Why are you telling me this?"

"Because what I've been seeing over these past two days is an awful lot like what I saw back home." He gave Garrett a grave look. "You mentioned the way this is playing in the media. There's that, and the moves that city hall and the brass are making, too. It all smells just the same."

Garrett lowered his head and shook it mournfully. "I didn't do anything wrong."

"That won't matter," Sherman said. "Did you see that last press conference?"

"No."

"The mayor is losing it. The eyes of the nation are on little old Spokaloo, and his seat is getting hot. Same for the chief. Public opinion is turning against you."

"He shot at *me*," Garrett whispered, "and those men attacked *me*."

"And the dope ain't yours," Sherman finished.

"It isn't."

"I believe you, man, but this ain't about truth. This is just like Chicago. It's about what plays. Who survives and who doesn't. And trust me on this one—when it comes down to it, those sons-of-bitches wearing suits will offer you up as a sacrifice to whatever gods rule the day."

Garrett took a deep, wavering breath and let it out.

Sherman reached out and clapped a strong hand on his shoulder and gave him a squeeze. "Sorry to have to speak such hard truths, brother. I didn't want you caught by surprise."

Garrett nodded his head. "Thanks, man."

"You got it."

"No one else…" he trailed off, surprised at how the words caught in his throat. "No one…"

"You don't have to say anymore." Sherman patted his shoulder and gave it another squeeze.

"You should go," Garrett said thickly. "There's no reason you should get caught up in this mess."

Sherman laughed ironically. "Hell, man. I've already been mistaken for you three times. I'm caught in this mess same as the whole entire country."

Garrett laughed with him. It wasn't quite a real laugh, but it still felt good. "Thanks," he repeated.

"You'll get through this."

"I will."

"Stay strong and stay safe."

"I'll do my best," Garrett assured him.

Chapter 35

Detective Wardell Clint parked around the corner from the barber shop and took the alley. He gave three sharp raps on the back door and waited. A few moments later, the elderly face of Delmar Oakley appeared through a crack in the door.

"You here to help?"

"That's my job description."

"Don't lip me, son. It's an honest question."

Clint looked at him evenly. "*He* called *me*. I'm here alone. What you want me to do, swear on a stack of bibles?"

Oakley scowled slightly but opened the door for him. Clint stepped through. Garrett sat nearby, looking like a trapped animal. Oakley closed the door and crossed his arms, standing protectively.

"You going to arrest me?" Garrett asked.

"Should I?"

"Why not? It already happened once."

"Not by me," Clint said, "but at some point, I might not have a choice."

Garrett looked suspicious. "How's that?"

"Part of the reason it took me so long to get here was because I was at the station. It looks like the department is putting you on administrative suspension until this thing with the drugs and the fight is completely investigated."

"Damn," Garrett breathed.

"Dale Thomas didn't call you?"

"I don't have my phone."

Clint's eyes shifted to the cell phone on the table in front of Garrett.

Garrett followed his gaze. "It's a pre-paid. I picked it up after they released me. I left my personal phone at the house when they...when they arrested me."

"Well, I'm sure Mister Union President is blowing up that other phone with messages."

"I guess I should've seen this coming."

"Probably."

"It's just...I thought they'd stand behind me. I've done everything right. And none of this is my fault. As soon as I get to be inconvenient, they abandon me."

"That's their way," Clint said.

"It's not right."

"Don't be naive."

Garrett looked at him, his eyes shining with anger. "I thought you were here to help me."

"I suppose I am. Look, all of this is moving too fast. Everyone's scrambling to cover their own ass, and no one is asking *why*. Why did any of this happen?"

"Timing. Bad luck."

"It may have started that way, but there's something more at work now. They are hanging you out to dry." He took out a stick of gum and popped it in his mouth. "The county is looking for you, too. They want to interview you about the shooting as soon as your seventy-two expires. Their lead detective, Harris, told me."

"Man, I can't talk to them right now. Not with all this other stuff going on. My head's all twisted around."

"Then don't."

"I have to. If I don't cooperate, then I look guilty. I'm screwed either way."

Clint said nothing.

"I don't know what to do," Garrett said. "I'm afraid to go home. I don't know who to trust."

"Talk to Dale Thomas. Or that high priced mouthpiece you had at first appearance."

"Wei?" Garrett considered. "Yeah, she might know the best thing to do."

"Or talk to both, but don't trust them completely. Don't trust anyone completely."

Garrett let out a long sigh. "Man, you are a depressing guy. Anyone ever tell you that?"

"If they did, I didn't bother listening."

Garrett chuckled slightly in spite of himself.

"Excuse me," Oakley said. "I have a question."

Clint turned his gaze to the barber.

"He asked earlier if you were going to arrest him. You said you might not have a choice. What's that mean?"

"It means that I think the prosecutor and those two clowns Talbott and Pomeroy will eventually get their act together and charge him for the assault, and for the drugs."

"It'll never stick," Garrett said.

"Maybe not. They'll charge it up either way. There's too much public pressure."

"Seems to me," Oakley said, his voice sound tired and angry at the same time, "we're still lynching black men in this country even today. The only thing that's changed is the rope."

Clint nodded in agreement. "It's an ugly thing," he said, "but it goes deeper than that."

"Deeper?" Garrett asked. "We talking conspiracy now?"

"Conspiracy is everywhere, if you look with a critical eye. I'm not talking about that. Black is one color that matters here, no doubt. There's another color in play, too."

Oakley gave him a perplexed look, but Garrett understood. "Blue," he said.

"Exactly." Clint was glad the kid was smart enough to see it. "City Hall has to worry about both issues. In some ways, the blue outweighs the black. The weight of the Philadelphia shooting, and every other police shooting in the country is part of what drives the response to yours. There's a lot of moving parts."

"I did my job," Garrett said, his jaw clenched.

He gave Garrett a hard, appraising look. "Look, I don't necessarily like you. I think you're a prima donna poster boy who played the game and got awful cozy with the white shirts along the way. However, I believe you. What they're doing to you isn't right. They don't care about figuring out the actual truth, and that flat out angers me. Something stinks about this whole situation and finding out the truth of the matter is the only way we figure out where the smell comes from. I don't give half a backward dump who gets what they got coming when that truth is discovered, even including you. I promise you this. I will find the truth."

"They say the truth will set you free," Garrett said quietly.

"I don't think we're gonna find that kind of truth."

Chapter 36

"I've been waiting to hear this for an hour and a half, Lieutenant," the chief said. "The mayor is climbing all over my ass. Tell me something good."

Farrell watched as Flowers swallowed nervously. Right then, he knew things were completely sideways.

"It's not good, sir."

Farrell should have known the answer to this before he and Flowers came to the chief's office. Things were breaking too fast, and he was cut out of the loop. He imagined he should feel lucky just to be in the meeting now.

Baumgartner clenched and unclenched his jaw. "Give it to me straight."

"We screwed up."

"We?"

"My detectives," Flowers clarified. "They got wrapped up in doing follow up and didn't get the paperwork done."

"Who?"

"Talbott and Pomeroy."

Farrell winced. He couldn't believe Flowers was throwing his men under the bus like that.

"Those are veteran detectives," the chief said.

"They are. However, this is a high-profile case, and Garrett's one of our own. It threw things off. They were focused on conducting follow up. Both thought the other one filed the charging request affidavit, and it fell through the cracks."

"That's a pretty major oversight!"

"I know."

Chief Baumgartner drummed his heavy fingers on his desk. "You're the commander of the Major Crimes Unit, aren't you?"

"Yes, sir."

"Ultimately, it is your responsibility."

Flowers blanched.

"And he walked," finished the chief. "It's your fault, right?"

"Yes, sir. Technically. But—"

"But nothing. Dan, if you can't run that unit, I will transfer you out and bring someone else in who can. Put you over at the garage in charge of making sure the hubcaps get polished."

Flowers swallowed. "Sir, our record—my record—we've done good work. This mistake—"

"Is massive. We're on the national stage here. Your detectives and their mistake makes us all look like Keystone Cops." He continued to drum his fingers.

Flowers remained silent. Farrell thought that was wise. The chief's temper wasn't something you wanted to invoke, and excuses, whether valid or not, were a frequent catalyst of that temper.

Finally, Baumgartner said, "I can't go to the mayor with 'mistakes happen.' How do we fix it?"

Flowers swallowed, obviously uncomfortable. "I…I think the best thing to do is let the investigation run its course. When it is completed, the prosecutor can decide whether or not charges are merited or not. They can direct file via affidavit. They don't need us to request charges. Technically."

"Technically?" the chief asked. "Normally, we do."

"Yes, sir."

"I wasn't asking," the chief snapped. "I've been on this job before you were a glint in the milkman's eye. I know how this place runs." He turned to Farrell. "Tom?"

Farrell thought about it before answering. "There's an advantage to what Dan is suggesting. It keeps us from appearing biased. If we request charges against Garrett, there's the risk of people thinking he's been persecuted because of his race. If we don't request charges, there's the risk of people thinking that it is a case of the police taking care of our own. Either way is bad for us."

"We just kick the can down the street," the chief said.

Farrell shrugged. He believed it was more like a game of Pass the Turd, but the chief's analogy worked, and the more you agreed with Chief Baumgartner when you could, the better things tended to go.

Baumgartner mulled it over, then shook his head. "I am so sick of politics."

Then you picked the wrong job, Farrell thought, but kept silent.

The chief heaved a heavy sigh. "Here's what we're going to do."

Chapter 37

Detective Cassidy Harris sat opposite SPD Officer Ray Zielinski. She activated her voice recorder, glanced at McNutt to make sure he was ready, then turned back to the officer. She knew Zielinski only by reputation, which was good. Truth be told, most of her experiences with SPD officers and detectives had been decent, and the agency seemed to have a lot of talent. That was part of what made dealing with Clint such a frustration. They could have landed virtually anyone else as a shadow and not had to worry about conspiracies or conflicts.

Zielinski was accompanied by Dale Thomas, the police union president. Harris didn't know Thomas, other than from his occasional media statement. He seemed affable, though it was clear he'd put on his game face for this interview.

Harris read the rote opening she always used to begin official interviews like this. She noted the date, the time, and who was present. She asked each person present to identify themselves and consent to being recorded so that anyone listening would know who was who. All three men followed her directions woodenly. With that out of the way, she launched into the interview.

"This interview is part of the ongoing investigation into the shooting death of Todd Trotter. Officer Zielinski, can you take me through the events as you recall them?"

Zielinski nodded, and began to describe how he responded to back up Garrett, then heard shots. Harris listened carefully, making an occasional note. Beside her, McNutt wrote nothing.

Her standard interview strategy was to walk the witness through the events as gently as possible the first time and elicit as much information as possible. Unless she absolutely had to, she didn't interrupt, only giving the witness mild nudges to keep the story rolling. If she encountered problems or issues in what she heard, she made note of them and circled back around to them rather than address them at the time.

This last piece drove McNutt crazy. He was like a pit bull in interviews, going for the jugular as soon as he felt like it was exposed. To his way of thinking, an interview was a battle to be won. Harris saw merit to his thinking when it came to a suspect interrogation, at least some of the time, but an interview was supposed to be a collaborative affair between the witness and the detective. For that reason, she'd asked McNutt to remain silent unless she specifically asked him to interject.

Zielinski didn't seem like a reluctant witness, but his guard was up. Maybe it was because Garrett was his friend and co-worker, or maybe this was just his "testimony" face. Either way, Harris could sense something there, below the surface.

Once Zielinski described arriving on scene and his interactions with Garrett, he stopped. Harris began circling back around to a few items of interest.

"You had your dash camera on, correct?"

"Yes."

"Is that standard?"

"It is for me."

"Is it automatic, though?"

"No," Zielinski said. "Whenever I hit my lights, I hit the camera, too. The button is right there. Besides, it's policy."

"Was Officer Garrett's camera activated?"

"How can he know that?" Dale Thomas interjected.

Harris shrugged. "I'm not familiar with the system." She looked at Zielinski. "Is there a way to tell?"

Zielinski shifted in his seat before answering. "Yes. There's a small red light that comes on when it's recording. You can see it through the windshield."

"Did you notice if Officer Garrett's light was on?"

"I didn't really notice it at first, but when he went back to get his flashlight, he turned it on."

"What did you think of that?"

"Okay," Thomas broke in again. "I'm going to stop you there. What he thought isn't a matter of evidence."

Harris gave Thomas a cool stare. "Counselor, you're free to express your objection by stating 'exception' for the record, but I can ask any question I see fit to ask. Officer Zielinski is a witness here, not a suspect."

"Witness or suspect, he has rights."

"I'm not violating them."

Thomas made a slightly pained expression. "Ehhh…you're coming awfully close."

"I'll answer," Zielinski said.

"You don't have to," Thomas told him.

Yes, you do, Harris thought, but she held her tongue.

"It's all right." Zielinski turned to Harris. "The answer is, I don't know why it wasn't already on."

"Why do you think?"

"Now you're asking him to speculate," Thomas argued.

Harris ignored him, keeping her eyes locked on Zielinski.

The veteran officer leaned back in his chair. He looked at her and McNutt and shook his head. "I don't know." He glanced at Thomas, then continued. "I've been thinking about this a lot today, and that's the best I can do. I don't know. What I do know is that Ty Garrett's been a good platoon mate for years. I know he takes his calls for service without complaining, and he does a good job on them. He's always there when I ask for back-up, and he knows tactics. He's a family man, and he cares about the community we work in. He takes it personally when someone does crime in East Central. In the last couple of days, it seems like everyone has forgotten about all of that." Zielinski paused, then added, "Me included."

"Officer—" Harris began.

"My guess is he forgot, Detective. He's human, just like the rest of us, and he forgot. He made a mistake."

Harris was quiet as she looked over at McNutt. He didn't meet her gaze, but he had a strange expression on his face, one that mirrored Zielinski's.

She heard a buzz and followed the sound to Dale Thomas' phone. The union president glanced down at the screen, then vaulted to his feet. "I've got to take this. I'll be right back." He answered on his way out of the room. "Hello? This is Dale."

When the door pulled shut, Harris turned back to Zielinski. She knew better than to try to continue the interview in the absence of the union president, but it didn't really matter. It was obvious to her that the interview was over.

"Thanks for coming in," she said. "I appreciate your honesty."

Zielinski gave her a tight-lipped nod before he rose and left the room.

Harris noted the time the interview concluded and snapped off the voice recorder.

"He's got a point, you know," McNutt said.

She considered reminding McNutt that he'd jumped on the "Garrett is dirty" bandwagon from the first moment they'd heard about the arrest for drugs, but let it go. Instead, she said, "Our responsibility is the shooting. Nothing more. We need to keep our investigation compartmentalized from whatever else is happening here."

"Which is what?"

"I don't know for sure," Harris answered.

Maybe I should ask Clint, she thought sarcastically.

Chapter 38

Ty Garrett stepped out the back of Oak's Barbershop and dialed the phone number Wardell Clint had given him. He'd waited long enough and had no doubt this call would be answered quickly.

Second ring. "Hello? This is Dale."

"Dale, it's Ty Garrett."

"Oh, man, am I glad to hear from you," Union President Dale Thomas said. "We've got to talk."

"Yeah, I know."

"You know?"

Garrett leaned against the building and stared at the ground. "I talked with Wardell. He told me about the administrative leave. They're hanging me out to dry, but I'm ready to talk to the county."

"Screw that, they've just filed the PC affidavit. Detective Pomeroy is getting the warrant signed now. Once that's done, they'll be coming for you."

"You're kidding me. I just had my first appearance and was released this morning."

"Word is Talbott and Pomeroy screwed up on the filing. The chief is on the warpath over this and blew up Flowers for it. He's using the affidavit and warrant to remind everyone this is his department, not the mayor's. Seems like you're getting dragged into some pissing match between him and city hall. Rumors are swirling that there could be some department realignments because of this."

Garrett pushed off the wall, his voice rising with anger. "That's not my problem. I hope heads roll since I'm the only one taking real heat in this whole debacle."

"Why don't you come to my office and I'll walk with you?"

"What are you talking about?"

"The warrant. Let's hit this head on."

"I'm not turning myself in."

"What?"

"You may have faith in this system, Dale. I'm fast losing it. I think I'm converting to the Wardell Clint vision of the world."

"Don't say that. We can figure this out."

"Keep thinking that, prez. Thanks for the heads up on the warrant. I'll be in touch."

Garrett walked back inside and found Delmar Oakley sitting at the table. The older man watched him with pursed lips. "You heard that conversation?"

"Most of it. Sounds like things just went from bad to worse."

"It most definitely did. I need to go, Oak. I can't stay here. Too many people know where I'm at now. They'll come looking and that means they'll be bothering you."

Oakley nodded. "I understand, son. Do you need anything from me? Some money?"

"I'm good with money, but I do need a favor, though."

"What's that?"

"You still got that snub nose in the drawer? The one under the cash register."

Oakley's eyes turned suspicious. "What do you need that for?"

Garrett shook his head. "I don't trust how things are working out. Someone is painting me into a corner. I've got a bad feeling about this."

"A gun doesn't solve anything."

"Then why do you have it?"

Oakley studied Garrett before nodding. "Okay," he said, then stood with a groan and walked out to the barbershop floor.

He talked with the other barber for a bit then he pulled open the drawer and discreetly removed the gun without the other barber noticing. When he returned, he handed Garrett a Smith & Wesson snub nose .38 and a box of shells. "I hope you don't need these."

Garrett opened the cylinder and saw six rounds inside. He put the revolver into the front pocket of his shorts and then looked around the kitchen area. He grabbed a small paper bag and put the shells inside. "I appreciate this, Oak."

"I've owned it for almost fifteen years and never fired it once," Oakley said. "I pray you don't have to use that."

"What the hell, T? I thought you were in jail?" the tall, white man said. His bald head and face were deeply tanned from the summer sun. He wore shorts, a white tank top, and flip-flops.

"Can I come inside?" Ty Garrett asked.

Derek Tillman smiled and waved him inside. "Oh, man, I'm sorry. I was surprised, is all. You've been all over the news lately."

Garrett had left Oak's barbershop through the back door and walked through the East Central neighborhood until he made it to an ATM near the corner of Sprague and Third. After he withdrew some cash, he placed a call to SpoCab and one arrived a few minutes later. When he slid into the back seat, he gave the driver an address in Liberty Lake, a small city east of Spokane. The cab took off immediately.

The driver, an Indian man, never made eye contact or conversation with him during the twenty-minute trip. When they arrived, Garrett paid for the ride with crisp twenties and walked up to the front door of the condominium.

Derek Tillman and Garrett had played high school basketball together. Tillman was good enough to get a scholarship at Eastern Washington University where their friendship continued to grow.

They walked through Tillman's condo and stopped at the television. Tillman had it turned to CNN which had a live update scrolling along the bottom of the screen along with the other headlines. One caught Garrett's eye. *Breaking — Spokane, WA—Arrest Warrant Issued for Police Officer Tyler Garrett.*

Tillman grabbed the remote and turned off the television. "I'm sorry about that."

"It's okay. I heard that it was coming."

"Let's go out on the deck," Tillman said with a jerk of his head toward the sliding glass doors

They sat on a couple of deck chairs overlooking the lake. "Want a beer?"

Garrett shook his head.

"Water?"

"I'm good."

"Destiny will be back in a bit. If there's something you want, I'll send her out for it."

Garrett raised his eyebrows. "Destiny?"

"She's the flavor of the week." Tillman smiled while using his hands to mime a set of large breasts. "Can't be tied down during lake season, you know that."

"She sounds like a stripper."

"How did you know?" Tillman said with a laugh. "She's perfect for this time of the year."

Garrett shook his head. "I don't know how you do it, D."

"It's the condo, man. Girls want to come out to the lake, ride the boat, and get drunk. They know the price of admission and I know my role. It's a symbiotic relationship while it lasts. After a while, they'll either trade up to one of the nicer houses on the lake or I'll push them down to the trailers. Either way, it's summer at the lake."

Garrett lifted his face to the sun.

"Enough about me, man. What the hell is going on with you?"

Garrett turned to Tillman and quickly relayed his story. When he was done, the two of them sat in silence. Eventually, Tillman let out a low whistle. "This is messed up, T. I mean, when you watch the news, it looks like you're the bad guy."

"That's how they're painting it. I make an easy target."

"That's some real crap." Tillman sounded indignant.

"It's a perfect storm," Garrett said. "First the shooting happens, then all the haters post my address on Facebook. That led to those two white power dudes attacking me. Then all this other stuff."

"It doesn't make sense."

Garrett said, "I'm getting set up. The way I've figured it, the guy I shot must be connected. It's the only thing that makes sense. From there, I don't know who is pulling the strings, but it involves dirty police."

"Here? I mean, I get it in L.A. and all, but…"

"There's a detective on the department I can trust. He's helping me figure this out, but I gotta disappear until we can do that. No one can know where I am, so I need a place to hide while we work things through."

"Where's Angie and the kids?"

"With her parents. I needed to know they were safe."

Tillman smiled and gestured toward the lake. "There's no sweeter place to hide than the lake, my friend. You can do it in style with lovely ladies and margaritas."

"I don't think Angie would approve," Garrett said.

"What she don't know…"

"How about a vacancy in one of your rentals?"

Tillman scrunched his face. "Sure, if you prefer that over this. Remember that rental house on Hoffman I bought? The one near the mall."

Garrett nodded.

"That's vacant, now. I just started turning it. If you want, you can stay there for a bit. There isn't anything inside, no furniture, I mean, but you can use it. I've got a sleeping bag you can take. There's a lockbox on the front door with a key inside for contractors. Code is 6969."

"That was your password in high school."

"Why change a good thing?" Tillman said with a laugh.

"I appreciate this, D."

Tillman's laugh faded. "Hey, man, I owe you. If you hadn't stood for me when that girl said what she said…" He trailed off, then shrugged. "I wouldn't have finished college, that's for sure. I'd be putting up jump shots in the penitentiary league, probably."

"She was out to get you. It was plain to see."

"Don't matter," Tillman said. "People might've believed her, 'cept for you speaking up for me. Saying what you said."

Garrett nodded that he understood. "People believe what they want to believe…" He motioned toward the darkened TV. "That."

"To hell with people. I know the truth."

"Thanks."

"You got it. Hey, are you *sure* you don't want to hang here at the lake?"

Garrett left the condo and walked over to a small, white Toyota pick-up alongside the road. Tillman had given him the keys to his spare rig, the one he used to do work around his rentals. Garrett promised to keep it safe and bring it back in a few days.

He opened the passenger door and tossed the sleeping bag in. He also put the small brown bag containing the shells on the floorboard.

"I took a chance and it looks like I won the lottery," a voice said behind him.

Ty slowly put his hands into shorts and straightened.

Detective Butch Talbott stared at him, his gun in his fist. "I was on my way down to that barbershop everyone knows you love so much. I saw you walk away and catch a cab. When I called the cab company, they were nice enough to tell me where they dropped you off. I guess they didn't want me coming down and digging through the records."

The door was between Talbott and him. "Where's your partner?" he asked.

"Does it matter?"

Garrett shook his head. "What game are you playing, Butch?"

"No game. It's been the same truth all along. I just took me some time to realize it. You helped me do that."

"How'd I do that?"

"You showed me I was replaceable."

"I don't understand."

Talbott waved his gun. "Very slowly, step out from behind the car door."

Garrett took a slow step to his right, exposing himself directly to Talbott. "You know people are probably watching us right now. I got myself jammed up by not taking that into consideration."

"It's okay. I'm not the one running from the law."

"I'm not running. I'm right here."

"Take your hands out of your pockets, Garrett."

Derek Tillman stepped out of his condo and hollered, "Yo! Is everything okay?"

Talbott looked at him and yelled, "Get back inside."

Garrett ducked and moved behind the open truck door.

Talbott saw the movement and fired twice, both rounds striking the open door. One round fully pierced the door, exploding the plastic armrest near Ty's head. Garrett freed the gun from his shorts, dropped to the ground and fired two shots upward at Talbott.

The detective stumbled backward before tripping on a landscaping rock. He crumpled to the ground and lay motionless.

Garrett quickly stood and looked around, searching for Detective Pomeroy. Not finding him, he ran around the truck, climbed into the driver's seat and started it. He glanced over to Tillman who was still on his porch, his eyes wide with shock. The tires chirped as the truck sped away.

Garrett drove eastbound on I-90, the opposite direction of where he wanted to go. It took him ten minutes to get to the Idaho border town of Post Falls. He stopped in the parking lot of a Super 1 grocery store and pulled out the disposable cell phone.

Wardell Clint answered on the second ring. "You need to stop calling me. The arrest warrant on you is official now, and Harris still wants to talk to you about the shooting as soon as—"

"I shot Butch Talbott."

"What did you say?" Clint's voice hardened.

"Talbott approached me. He drew without provocation and fired two shots. I returned fire."

"It's time to come in, Garrett."

"I don't know who to trust."

"I'll protect you," Clint said. "We have to get to the bottom of this mess and figure out who else is involved."

"Man, I trust you, but I don't believe you can protect me from this system or whoever is behind it."

There was a brief silence on the phone before Clint asked, "Where did this shooting occur?"

"Listen for the call, Detective. You'll know it when you hear it."

Chapter 39

Detective Clint rolled up to the crime scene, parking as close as he could get. He didn't care about stealth or getting a flavor for the scene. This wasn't going to be his case. It wasn't even inside his jurisdiction.

He spotted the Liberty Lake PD cruisers scattered around the block, and several state patrol vehicles tucked neatly against the condo, just outside the yellow tape. A crowd, small by Spokane standards, had gathered at the outer perimeter. People craned their necks for a glimpse of what was happening a half block away.

Clint wished Garrett had simply told him the shooting happened in Liberty Lake. If he hadn't flipped to "all-scan" on his radio, he'd have missed the call. Then he wouldn't have known about this until the media got its first, and likely wholly inaccurate, reports out there.

He pushed his way through the small crowd to the outer perimeter. He recognized the patrol officer with a clipboard that was guarding the tape as former SPD. Jerry Anderson was five feet ten inches tall and almost as broad. One might think that there was nothing but fat underneath that uniform, but Clint knew better. He'd worked with Jerry more than once and seen him in action. The man had the strength of a bear. Maybe a bear just about ready to winter, but still a bear. When the pace of the work in Spokane didn't mesh with his laid-back attitude toward life, he lateraled to Liberty Lake. Clint hadn't seen him since.

Jerry spotted him right away. His face broke into a smile, though part of it was obscured by his thick beard. "Wardell?"

Clint held out his hand. "Hey, Jerry."

Jerry took his hand and shook it vigorously. "Hey, man. Good to see you." Then he paused. "Uh, why are you here?"

Clint avoided the question. "You guys handling the investigation?"

Jerry hesitated, looking around. Then he motioned with his head for Clint to come closer, raising the yellow tape as he did so. Clint came into the crime scene and the two walked a few paces away, out of the gawkers' earshot.

"This is some bad mojo," Jerry told him. "The DOA is a cop. One of yours."

"Butch Talbott."

"I don't know his name, but Alan said it was definitely SPD." Jerry looked at him. "Wait. How do you know who it is?"

"They called me in to consult," Clint lied, feeling a twinge of shame at the deception. If Jerry had a single evil bone in his body, Clint was pretty sure it was a small one. But his immediate need overshadowed his relationship with Jerry.

"Alan asked for help?" Jerry said doubtfully.

"He called in state, too," Clint pointed out.

"Yeah, I suppose. But that's the OIS protocol."

Clint shrugged.

Jerry mulled it over for a second, then scratched Clint's name and the time on his crime scene log. He pointed to a gaggle of men most of a block away. "If you couldn't already tell, that's your guy there."

"Thanks, Jerry."

"No worries, man. Good to see you."

Clint gave him a comradely clap on the shoulder and headed up the street. As he drew near, he recognized some of the players. Alan Rogers was the Liberty Lake major crimes detective. As far as Clint was aware, the small city only had one, and he tended to work a lot of property crimes to fill his time. Clint only knew of him passingly and from what he'd seen, the guy suffered from the jurisdictional equivalent of small man's syndrome.

He didn't recognize two of the men in suits but figured them for State Patrol detectives. The chief of the Liberty Lake Police Department stood slightly apart from the other three, on his cell phone. Next to him, Clint was surprised to see Captain Tom Farrell.

It was Farrell who spotted him first. The captain's eyes narrowed, and he broke away from the group to approach him. "What the hell are you doing here, Ward?"

Clint didn't bother correcting him on his name. "I heard the call on the radio. Thought it might be important that I see what was what." His second lie, but this one was easier than the one he told Jerry.

"What, do you scan all police frequencies?"

"Don't you?"

Farrell looked at him, considering. Clint let him, knowing his reputation would work in his favor here. Finally, Farrell said, "What made you think you needed to know something about this?"

"Come on, Captain. SPD detective gets shot? With all that's been going on this week?"

"How'd you know who the victim is? That didn't go out over the air."

Clint smiled mildly. "Captain, we both know that ComSec is pretty weak, especially when you get multiple jurisdictions involved. The word is out there, and I heard it."

Farrell scowled, but didn't argue the point.

"What does it matter?" Clint continued. "I'm here. Let me help."

Farrell shook his head. "No. Absolutely not. Not even in an advisory role. This is the Lake's jurisdiction, and state is assisting. There has to be clear lines of demarcation here, to protect everyone."

"You're sounding more like a politician every day, Captain."

"Screw you, Ward."

"It's Wardell," Clint said easily, glad to see Farrell was stressed by all of this. "But that don't matter. Just tell me this—do we know who the shooter is?"

Farrell stared back at Clint for a long while. Clint could almost see the gears grinding behind his eyes as he thought through his response. When he finally spoke, his voice sounded slightly calmer. "I'll brief you, but then you have to do something for me."

"What is it?"

"You go brief Harris on everything I tell you. State and Liberty Lake PD don't want her or McNutt coming out here complicating things."

Clint agreed. "It's the least I can do."

"That's probably the truth of it," Farrell said, a little sharply.

Clint didn't react.

"There are several witnesses," Farrell continued. "All of them saw Talbott approach a male, most likely black, getting into a small white truck. Talbott pointed a gun at the other guy, then shot at him. The other guy shot back, hitting Talbott."

Clint glanced over to the group of men huddled around the body on the ground. "What about Pomeroy?"

"Not here, as best we can tell. He went home after he filed the PC affidavit, and he didn't answer his page yet."

"He got an arrest warrant but went home while his partner went hunting? That seems strange," Clint observed.

"Talbott is more dedicated, I guess."

Clint raised an eyebrow at Farrell's comment. Farrell failed to bite, so he asked, "And the black male?"

"It's gotta be Garrett," Farrell said.

"Because he's black?"

"Oh, Christ. Will you dump that garbage?" Farrell shook his head in anger. "You know, when you take a real problem like racism and you play it over and over again where it *isn't* a factor, all you do is take away from the actual problem. It's like the boy who cried wolf."

"Glad to know you're such an expert on race issues, Captain."

"I'm an expert on human behavior. Right now, you're being difficult on purpose. Knock it off."

Clint raised his hands in an easy gesture. "I'm just trying to find out if we made a positive ID on Garrett or if we're going on assumptions here."

"First, there is no *we* in this situation. It's Lake and State. Second, it's neither of what you said, but something in the middle."

"That's too vague for me to understand. What does it mean?"

"It means that they haven't had time to show any photo lineups to the witnesses yet, so officially the suspect is unidentified. But—"

"Whoa. Suspect? I thought you said Talbott fired first."

Farrell sighed. "We'll circle back around to that, all right? Can I finish answering one of your questions before we go down a different rabbit hole?"

"Yes, sir."

"No one has looked at a six-pack of photos to pick out Garrett yet, but state is hopeful one of them will be able to pick him out. The fact that he was on TV may actually help."

We all look alike anyway, Clint thought, but held his tongue. He knew that if the witness admitted to seeing Garrett on TV, an attorney of Pamela Wei's caliber stood a good chance of getting the ID tossed as tainted.

"The other witness is Derek Tillman. He and Garrett went to school together. He's been dodgy, asking for a lawyer right away, but we think Garrett came to him for help."

"Did he help?"

"He wouldn't say. He wouldn't even confirm Garrett was there, but one of the neighbors said that the truck the guy was getting into when Talbott engaged him belonged to Tillman. Based on that, I'd say the answer to your question is yes."

"Did Tillman say anything else?"

"Unless something has changed since Rogers first talked to him, all he'd say is that he saw a white guy point a gun at a black guy, that the white guy shot first, and the black guy shot in self-defense."

"Hunh. Is Rogers still with him?"

Farrell glanced around, then spotted Tillman sitting alone on the low porch of his condo. He motioned with his head. "Doesn't look like it. Tillman's the tall white guy in the shorts and sandals."

Clint followed his gesture. "John Stockton meets Jimmy Buffet," he said.

Farrell let out a snort. "That's actually pretty funny. I didn't realize you had a sense of humor."

"I'll be right back."

"Hey—"

Clint walked purposefully toward Tillman, half-expecting Farrell to grab him by the arm, but the captain let him go. As he approached Tillman, he saw a man with a lean, athletic build, sitting with his elbows on his knees, cradling a bottle of water. He looked up at Clint.

"I got nothing more to say until my lawyer gets here," he said.

"When, pray tell, will that be?"

"He's on his way."

"On his way, huh? A lawyer who does house calls."

"He's a friend of the family."

"Fair enough. Then, are you under arrest and no one told me?"

"Why would I be under arrest? I'm a bystander."

Clint settled onto the stoop next to him. "Well, you're more than that, aren't you? Officially, I guess you're still a witness, albeit an uncooperative one. That could change, depending on what they find out in the next hour or so."

"What's that supposed to mean?"

"You know what rendering criminal assistance is?"

Tillman's eyes flared open, then narrowed. "If it means what it sounds like, I think so."

"Good, then you can't plead ignorance later on. See, if they find out you knowingly helped Garrett while he was a fugitive from justice, then that's the charge they've got on you. At that point, you *will* need a lawyer and not the imaginary one you ain't called yet."

Tillman didn't answer, but Clint could see he'd guessed right.

"Look, I'm going to level with you, Derek. I'm SPD. Not Lake police, not state. This is their show. If they connect the dots here, they'll think Ty shot a cop while on the run."

"The other guy shot first. I saw it."

"I believe you."

"Ty's innocent. This is…it's a perfect storm."

"I've thought the same thing exactly, but things are only going to get worse for Ty. I want to bring him in safely. Help him through the process."

Tillman eyed him warily, as if considering something, but then he just shook his head. "I can't help you. I wish I could, but I don't know if you're the one I can trust."

"I am."

"I don't know that."

Clint looked left and right to make sure no one was listening. That was when he spotted Alan Rogers striding angrily in their direction. He needed to close this out. He slipped his business card in between Tillman's foot and his sandal. "Derek, I'm only here because Ty called me right after this happened. He trusts me, and I need you to trust me, too."

Tillman shook his head again. "I don't trust cops. Ty was the only decent one I ever knew. I've got nothing else to say to you."

Clint pointed to his card. "If you change your mind."

"I won't."

Clint exhaled, defeated. He rose and headed back toward Farrell.

Rogers intercepted him. "What are you doing talking to my witness?" he barked.

"Exchanging barbeque recipes," Clint said, not slowing down.

"I want you out of my crime scene. Now!"

"Pound sand," Clint growled, but kept walking.

When he reached Farrell, the captain grabbed him by the arm and tugged him away from the gathered investigators. The state detectives looked on dispassionately, but the Liberty Lake chief glared at him. Farrell hauled Clint toward the crime scene tape. After a moment, Clint shrugged out of the hold. "Don't touch me."

"Then move your ass."

The two men walked silently toward the edge of the yellow tape. Jerry lifted the tape, giving Clint a look of concern. Clint didn't meet his gaze, but instead kept walking past him and through small crowd of civilians. Neither he nor Farrell said a word until they reached Clint's car. Then Farrell broke the silence.

"That was stupid," he observed.

"Rogers is small time. He mostly investigates shopliftings and drunk boaters."

"It was still stupid." Farrell was quiet for a beat, then said, "You know about the arrest warrant, right?"

"Yes."

"Garrett is on the run. This is blowing up."

Clint met Farrell's gaze and held it. "What do we really know, Captain? All we've got are a bunch of unanswered questions, even going back to the shooting on Sunday. Things have been happening so fast that events have outpaced our ability to make sense of them, or even compile the facts. Hell, the shooting that started all of this is three days old and we haven't figured it out yet. How can we know what we're dealing with considering everything that's happened since?"

"What I've got is a soup sandwich," Farrell said. "I've got one cop who shot another cop."

"Witnesses say Talbott shot first."

"Witnesses are notoriously unreliable. You know that."

"Sometimes," he admitted, "but usually not when they all see the same thing." He paused, then added, "A lot of other people are prone to seeing the same thing when they look at Garrett. They see black."

"I thought we covered that."

"Oh, yeah. I forgot you're the expert."

"Why do you always have to poke the bear?" Farrell asked. "It's like you have oppositional defiant syndrome or something."

"I'm just saying that when the powers-that-be are deciding who to believe and who not to believe, the fact that Garrett is black and Talbott is white comes into play."

"What comes into play for me is who is under indictment, and who isn't."

"Captain, what if that's the problem here?"

"What the hell does that mean?"

"What if Talbott was dirty?"

Farrell rolled his eyes and sighed. "Another conspiracy theory? Do you ever stop seeing shadows in every bush?"

"You're willing to believe Garrett is dirty, but not Talbott? What's the difference?"

Farrell started to answer, then thought better of it and closed his mouth. "I don't have time for this."

"Think about how we got here. If Talbott planted those drugs at Garrett's house, it drives all of the events since then. If that's true, and Garrett doesn't want to come in, can you blame him? I wouldn't, either."

"You're not the best benchmark for reasonable behavior, Ward."

"It's Wardell, Captain. You can stand there and insult me all you want. I don't hear you responding to the logic of what I'm saying, though."

"That's because it isn't logical. It's full-on JFK-was-killed-by-the-CIA-because-the-aliens-in-the-Illuminati-ordered-it conspiracy theory."

Clint gave him time to settle down, then asked, "You're an educated man, right?"

"Yeah, I've got my master's degree. What about it?"

"Be open-minded for a minute. *If* Talbott planted the drugs, doesn't everything that follows make sense?"

Farrell waved a hand. "Sure, I guess, but that's a monumental *if.*"

"Garrett being dirty wasn't just as unlikely?"

"Look, Wardell. A lot of things are possible in this world. Contrary to what goes on behind those glasses of yours, most of the time what happens is exactly what it looks like. I'm talking Occam's razor. All things being equal, the—"

"The simpler explanation is the more likely," Clint finished. "I know the law of parsimony. I also know that the world is a complex place full of complex people. When you multiply complex times complex, you get a lot of possibilities squared."

"In my experience, the simplest explanations almost always end up being what happened."

"Or what we're led to believe happened."

Farrell threw up his hands in frustration. "Enough philosophy. You can theorize all you want. As far as I'm concerned, it comes down to one thing. Innocent people don't run."

"They do if they don't think they can get a fair shake." Clint frowned. "And you claim to be an expert on race issues."

Chapter 40

Ty Garrett walked through the north Spokane neighborhood. The late afternoon sun beat down on him as he hurried to his destination. His mind ran through various schemas on how the rest of the day would play out. Amid the visualizing of outcomes, Garrett would occasionally break into a jog to make up distance.

He had parked the pick-up in Post Falls, Idaho, in a grocery store parking lot. After calling Wardell Clint, he immediately called SpoCab and asked if they had a cab close enough to Post Falls that would be willing to pick him up. The dispatcher checked, found one in Spokane Valley, and told him it would be there in fifteen minutes.

Garrett used that time before the cab arrived to call Angie.

"Hey, baby," he said, trying to sound calm.

"Where are you?" Her voice was panicked. "What is this phone number?"

"It's a pre-paid cell. Mine is at home. I didn't get to take it with me."

"Have you seen the news? They issued a warrant for your arrest."

Garrett nodded to no one and gripped the truck's steering wheel. "It's okay, Ang. I'm going to get it all figured out. I'm working with Wardell."

"Wardell Clint? The detective who sees black helicopters everywhere? You're kidding me, right?"

"No. He believes I'm innocent. He'll get this straightened out."

"Baby, that man isn't right. Who knows what he thinks? Or how he thinks?"

"He's the only friend I've got in the department now."

Garrett steered the conversation away from him and to the kids. When the taxi arrived, Garrett said, "I love you. Don't believe what you see on the TV."

"What does that mean?"

"It means someone is trying to bury me, Ang. I'll get through it. I may not talk with you for a bit, but I'll be okay."

"You've got me worried, Tyler." She always used his full name when she was upset.

"I have to go, baby. I love you. Kiss the kids for me."

He ended the call, exited the truck and ran toward the cab.

The taxi dropped him off in a neighborhood at least a mile from his final destination. He would walk the rest of the way. It didn't seem that the driver recognized him, and he paid in cash, but Garrett figured that if the man was ever approached by a detective, the best information the driver could provide would be some random neighborhood.

Garrett slowed as he approached his destination, his mind feverishly spinning. The zip code he stood in was the poorest in Eastern Washington. The neighborhood was built post-World War II and the majority of houses had fallen victim to absentee landlords and tenants who didn't respect their homes.

Many of the cars along the street were in the same state of disrepair as the houses. However, in front of one house was an immaculate purple 1962 Chevy Impala. Its frame had been lowered to the ground and it looked freshly washed and waxed.

Garrett turned on the sidewalk in front of the Chevy and headed toward the house. He dropped the brown paper sack he was carrying on the front porch, opened the door, and stepped inside with his right hand inside his pocket.

An overweight Hispanic man in khaki shorts and white T-shirt sat in a recliner while a woman wearing a tight-fitting dress with heavily applied make-up lounged on the nearby couch. The dress had ridden slightly up her hips and revealed that she wasn't wearing any underwear. There was a bong and a bag of marijuana on the table in front of them.

They were watching *Star Wars* on a big screen TV with the sound turned up.

The man saw Garrett enter the house and he moved to stand but fell back into his chair. He laughed at himself and shook his head.

Garrett watched until the man composed himself. Finally, he lifted his chin toward Garrett a couple times in a greeting and then thumbed toward the back of the house.

The woman, who looked in her late twenties, watched Garrett with her droopy eyes. She smiled lazily at him. "Hey," she said, dragging the word out.

Garrett ignored her and walked to the back of the house.

He pulled the gun from his shorts and opened the bedroom door quietly.

A small Hispanic man with tattoos on his back was on top of a pink-haired woman. She was moaning loudly. Garrett hadn't heard their noise from the front of the house due to the loud explosions from the movie.

Garrett closed the door and moved to the side of the room allowing him to see if the door opened.

Finally, Garrett said, "'Nesto."

Ernesto Ocampo rolled over, exposing himself and the naked young woman underneath him. Both focused on the gun in his hand. Ocampo's pock marked face was in stark contrast to the blemish-free face of the teenager with him. She looked barely eighteen years old to Garrett.

Ocampo nudged the teenager and said, "Get out."

"No," Garrett said, flatly. "She stays."

Ernesto pushed himself back against the headboard and spread his legs, further exposing himself to Garrett. "Why are you here?"

The young woman also pushed herself against the headboard and covered herself with a pillow. Her eyes were locked on Garrett, but he ignored her, instead focusing entirely on Ocampo.

"Are you setting me up?" Garrett asked.

Ocampo smiled, revealing extremely white teeth. "Why would I do that?"

"I don't know. I'm trying to figure things out."

"I think you got it wrong, *ese*."

The teenager said, "You're the guy on TV, right?" She looked to Ernesto.

"I guess you're famous," he said with a shrug.

Garrett shook his head and said, "I never wanted to be."

Chapter 41

Detective Wardell Clint hesitated at the edge of the garage door for the house. He'd approached from the side, walking through the front yards of the neighboring houses. When he spotted the maroon detective's car through the garage window, he was glad for his caution. Sidling up to the front door, he listened and didn't hear anything. No TV, no music, no movement.

Standing to the side of the door, he depressed the doorbell. The chimes were old school, nothing fancy, just a quick *ding-dong*, so Clint hit them again. He watched through the small window in the door as a figure approached.

Pomeroy, Clint confirmed with a glance. The drooping mustache would have given it away, even if all he'd seen was the profile. The detective wore a pair of jeans and a black polo shirt. There was no badge on his belt, no gun that Clint could see, and his hands were empty.

Pomeroy hesitated, standing in his living room and staring at Clint through the small window in his front door. He rubbed his mouth nervously.

Clint gave him a slight wave but kept his expression neutral.

He waited.

Whatever internal discussion Pomeroy was having reached its conclusion, and he ambled toward the door. He opened it up, and eyed Clint warily. "What's up, Ward?"

"It's Wardell. We need to talk."

"Talk about what?"

"About how messed up your life is about to become if we don't."

Pomeroy swallowed, but put on a brave face. "That's sounds like some real deep-dive conspiracy crap, Clint. Listen, I'm done for the day, so—"

"Talbott's dead."

Pomeroy took a long wavering breath. "I...I know. I saw the news."

"The bosses ain't been calling you?"

"My phone died. It's charging in the kitchen."

"Pager died, too?"

Pomeroy frowned. "I don't carry that leash when I'm not next up on the wheel. Besides, why we even still have pagers is beyond me."

Clint glanced over his shoulder to see if anyone was watching and to make a point. Then he turned back to Pomeroy. "Listen, man. You really want to have this conversation on your front porch? Neighbors and all?"

Pomeroy considered, then stepped aside to let Clint enter. Clint walked into the living room, then turned to face Pomeroy as he closed the front door.

"Say what you gotta say," Pomeroy said, "and then leave me alone. I...I gotta go check on Carrie."

"Talbott's wife?"

Pomeroy nodded. "It's the least I can do. Butch was my partner."

Clint nodded. "He was a real piece of work, your partner."

Emotion flashed across Pomeroy's face, but to Clint's eye, it wasn't strictly anger. He saw some fear in there as well.

Pomeroy pointed his finger. "Watch how you talk! Don't talk bad about him."

"I'm just talking facts. Facts you better get your head wrapped around."

"Like what?"

"Like he tried to shoot Ty Garrett a few hours ago. Why do you think that is?"

"That son-of-a-bitch shot *him*!" Pomeroy yelled, pointing his finger again, and jabbing for emphasis this time. "He's dirty. He killed Trotter, shot him in the back. He was dealing drugs, and now he murdered Butch. He's a lowlife menace, a damn n—"

He stopped abruptly, staring at Clint.

"A damn what?" Clint asked evenly.

Pomeroy wiped his mouth again. "He's dirty," he said finally.

"Dirty, huh?" Clint repeated.

Pomeroy nodded.

Clint took a deep breath and let it out audibly, giving Pomeroy a hard stare. He wasn't certain of the next piece, or at least he didn't want to be, yet he forged ahead, because that was what he did. "That house where the shooters were, it's up for sale. Did you know that?"

Pomeroy shook his head, but Clint could see he was lying. It never failed to amaze him how bad most cops were at lying. He always thought people that were good at detecting lies might be better at telling them.

"Of course, you do," Clint said. "Your girlfriend Kayla Trent is the realtor. That's connection one."

"Connection? What the hell?"

Clint kept rolling. "Two shooters." He held up two fingers. "You and Talbott. That's connection two."

A wild panic flashed in Pomeroy's eyes, and that was when Clint knew for sure. He kept his body loose and prepared to go hands on or draw his pistol if Pomeroy made a sudden move. The detective just stared at him, sputtering, "This…this isn't happening."

"Talbott just happens to find drugs in Garrett's house while you're there, too. That's connection three."

"We were sent there to interview him on the assault! Ask Flowers!"

"He dirty, too?"

"No, he's…" Pomeroy stopped. "Screw you, Ward. You don't know anything."

"But I do. I know Talbott's duty day ended but then he followed Garrett out to Liberty Lake and tried to murder him. That's connection four."

"He was working overtime. What, you never logged OT to close out a case?"

"I think he was trying to close out Garrett, pure and simple."

"You're crazy."

"I'm just talking facts, like I said." He counted off on his fingers. "One connection is a coincidence. Two connections, maybe an anomaly. Three is a pattern. And four? Conspiracy. These are the facts."

Pomeroy rubbed the corner of his mouth with the back of his hand. "You're spouting complete nonsense. Everyone knows you're paranoid, man. No one is going to believe a word of this crap."

"Maybe, but there's more. See, Talbott didn't die on scene."

Pomeroy's eyes narrowed with suspicion. "I hadn't heard that."

"They took him to Valley General. A Liberty Lake cop rode in the wagon with him. You remember Jerry Anderson?"

Pomeroy shook his head.

"Former SPD. Sharp guy. He talked with Talbott all the way to the ER. It seems that Butch knew he was going to die. He could sense it. Sometimes they can, you know? And he wanted to unburden." Clint paused dramatically, then asked, "You at all curious about what he said?"

Pomeroy's hands were trembling slightly. He made fists to stop them. Clint could see a sheen of sweat on his gaunt face. "What?" he asked, sounding as if the question came out against his will.

Clint smiled then. Not a friendly smile, but a knowing one. "Come on, Justin. You already know, don't you? He spilled it all."

"How do you know?"

"I went to the hospital first. It was closer than the crime scene, anyway. Jerry told me. As soon as the staties get things wrapped up at the crime scene, they're going to get to the hospital, too, where they'll hear the same thing I did. Won't be much longer after that before they come to see you, don't you think?"

Pomeroy shook his head. "Talbott's a liar. I…I don't know what he was into. We were never that close. He—"

Clint moved smooth and fast, surprising Pomeroy. It took him barely more than a second to have his grip and to twist Pomeroy's wrist and arm into a two-point leverage hold. The thin detective was more flexible than most, but Clint found his range of motion easily enough and applied pressure.

Pomeroy sank to his knees, letting out a cry. "Ouch! Let me go!"

"Tell the truth," Clint urged. "What were you and Talbott into?"

"Nothing!" Pomeroy protested.

Clint cranked down, eliciting another yell from Pomeroy. "The truth," he repeated.

"Okay, okay, okay!"

Clint eased off just a touch, keeping Pomeroy at the edge of discomfort. "Talk."

"Garrett turned on us," Pomeroy said.

"What?"

"He turned on us. He was cutting us out."

"Liar," Clint raged. He leaned into his grip and applied more pressure.

Pomeroy howled in pain.

"Don't you lie to me!" Clint told him.

"I'm not! Please, stop!"

Clint let up slightly. "Tell the truth. Stop trying to drag a man down."

Pomeroy stared at him with panic-filled eyes, grimacing in pain. "That is the truth," he grunted through clenched teeth. "You can break my arm if you want, but it'll still be the truth."

Clint's mind was reeling. *This wasn't true.* He guided Pomeroy to an overstuffed chair and pushed him into it. Pomeroy collapsed onto the cushion, then righted himself, rubbing his wrist and rolling his shoulder.

"That hurts," he protested weakly. "You tore up my rotator cuff or something, man."

"Tell me everything." *It can't be true.*

"I want immunity."

Clint drew his pistol and leveled it at Pomeroy's face. "I don't give a damn about law or charges here. I want the *truth*! Now, you give it to me straight or one more person is going to die today, I swear to Christ."

Pomeroy swallowed. "None of this...none of this is admissible."

"I give you the impression I'm building a case here?" He leaned forward slightly, bringing the barrel closer to Pomeroy's face. "Now, you are going to tell me *everything*."

Pomeroy drew a shuddering breath. "All right. All right." He swallowed, his eyes flicking between the barrel of the gun and Clint's face. "It was the three of us that were in on it. Butch was still SWAT when Garrett came on the team. Somewhere back then, the two of them cooked up the idea of hitting dealers for their cash. It's not like they can call the cops about it, right? Butch brought me in after we'd been partners for a couple of years and he knew he could trust me."

"How'd you pick the dealers?"

"Guys talk. We'd pick up things from the narco detectives, or through SWAT operations. Even after Butch left the team, Garrett heard stuff, but mostly, we got the info from 'Nesto."

"Who?" Clint demanded, not believing what he was hearing.

"Ernesto Ocampo? He's a mid-level dealer in Northeast. He'd clue us to the best houses. We'd hit the place and score the cash, and he'd get rid of some competition."

"How'd you get with Ocampo? You bust him?"

Pomeroy shook his head. "No, man. He and Garrett went to school together."

"*Garrett* brought him in?" Clint stared at him, incredulous.

"That's what I'm telling you. It was Garrett. He'd get the info from 'Nesto, fill us in and then we'd take the place. Did four or five rips a year, plus some smaller shakedowns. We put a few people on the bus to Seattle or Portland, too. Things were going good. We were making some money. Then Garrett turned on us."

Clint shook his head, as if he could somehow deny the words. "How?"

"He was cutting us out with Ernesto. He was going to do the rips on his own or use someone from Ernesto's crew."

"You're lying!" Clint shouted, jabbing the gun at him as spittle flew from his lips. "You and Talbott are dirty and you're trying to put it on this man because he's an easy target!"

Pomeroy held his hands up in surrender. "It's the truth, man. I swear."

"Stop lying to me! I'll shoot you in the face!"

Pomeroy let out a sound that was somewhere between a moan and a whimper but said nothing. He shrank back into the chair.

Clint stood still, staring at the pitiful man in front of him. He noticed the tip of his barrel was wavering, so he lowered the gun to his side. In that moment, he felt his cell phone vibrating. He reached into his pocket and answered it, not taking his eyes off of Pomeroy.

"Clint."

"This is Flowers. Where are you?"

"Working."

"Well, last time I checked, you work for me. Drop whatever you're doing and get over to the address I'm about to text you. There's been a quadruple homicide in a house, and we need more investigative support."

"I'm not up on the wheel."

"To hell with the wheel!" Clint could hear the frustration in the lieutenant's voice. "One of my detectives is dead. I'm trying to get people in to supplement, but no one is answering. We're hurting for bodies. I need you over there, now. That's an order."

"Copy that," Clint said. "Send me the address. I'll be en route."

Flowers severed the connection without another word.

Clint slid the phone back into his pocket. "We're not done here," he said to Pomeroy. "I'm coming back to finish this interview, and you better be here."

"I'm heading over to see Carrie," Pomeroy said.

"That can wait. I'm coming back, and when I do, you better be here. And stop telling me these lies. I want the real truth. You better own up."

Pomeroy shook his head. "I'm not lying. I wish I was, but I'm not."

Chapter 42

Clint didn't wait for the patrol officer to finish writing his name on the crime scene log before heading into the inner perimeter. He spotted Bo Sherman in uniform at the front door to the house. He wasn't sure if the big man was waiting for him or guarding the door.

"What's up?" he asked. "Who's lead?"

Sherman shrugged. "I don't know how you all work that. Marty Hill is already inside, along with Detective Hollander. I forget her first name."

"Leanne," Clint said.

"Sure," Sherman said. "All I know is she's old as dirt and has about the same personality, my man."

Clint nodded. That sounded about right. "You logging entry?"

"Nah. I'm just an overpaid bouncer right now. You can pass, my brother."

Clint gave him a short nod and went through the door.

Inside, he found Marty Hill carefully scanning the living room. Leanne Hollander was squinting at a still body, probably examining the wounds. Clint caught Hill's attention. "How many?"

Hill pointed to the body Hollander was examining. "Hispanic male, gunshot wound. On the other side of that chair is a smaller female, also deceased, also gunshot wound." He pointed toward the back of the house. "Two more in the bedroom. Hispanic male, single shot to the forehead. That one's pretty gruesome. Blood and brain spatter all over the wall and headboard. Final victim is a juvenile female, also a single shot. Hers was execution style, behind the ear."

Clint nodded that he understood. This one was going to be a lot of work, which was a problem. He had to find a way to get back to Pomeroy soon. "Got any ID?"

"Still trying on the juvenile. Chubby over there is Jorge Salazar. He's got a sheet, but not too long. The woman is Galina Herrera. Couple of possession pops, nothing big. The guy in the bedroom with the juvenile female is a little rougher. His name is…" Hill consulted his notepad. "Here it is. Ernesto Ocampo."

Clint felt the air go out of his lungs as if he'd just been kicked in the stomach. He wanted to cry out against the information but knew it would do no good. Reality was what it was. All of the pieces had fallen into place with a resounding click.

"You okay, Wardell?" Hill asked.

"Fine, Marty." He cleared his throat. He needed some air, so he could think. He might have been played a fool, but the play wasn't over yet. "What do you need from me?"

"You want to make sure that the canvass is rolling? After that, we can plug you in here."

"Perfect." Clint turned and left. He didn't say anything to Sherman as he passed. When he got to his car, he put his hands on the trunk and leaned forward, taking a few deep breaths.

How could I be so stupid?

He had to fix it. He should have seen it coming, and he didn't, so he had to fix it. But how?

The correct thing to do was pull Detective Hill aside and tell him everything. Garrett was a suspect in these murders, and he deserved to know. Marty Hill was one of the few detectives that Clint thought was both a stellar detective and a decent person. He shouldn't keep this from him.

Yet what did he have? Pomeroy's inadmissible confession? He needed corroboration first. Pomeroy would fold when the investigators hauled him in for questioning. He'd get his immunity, or at least something that passed for it. Without some kind of corroboration, all he had was one dirty cop's statement against another, and what? The coincidence that Ocampo and Garrett went to the same high school? That didn't mean anything. There were five high schools in Spokane. There was a twenty percent chance that Garrett went to high school with anyone who graduated three years before or after him.

He looked up, taking another deep breath and trying to clear his head of all the anger and bitter, dark betrayal roiling around inside. He saw a female patrol officer interviewing an elderly white female two houses away from Ocampo's. She was making notes and nodding her head frequently while the woman spoke and pointed in the direction of the house.

Clint walked toward them. The patrol officer noticed him as he came up the walkway and motioned for the woman to wait. She met him halfway down the walk. Clint glanced at her nametag and read Mixon.

"Paula Mixon," he said.

"Yes, sir."

He'd never met her, but he'd read several of her reports. She was solid, and thorough. "What do you have?"

She motioned toward the woman. "Her name's Nona Henry. She may have seen the shooter."

"How's she know?"

"She saw him go in, heard some shots, and watched him come out."

"From where?"

"Her kitchen window."

"Did she see a gun?"

Officer Mixon shook her head. "She got a good look at him, though."

"Description?"

"Black male. Thirty-ish. Handsome."

Clint glanced over at Nona Henry, who was watching with mild concern. He noticed she was wearing glasses. "How old is she?"

Mixon consulted her notes. "Eighty-two."

"How's her eyesight?"

"I don't know. I didn't ask."

Clint brushed by her, heading toward Nona. She noticeably pulled away from him as he approached. He didn't see personal animus in her eyes when he looked there, only whatever fear and bias she and most of her generation soaked in just from living life. "I'm Detective Clint, ma'am."

Nona glanced over at Mixon and then back to him. "Hello," she said uncertainly.

"How's your eyesight, ma'am?"

"Pardon?"

"How well do you see?"

"Oh. Well, I suppose fair enough. I can still drive if I have to, though I don't like to. Usually my son will—"

"Ma'am, I need you to listen to me. I'm going to be back in a couple of hours to show you some photographs, to see if you can pick out the man you saw next door. Are you able to do that?"

"I believe so, but I was talking to that nice lady officer before."

"She's helping me," Clint explained. He handed her a card. "From now on, it's important that you don't talk to anyone but me, all right?"

Nona took the card with bony fingers. "Well, if you say so, but…"

"Thank you, ma'am. You can go back inside now." Clint turned away and walked toward Mixon. He held out his hand. "You have her horsepower there?"

"Huh?"

"Her name, DOB, all of that. In your notepad."

"Oh. Yeah, it's here."

"Let me have it. I'll finish up with this witness."

Mixon tore off the page and handed to him. "Detective Hollander told me to bring it to her."

"I'm helping her. You're all good, Officer. Go ahead and hit the rest of the block." He handed her a card. "My cell number is on that. Let me know if you get any other good witnesses."

Mixon took the card and put it in her shirt pocket without looking at it.

Clint didn't wait for her to ask another question. He headed back to his Crown Vic, got in, and headed toward the station. Once his phone was synced up to the Bluetooth, he placed the call. He didn't like using a phone, much less a cell, but it was unavoidable.

The phone range twice before it was answered with a terse, "Captain Farrell."

"Captain, this is Clint. I need to talk to you."

"We are talking."

"In person."

"All right." Farrell sounded cautious. "Is this regarding the county's investigation?"

"Yes," Clint said, figuring that was close enough. "I'm going to be near the station soon. Meet me in the parking lot at the Veteran's Memorial Arena. Just you."

"Just me...? What's this about?"

"Better if I give it to you in person." Clint hung up before the captain could answer. He parked a half block away from the Public Safety Building and took a side entrance. Instead of going to the SPD investigative wing, he slipped into the sheriff's detectives' bullpen. There was no sign of Harris or McNutt. Clint shrugged that off. He could go to them later if it made sense to do so. Quickly, he made use of the ident mugshot computer system at an empty desk, glad for once that the city and county shared the same software, so his login and password worked. He created a six pack of photos that included Ty Garrett's recent booking photo and printed off several copies. Then he slipped out of the sheriff's office area and made his way back to his car.

Captain Farrell was waiting for him when he pulled into the empty arena parking lot. Clint car-sided him, pointing his car in the opposite direction and putting their driver's side windows next to each other.

"What is this all about, Clint?"

"It's bad, Captain. Real bad."

Chapter 43

Garrett leaned forward and rested his head against the passenger seat in front of him. He was exhausted.

The taxi driver, a heavy-set woman with frizzy hair, asked, "You okay?"

"Yeah."

"You're not going to throw up, are you?"

"Not drunk. Just tired."

"Okay," she said, "but if you throw up, I'm charging you extra."

"Sounds fair," Garrett said and left his head against the seat.

Carly Simon's "You're So Vain" played through the radio while the woman hummed loudly along with it.

Garrett opened the brown paper bag between his feet before pulling the gun from the pocket of his shorts. He kept it low where the woman couldn't see it. Quietly, he opened the cylinder of the gun and shook out the empty shells into his hand. He placed them into the bottom of the bag and lifted out the box of shells.

After removing six of them, he carefully wiped each one with his shirt before pushing them into their corresponding chamber. Garrett closed the cylinder and tucked the revolver back into his pants pocket. He then closed the box of shells and put them back into the bag.

He leaned back and stared ahead.

It was then he realized he smelled of body odor.

Garrett had taken a cab to a small neighborhood shopping center in the northwest part of town. The stadium the high school football teams played in was to the north. He stood in the parking lot until the taxi drove away, making sure she was out of sight before moving.

Time was not on his side and Garrett ran the half mile to his destination like he was taking the SWAT test again. He left nothing on the table.

When his mind wandered, Garrett focused solely on the present. Inhale for two steps, exhale for three steps. Exhaustion was replaced with awareness. He was a block away from his objective and he slowed to a walk. His eyes scanned the well-manicured neighborhood. As he rounded the corner of the house, he peered into the garage and saw a maroon detective's car.

Garrett had the revolver in his hand and by his side as he confidently walked to the front door. As he approached the concrete front steps, he dropped the brown bag into the flower bed. With two quick steps, he was at the door. He turned the doorknob, surprised that it opened.

Justin Pomeroy was at the kitchen sink filling a glass with tap water. "Is that you, Wardell? I saw you through the window. I didn't think you be back so fast."

Garrett closed the door and quickly moved into the house.

When Pomeroy saw him, he froze. The glass of water hovered in front of his face, his hand shaking.

"Clint was here?"

"No," Pomeroy said, slowly lowering the glass to put it on the kitchen counter.

"You're the worst liar on the department, Justin. That's why Butch liked you. He could trust you because he always knew when you were lying."

"You killed Butch."

Garrett ignored him. "What did you tell Clint?"

"Nothing."

"I said you're a poor liar. Just stop. Did you tell him about us?"

Pomeroy pursed his lips until Garrett leveled his gun at him. Pomeroy nodded.

"What about Ocampo?"

Another nod.

"Did you tell him about the jobs?"

"Some of them, but nothing in detail."

"He's got enough, Justin. Was it you and Butch in the house that night?"

Pomeroy stared at him.

"Trotter? He was working with you?"

Pomeroy continued to stare, but the little ticks he made with his eyes when Garrett hit on the truth gave him away.

"You knew I patrolled East Central, didn't you? Everybody knew I protected that neighborhood. I made myself an easy mark." Garrett nodded as he thought the problem through. "Damn."

Pomeroy swallowed and licked his lips.

"That night. Trotter didn't stop right away because he was going to run, like I thought. He didn't stop because he needed to bring me to you and Butch." Anger flashed on Garrett's face.

"You should stop all this, Ty," Pomeroy said. "I told Wardell everything. There's no way out."

"You're wrong," he said, his mind running as his eyes scanned for a solution.

Pomeroy turned his hands palm up, surrendering. "How about this? I'll recant my story with Clint. I'll tell him that I made it up. He had a gun on me, for Chrissakes. I'll say that Talbott was dirty, and I was only trying to bring you down. I'll take the heat."

Garrett pointed to the counter. "Pick up a knife."

Pomeroy glanced at a block of knives near the sink. "You'll shoot me if I do."

"I'm going to give you an option."

"Option for what?"

"You can either go peacefully or you can go violently." He leveled the gun at him for emphasis. "It's your choice, but everything ends today."

Pomeroy had difficulty swallowing and reached for the glass of water.

"The knife, Justin, or I'll end it now."

Pomeroy lowered his hand and tears filled his eyes. Finally, Pomeroy reached over the counter and pulled a knife from the block, holding it in his fist. Even though Pomeroy had a look of resignation, Garret's hand tightened on the gun, but his finger remained calm on the trigger.

The thin man stared at the knife. "Does it really come down to this?"

Garrett didn't respond. He knew that Pomeroy was working it out in his head.

Finally, Pomeroy looked at him and asked, "Can I sit down?"

Garrett nodded.

Pomeroy sat on the tile floor and pushed his back against the doors underneath the sink. He held the knife over his left wrist, his hand shaking again.

He lowered his hand and looked up at Garrett. "I'm scared."

Garrett sneered, took a step forward and lifted the gun.

"Wait!"

Garrett stopped.

"Wait, damn it, wait. Come on, Garrett, haven't you ever been scared?"

"Plenty of times. The night you shot at me comes to mind."

Pomeroy stared at him. "We used to be friends."

"Start cutting or I shoot, and it's done. You can get a couple more minutes your way."

Pomeroy stared at the knife for another moment before pulling it deeply across his skin. Red immediately flowed.

"Vertically next time," Garrett said. "And it better be deeper than the one you just did, or I'm done."

Pomeroy looked up with sudden hatred in his eyes. However, the anger quickly faded, and he switched the knife into his other hand and dug deeper with the knife wincing and whimpering as he did.

Blood flowed from the two wounds on Pomeroy's arms. Garrett stepped back and grabbed a chair from the kitchen table. He set it down in front of Pomeroy.

"I didn't think it would end this way," the detective said.

Garrett nodded in understanding.

Pomeroy began to cry, and Garrett watched him, waiting for the man to get up and do something to save himself. More than five minutes passed, and Pomeroy faded considerably, but Garrett was antsy to get moving. A significant amount of blood from Pomeroy's wrists had pooled around his buttocks and thighs. However, he knew he needed to wait.

"I wish you wouldn't have told Clint about Ocampo," Garrett said.

Pomeroy slowly lifted his head, a dull expression on his face.

"Because I just killed Ernesto."

With effort, Pomeroy widened his eyes.

While he watched Pomeroy's life trickle away, Garrett remembered.

When Ernesto Ocampo told Garrett that he was famous due to the amount of television coverage, Garrett replied, "I never wanted to be."

"That's too bad, *ese*. It's with you now."

"How do we get out of this?" Garrett asked.

Ocampo shrugged. "There is no we. There's only you. You're the *mayate* who got yourself into this mess. You figure your own way out."

Garrett blinked several times. "What did you say?"

"I said you need to figure your way out."

"*Mayate*," Garrett said, his lip curling.

Ocampo shook his head. "I didn't say that."

"It's a beetle that rolls its dung everywhere. The first time someone called me that I went home and looked it up. I've never forgotten it."

The girl looked between Ocampo and Garrett.

"I've been on the street for a decade, Ernesto. I know all the sneaky ways people call me a nigger."

Garrett quickly raised his gun and fired one shot, hitting Ocampo in the head, killing him instantly.

The teenager screamed and rolled from the bed. She huddled in the corner, her eyes not meeting Garrett's. He took care of her quickly. She wasn't involved, but he couldn't leave behind a witness.

When he slipped out of the room, the volume on the television had been muted. He leaned quickly around the corner to see the fat man standing at his chair with his gun held between both hands. He fired three shots, all of them smashing into the wall next to Garrett.

Garrett brought his weapon up tightly to his chest, leaned quickly out, and fired two shots. The big man squealed and went down.

When Garrett entered the small living room, he realized the woman wasn't on the couch. He looked around hurriedly for her. The front door was still closed. Garrett turned around and saw a back door on the opposite side of the kitchen.

Garrett stepped into the kitchen and the woman leapt at him with a butcher's knife in her hand. Garrett jumped out of the way, hit the couch, and tumbled over it, landing on the coffee table. He regained his footing just as the woman cleared the couch with her hand in the air, the knife ready to strike. Garrett fired two rounds and the woman went down.

Six rounds fired. The revolver was empty.

He tucked the gun in his shorts and lifted the cushions on the couch. Under the third one he found multiple packets of powder. Garrett found an old napkin near the fat man's chair and grabbed it. Using the dirty napkin, he picked up a couple of the packets and put them in his pocket. He then tucked the cushions back into place. He quickly stepped outside, picked up the brown paper bag from the front porch, and hurried away.

Now, Garrett stood and stared down at Detective Justin Pomeroy. He wanted to move closer to check for vital signs, but he risked stepping into his blood. From enough experience, he knew the man was dead or as close to it as possible.

"You were weak," Garrett said.

Garrett pulled the dirty napkin from his shorts. Carefully, he extracted the two packets of powder from his pocket, ensuring his fingerprints wouldn't be added to the plastic. He thought about a hiding place for them where someone may find them. However, he worried that detectives wouldn't search deep enough if it they believed Pomeroy's death was a suicide. Finally, Garrett decided that obvious was best and dropped the packets into the blood next to Pomeroy's hand.

When he was done, he rubbed down the knob with his shirt and pulled the door closed.

Calmly, he walked out of the neighborhood. When he was a block away, he broke into a run.

Chapter 44

Several blocks away from Pomeroy's house, Garrett began to breathe easy again.

He walked through an alley and slowly, methodically began disposing of the brown bag and its contents. In one can, which was nearly full of trash, he disposed of the empty shells.

Another block away, he entered an alley. He found another can nearly full, and poured the remaining rounds in, although he saved the empty box, the white tray the rounds had sat in, and the brown paper back. Garrett continued to walk as he tore apart the cardboard box. He tossed it into a can and continued walking.

Using his shirt, he wiped any fingerprints from the white tray and carefully tossed it into another can along with the brown paper bag.

Garrett soon arrived at a Walgreen's pharmacy. Inside, he grabbed a handcart and moved through the store. He tossed soap, toothpaste, and a toothbrush into the cart. He added a small hand towel and washcloth. He found a clothing section. He grabbed a green and gold t-shirt and sweats that promoted the local high school. They were the only things that would fit him. It took him a minute to find the last thing he needed, but he soon found a multi-head screwdriver.

The cashier was a young woman with a full-sleeve tattoo on her right arm and a bored expression. As she reached the toothpaste, Garrett asked, "Can I get an extra bag?"

She shrugged and continued scanning his items.

He was out of the store in less than five minutes.

Finding a quiet place in a neighboring alley, he pulled the gun from his pocket and sat with his back against a dilapidated garage. He unloaded the six rounds inside the cylinder and dropped them into the empty bag. He then removed the multi-head screwdriver and set to work on the revolver. He unscrewed the grips and tossed them into the empty bag. Next, he undid the screws holding the side plates which also freed the cylinder. It took him only a few minutes and the entire revolver was completely dismantled. Garrett tossed the screwdriver in the bag and was on the move again.

As he walked, he dropped several screws. Another block, he tossed the grips into a trashcan. He repeated this process until he had only the frame and the cylinder left. These two items he took care to wipe down before disposing. He dropped them both into trashcans several blocks apart.

Finally, he tossed the screwdriver and bag away.

He stepped out of an alley, opened his phone, and called for a cab.

The hot water pelted his frame. He had the water turned as high as it would go. The cab had dropped him off a couple blocks away from Derek Tillman's rental house. Just as Tillman said, there was a lockbox on the front door with a key inside. The house was completely empty.

However, the hot water worked and that was all Garrett needed.

He quickly scrubbed himself with the washcloth, paying particular attention to his hands.

When he was done, he wiped himself down with the hand towel. After brushing his teeth, he put on the new sweats and T-shirt.

With attention, Garrett collected the items he'd brought into the house and put them back into the plastic bag. He secured the house, placing the key back in the lock box.

Two blocks away he put the bag into a trashcan in an alley.

He stepped onto a corner and called for another cab. It only took a few minutes for the cab to appear. As it approached,

Garrett opened his pre-paid phone and snapped it in two. He dropped it on the street and stomped it until it broke in pieces.

Garrett climbed into the back of the cab and gave the driver his home address.

He leaned back, and a wave of exhaustion rolled over him.

When the cab arrived at Garrett's house, the driver said, "We're here," waking him from his sleep. He'd been out for ten minutes.

Garrett saw a county patrol car sitting in front.

"Looks like you've got a visitor," the driver said.

Garrett paid for the ride and climbed out, not bothering to engage in conversation.

He approached his house, ignoring the deputy posted out front.

A car door opened, and a deep voice yelled, "Sir!"

Garrett turned.

"Are you Tyler Garrett?" the deputy asked.

Garrett nodded, wearily.

"I'm Deputy Douglas. I've been assigned to bring you to the station for an interview with Detective Harris."

He nodded and walked slowly toward the deputy, a tall skinny man who barely looked out of college.

"Sir, I need to pat you down before I put you in the car. I hope you understand. Regulations."

Garrett nodded and put his hands on the back of his head. The deputy quickly patted him down and then opened the back door of his patrol car.

He climbed in sideways, laying down on the backseat.

The deputy watched him settle in before shutting the door.

As the car pulled away, Garrett was rocked to sleep.

Chapter 45

Clint parked in front of Nona Henry's house. He got out of the car carrying the thin manila folder containing the six-pack of photos he'd created at the Public Safety building. Before he'd even closed his car door, a voice cut through the night air.

"Clint! What the hell?"

He turned to see Detective Hollander stalking toward him, her face twisted into a hostile sneer. Marty Hill followed, though his expression was more disappointed than angry.

"Flowers sent you here to help us out. Where have you been?"

"Farrell called me off for something else."

"Something else?" Hollander snapped. "What the hell could be more important than a quadruple homicide?"

Clint tapped his collar where the white shirts wore their rank insignia. "Hey, I see the gold, I do what I'm told."

"Yeah, you're a real paragon of service and virtue."

He spread his hands peacefully. "I'm off the case, sister. Sorry."

Hollander shook her head. "This is wrong." She turned and strode away toward the crime scene.

Detective Marty Hill hesitated, then said, "We could have used your help, Wardell. Still could, actually. It's a mess, and we don't have anything yet."

"Sorry."

"Yeah." He glanced at the file folder under Clint's arm. "If you're off the case, why are you back here?"

"Gotta talk to a witness. Some unrelated information came up during canvass."

Hill nodded slowly. "Some unrelated information? Just two houses away from our scene? This important information just happens to fit into some other case, one that trumps a quadruple homicide in terms of importance? Must be a hell of a case."

"Captain trumps lieutenant, Marty. That's all I know."

Hill pursed his lips. "You know I respect you, right? A lot of these other guys out here, they don't. They think you're crazy, or paranoid, or whatever. I know what kind of detective you are. When they get all ramped up talking smack about you, throwing around 'Honey Badger this' and 'Honey Badger that,' I'm one of the few people around this place who sticks up for you."

Clint stared back at him, expressionless. "So?"

"So, don't insult me, Wardell. Do what you have to do and shut up about it but have the respect not to lie to me."

Clint didn't reply, and after a few moments, Detective Hill turned and walked away. Clint watched him go, seeing the slight limp of an athlete with old injuries catching up to him, feeling the aura of disappointment and anger coming off the veteran detective in waves. He realized that Marty Hill was one of the closest things to a friend he had in the department. Hell, in his life. A small knot of emotion rose in his throat, but Clint pushed it down. He didn't have time for it now. He'd have to find a way patch things up with Marty later.

He turned and headed toward the house.

Nona Henry came to the front door in her robe, her hair down around her shoulders. "It's a little late," she scolded him.

"Justice knows no clock," Clint told her, and that seemed to work. She invited him inside and they sat down at her kitchen table.

Clint carefully instructed her on what to expect. "I'm going to show you what's known as a photo montage, Mrs. Henry. There will be six photographs of men, two rows of three across. Now, these men will look somewhat similar, and that's on purpose. If you recognize the man you saw go into and leave your neighbor's house earlier today, I want you to point to him. If you don't see him in any of these pictures, it's okay for you to say so. You need to be sure, so take your time."

"I understand, Officer."

Clint didn't bother correcting her. Instead, he turned over the photo montage. Six black faces stared up from the page. All of them were booking photos, and he'd chosen men who resembled Garrett at least a little. He paid particular attention to keeping the skin shade plus or minus a degree, knowing the statistics that said a white person tended to pick the darker skinned suspects if unsure.

Nona Henry scanned the page for a long while, taking time at each photograph. Then she looked up at Clint. "Can I choose now?"

"Absolutely."

She pointed a bony, aged finger at the number five position. "I believe it was him."

"How sure are you?"

"I would never accuse anyone if I wasn't sure, young man."

Clint allowed himself a smile. "Fair enough, but percentage-wise, how sure are you?"

She considered, then said, "Ninety-eight percent."

Clint handed her his pen. "Will you circle your selection and initial next to it?"

"Of course." Nona took the pen and drew a circle around Tyler Garrett's face, and scrawled her initials.

Clint thanked her and left as quickly as he came. Once in his car, he pulled away from the crime scene before he had to face any more of Hollander's righteous anger or Hill's disappointment. He dialed his cell phone, and Farrell answered almost immediately.

"Positive ID, Captain," he reported.

Farrell sighed with something that sounded like a mixture of relief and dread. "And she's a solid witness?"

"Maybe not all by herself. She's elderly, and we both know what defense attorneys can do with that. She'll corroborate Pomeroy's statement, though. It'll be enough."

"All right get back here and let's talk strategy."

"I thought we already had one. Get the ID, and then I bring in Pomeroy to talk. After that, we call state and turn it all over."

"Things have changed. County picked up Garrett for his shooting interview. When that's over, they'll have to book him on the warrant we issued. I want you to go at him as soon as they're finished. We need to lock him into a story before he lawyers up."

Clint nodded. It was a good plan, though it felt strange to be exercising it against a cop.

He isn't a cop, Clint reminded himself. He's a criminal with a badge.

"I'm on my way," he told Farrell.

Chapter 46

The day had been full of cat and mouse intrigue. The tension was excruciating.

Cody Lofton felt like he was in junior high school again and that truly bothered him. Amanda Donahue had gotten under his skin with the simple act of holding his hand at yesterday's press conference. It had thrown him off all day.

Lofton reminded himself that this was one of the many reasons why he preferred women younger than Amanda. Above all else, he was always in control. They held no allure in conversational aspects and he didn't feel an affinity toward them beyond the physical. Once he'd used them, he was free to move on from them, both in body and in spirit. It was easy to forget them.

With Amanda, however, Lofton felt suddenly upside down. Initially, she was a nobody, just the attractive new assistant to the mayor. Then she became a threat with her recent behavior and now, out of nowhere, she was...something. Lofton couldn't put his finger on exactly what she was, but she continued to smile at him and find reasons to be near him.

Is she playing a game with me, he thought?

He couldn't tell and that pissed him off. It also excited him.

The mayor had been away from city hall most of the morning and all afternoon at a new wing dedication ceremony at Fairchild Air Force Base. It was something Lofton hadn't needed to attend and so his schedule was open. It should have given him time to focus on the media storm still surrounding Ty Garrett, except Amanda found reasons to continually interrupt.

She wore a white plunging draped dress with strappy high heels. Her hair was pulled back into a bun and she wore cosmetic glasses. Maybe she wore contacts before and the glasses are real, Lofton wondered. Whatever the reason, the effect was intoxicating and that was before she stood next to him with her perfume.

He couldn't focus. He tried watching the news to get a handle on which way the winds were blowing, but he couldn't stay present. His mind kept wandering back to her.

Lofton pushed back from his desk and stood. Then he dropped to the floor and did a push-up, slowly down for a five count and back up to the starting position. He continued this process until he was nearing thirty, the pain was now excruciating. He hadn't thought about her for nearly twenty push-ups.

"Are you showing off?" a voice asked.

Lofton turned his head and saw her. His arms suddenly trembled, his concentration waned, and he flopped to the floor.

"Did I do that?" Amanda asked, playfulness in her voice.

He rocked back to his knees before standing. "I was at my limit," Lofton said out of breath.

Amanda smiled broadly and then said, "Chief Baumgartner is on line two."

"Tell him I'll be with him shortly. Want to catch my breath."

He watched her walk away and chided himself for losing control and letting her mess with his head.

Lofton tucked his shirt back into his pants and straightened his tie. He reached for the desk phone but stopped. He saw a blinking blue light on his cell phone. With a quick swipe of his thumb, the phone lit up. It was a text message from Lieutenant Dan Flowers.

Unknown DB in LL. Believed to be SPD. Don't know more. Still developing. Will update as I learn more.

Lofton knew a DB was short for dead body, but LL? He'd never seen that abbreviation from Flowers before. *Believed to be SPD.* What did that mean?

He picked up the telephone and heard Baumgartner's voice. "Lofton, where's Sikes?"

"Out at the base. There was a new wing dedication this afternoon. I'm expecting him anytime."

"Son of a bitch."

"What's going on, Chief?"

"One of my detectives was shot and killed earlier in Liberty Lake."

LL. Liberty Lake, thought Lofton.

"Who was it?"

"Butch Talbott."

Lofton wrote the name down, so he could brief the mayor.

"What was he doing out there? Was he on a case?"

"I'm not sure. Information is slow in coming. It's going through State Patrol and Liberty Lake PD before it filters back to me. I'm pretty pissed by the lack of communication. Farrell has been out there on and off through the day, trying to keep tabs on it."

"Where are you?"

"I'm in Ocean Shores, on the coast," Baumgartner said. "I drove over this morning for a long weekend with my girlfriend. We're packing the car back up and heading out in a bit. I'll be home in the early hours. See if you can get the mayor to meet with me tomorrow and send me a time. I'll make it work."

The line went dead.

Lofton stared at the phone in his hand. A dead cop. Lofton didn't know the last time the city had heard those words.

Amanda showed up and leaned against the doorframe. "How was the chief?"

Lofton looked up and her smile faded.

"What happened?" she asked. "Is everything all right?"

"Cody! Amanda! My office!" Mayor Sikes called out to them, his voice full of excitement.

Amanda hesitated, waiting for Lofton to nod before heading toward the mayor's office. Lofton hung up the phone and grabbed the piece of paper with the detective's name written on it.

When he walked in, the mayor was eyeing Amanda's outfit, but her look was non-committal. There were no wide eyes nor parted lips from her. She was all business with Sikes. A part of Lofton noticed, but it wasn't the part currently in control.

"God, I love the Air Force," Sikes said excitedly, taking off his jacket and loosening his tie. "Those guys know how to do a ceremony right. Classy folks all the way around. We can definitely learn a thing or two from them on how to promote an event." His smile faded when he saw Lofton. "What the hell is your problem?"

Lofton handed him the piece of paper.

The mayor glanced at it. "Who is Butch Talbott?"

"He's a Spokane Police Detective. He was shot and killed in Liberty Lake earlier today."

Amanda reached out for Lofton, but quickly pulled her hand back.

"What happened?" Sikes asked.

"They don't know yet, sir. Baumgartner just called me. He's on the coast—"

"What the hell is he doing on the coast?"

"He went to Ocean Shores for the weekend with his girlfriend, but he cancelled their plans and is on the way back now."

"What kind of leadership is that? That's a selfish move on his part. I'd like to get away from this crisis for a little bit, too, but you don't see me doing it."

Like spending the day at the air base for a dedication ceremony, Lofton thought.

"We've still got the Ty Garrett situation going on and the chief is playing hooky," the mayor groused. "I would have expected more dedication from Baumgartner."

Lofton shrugged. "His people are handling things, sir. Besides, the county should be finalizing Garrett's investigation. I don't think there's much he can do on Garrett's behalf right now. He did ask for a meeting tomorrow."

"I would never go out of town at a time like this," Sikes muttered. "What was he thinking?"

Lofton glanced at Amanda who stared straight ahead. A slight curl of disdain was on her lip.

"No," Sikes said, shaking his head. "I won't meet with him. Tell him I don't have time."

"Sir?"

"I'm going to teach him a lesson. When we're in the middle of a giant mess, you don't take a break," Sikes said, pointing his finger at him.

"There's a dead officer. You need to meet with him."

"Really?" Sikes face turned red. "People are targeting our cops and he's on vacation? Maybe he's the reason everything has gotten this far out of hand."

Lofton tilted his head and asked, "What?"

"Are you so dense you can't see what's happening, Cody? Tell me you see it, Amanda."

She shrugged and shook her head.

Sikes smacked his desk. "Look! Less than a week ago one of our best cops is ambushed. The best reason we've heard up to now is because he's wearing the badge."

We haven't heard that, Lofton thought.

"Then a highly decorated detective like Butch Talbott is gunned down in Liberty Lake."

Highly-decorated? We don't even know who Butch Talbott is.

Lofton made eye contact with Amanda who shook her head. Worry was in her eyes.

"Which officer is next? We need to put our officers on alert."

"I'll take care of it," Lofton said, hoping to end the discussion.

"Then we need to get out in front of it with the media."

Sikes was so wound up that he wasn't thinking things through. Lofton didn't like what pressure had revealed about his boss. "Nothing has been released about this yet, sir."

The mayor studied Lofton. "All right, I see your point, but I don't want to get caught off guard like we were with the Garrett situation. I want you to work on this tonight. Get some ideas down on paper. Let's meet in the morning and come up with a plan."

Lofton pursed his lips and nodded. There was no sense in arguing. He just wanted to be out of the office.

"Amanda, can you work late with me tonight? I've got several things I want to put into action after my day with the base commander."

Amanda shook her head. "I'm sorry, sir. I have plans tonight."

Disappointment ran across Sikes' face, but he shrugged it off before dropping into his seat. He then ignored them both since neither served a further purpose.

Lofton headed to his office where he gathered his laptop and notepad.

"Need some help?" Amanda stood in his doorway with her purse over her shoulder.

"No, I'm fine. I'm going to work on this from home."

"That's where I was offering to help," she said.

Chapter 47

As far as Harris was concerned, the interview with Garrett was going well. Despite all of the distractions, Garrett seemed at ease and focused. He answered each of her questions in a timely, thoughtful, and genuine way. Since most of her experience was interviewing emotional victims and witnesses or reluctant suspects, this was a welcome change.

"We've been going for a long while," she said, glancing at her phone for the time. "It's getting close to midnight. Do you want to take a break?"

Garrett shook his head. "No, I'm fine. Thanks for the water, though."

She nodded in acknowledgment, then glanced at Dale Thomas, the Police Union President, with the same question, unspoken this time. From his seat beside Garrett, Thomas gave his head a succinct shake. He'd barely said a word since they started, which added another item to her list of reasons why this was going so well.

Harris checked for the fifth time to make sure the recorder was working. McNutt was recording on a secondary device just to be certain. Thomas had his own recorder sitting directly in front of Garrett. The four of them were the only ones in the room, which wasn't how she initially envisioned the interview. Garrett had declined any representation by a criminal attorney, and the late hour made it easier to keep out any spectators. She'd fully intended to order out all non-essential personnel, but wondered how much pull that would have if the sheriff or the chief insisted on sitting in.

"Well, we're close to finished anyway," she said. "I just want to review a few key points for confirmation."

Thomas broke his silence. "These will be questions he has already answered?"

"Yes, mostly."

"Then why ask them again?"

"Like I said," Harris said. "For confirmation."

Thomas leaned back, looked over at Garrett and shook his head.

"It's all right," Garrett said. "Whatever you need." He swallowed, some emotion playing on his face. "It feels good to finally be able to talk about it."

Harris let that sentence sit by itself for a moment, then glanced down at her notes. She found her bulleted list for her final recap and started down it.

"Did you know Todd Trotter?"

"Only as an occasional name that came up in patrol work. I don't think I'd ever stopped him or dealt directly with him, though I guess it's possible he might have been present on a call I took or something."

"But no direct contact?"

"Not that I can think of."

"That night, why did you stop him?"

"Reckless driving. He shot out of a side street through a stop sign and almost caused a collision."

"Any idea why he didn't stop immediately when you activated your emergency lights?"

Garrett leaned forward, looking her directly in the eye. "At the time, I thought he was trying to decide whether to bolt or not. Now that I've had a chance to think about it, I think he was purposefully leading me to that spot."

"Why?"

"So that whoever was in that house could ambush me."

"Why would someone ambush you, Officer Garrett?"

Garrett shook his head. "I don't know. Maybe because I arrested them in the past. Maybe it has nothing to do with me personally, just the badge. Or maybe because of my color.

That's why those other two came after me a couple of days later."

"Are you saying that the fight you got into is somehow related?"

"I'm saying I don't know. No one knows. That's the hard part." Garrett grimaced. "I wish we had the answers to some of these questions. It would show people the truth about me."

"Going back to the situation right after the vehicle stop," Harris said. "You said Trotter got out of the car and confronted you. Did he advance toward you?"

"Only a couple of steps. Then he stood there and yelled at me. He was very agitated."

"What did you do?"

"I told him to get back into the car. He didn't listen, though. Then he reached behind him, like he was going for a gun or something."

"Or a wallet," McNutt said.

Garrett nodded. "Yeah, could be. I drew my gun anyway, because at that point, I didn't know."

"If he came out with a wallet?" McNutt asked.

"I'd have been really glad," Garrett told him, "but he didn't. Shots were fired, and I couldn't tell from where. In my mind, the suspect at the car was shooting at me, so I returned fire. After he went down, the shots continued. I was finally able to determine that they were coming from the house across the street."

"When you fired at Trotter," Harris asked, "What was he doing?"

"I thought he was shooting at me," Garrett said.

"He was facing you?"

"Definitely," Garrett answered, his tone sincere and certain. "When I made the decision to fire, he was facing me. It was a split second after I saw him reach behind his back, and shots were hitting my car. I feared for my life, and it was my reasonable belief that he was the source of the threat. I didn't realize I was being ambushed at the time."

"When did you know there was more than one person shooting at you?"

"I don't remember exactly. Everything happened so fast."

"Are you aware that Mr. Trotter was hit in the back with your round?" Harris asked.

Garrett gave her a small, rueful smile. "Kinda hard not to know that, after all the media play it got."

"Can you explain that?"

"All I can think of is that between the time I saw him facing me and decided to shoot and when my finger actually pulled the trigger and the bullet was fired, he turned away." Garrett lowered his eyes and shook his head. "It looks bad to people, I know. He was facing me when I perceived the threat and chose to respond with deadly force."

"After those initial shots hit your patrol vehicle, why didn't you immediately call for back up?" Harris asked him.

Garrett heaved a sigh. "I wish I had, but it happened quickly. All I could think of is that they had the tactical advantage, and I had to act right away."

"Is that why you charged at the house, too?"

"Looking back, that was just stupid on my part. Stupid, SWAT bravado. My blood was up, you know? Someone was trying to kill me, and the threat was coming from the house. When the shots let up, I decided to take advantage of the lull and take the fight to them. Aggression wins fights."

Next to her, McNutt smiled slightly.

"Let's move forward to when you and Officer Zielinski were scanning the scene. According to him, you didn't turn on your dash camera until you went to get your flashlight from the car."

"That's true. Ray would never lie."

"We have the video as well," Harris said.

"Your point, Detective?" Thomas asked.

"Why didn't you turn on the dashcam?"

Garrett looked mildly sheepish. "I forgot. Everything jumped off so fast. His bad driving, and then trying to catch up to him. He wasn't stopping right away, so I was updating dispatch. I usually punch the button for the camera at the same time as I hit the overhead lights, but I forgot. Once I forgot, it just wasn't on my mind anymore until I was with Ray and came back to the car to get my flashlight. I realized it was off, so I turned it on." He shrugged. "It was an honest mistake, but I figured better late than not at all."

Harris opened her mouth again, but Thomas raised his hand to stop her. "Detective, you went over all of this in great detail earlier. It's after midnight and we're deep into our third hour here. Officer Garrett has cooperated fully. His answers have been the same each time you've asked them because he's told the truth. Is there any reason we can't call an end to this interview at this point? I think all of your questions have been asked and answered, have they not?"

She glanced down at her notes one last time. There was a check mark next to each of her questions. Some had two or three, indicating she'd come at the question multiple times in different ways. Garrett's statement had been clean, and it meshed with everything she knew about the incident until now. She didn't know about the additional issues he was dealing with and had purposefully compartmentalized them during the interview. What happened after the shooting had no bearing on what happened during the shooting. And her sense of it was that Garrett was getting a rough ride that wasn't his fault.

"I think we can call it quits," she agreed.

Both she and McNutt stopped their recordings, and Thomas did the same. When he and Garrett stood, Harris cleared her throat.

"Uh, there's one last piece of business," she said.

Both men looked at her.

"The SPD warrant," Harris explained, slightly embarrassed. "We, uh, we have to arrest you on it and book you into jail."

"Of course," Garrett said. "I understand."

"I'll walk over with you," Thomas said.

Garrett shook his head. "No need. Just do me a favor and call Wei for me."

"All right. I'll come see you tomorrow, too."

"You bet."

Thomas looked around the room, then excused himself. When he opened the door, a pair of uniformed deputies stood outside. Thomas gave them a nod and left.

Harris waved in the deputies. One of them unsnapped his handcuff case. The metal cuffs rattled as he removed them.

Garrett stood without a word, turned around and extended his wrists behind him. The deputy ratcheted on the handcuffs, then set the double lock mechanism so they wouldn't tighten further. Gently, he guided Garrett toward the door.

"Ty?"

Garrett turned toward her.

"Thanks for being honest," she said. "Makes my job easier."

He shrugged. "I gotta tell the truth, man."

"I appreciate it. And…" She glanced at the deputies who had him custody and then back to Garrett. "For what it's worth, I'm sorry."

THURSDAY

The police must obey the law while enforcing the law.
—Earl Warren, 14th Chief Justice of the United States
Supreme Court

Chapter 48

It was eleven minutes after midnight when Detective Wardell Clint spotted them coming down the hall. He knew because he'd been looking at his watch every few minutes for the last hour, waiting for the county to finish their interview with Garrett. He wanted to intercept them before they booked him and get Garrett into an interview room while he was in the habit of answering questions. A night in jail sometimes had a sobering effect on a person's willingness to talk. For some, it loosened the tongue. Others, it hardened their resolve. Clint was all but certain Ty Garrett fell into the second category.

The two deputies that flanked Garrett were unknown to him, but Clint wasn't sure they'd say the same of him. He knew he had a reputation and that it drifted over to the county side, too. Hopefully, it would work for him and not against him.

Clint waited until they were close, then intercepted them from the side so that Garrett would have less opportunity to say anything to them. He held up his badge for them to see.

"Detective Clint, deputies. Is he under arrest on my warrant?"

The deputies exchanged a look. The older one said, "I don't know whose warrant it is. It's an SPD warrant for drugs and felony assault. We're booking him into jail."

"That's my warrant," Clint lied. "You can transfer custody to me."

The deputy shook his head. "No. We're booking him. If you want to talk to him, set it up through jail."

"Deputy, this is my warrant, and my case. I have the authority here."

"Your authority over me is nonexistent," the deputy said. "I take orders from the sheriff, not some…detective."

Clint read the tea leaves and changed tactics. "Where's the gun?" he asked Garrett.

Garrett surprised him by answering. "What gun?"

"The one you shot Talbott with."

"I never shot anyone."

"You shot Talbott," Clint said, not believing what he just heard. "You said it was self-defense."

"Don't put that on me. I've had enough of people putting things on me that I didn't have anything to do with."

"You called me and told me that," Clint insisted.

Garrett fixed him with a cold stare. "I called you and asked how the investigation was going. Man, I think you're losing it."

"That's enough." The older deputy guided Garrett past Clint. "Detective, you need to step aside."

"You shot Ocampo, and those others," Clint said, ignoring the deputy and keeping pace. "Where is the gun?"

The younger deputy put himself between Clint and Garrett. "You need to stop."

"I've got a witness, Garrett!" Clint shouted past him.

"You're crazy," Garrett replied evenly, without turning his head. "Everyone knows that."

Chapter 49

Lieutenant Dan Flowers parked in the driveway and walked straight to the front door. He could feel his jaw clench in irritation and forced himself to let it relax. He didn't like being kept out of the loop, and whatever Captain Farrell was doing, he was definitely not in the loop about it. First, he called Clint off a quadruple homicide for some secret squirrel mission, leaving Hollander and Hill shorthanded. Both were solid detectives but there was a ton of work at the scene. He didn't understand what could be more important right now in the life of a homicide detective than working that case. Double homicides were rare enough. A quad? Detectives went an entire career without encountering one.

He definitely didn't understand why he was the errand boy sent to fetch Detective Pomeroy to bring to the station. The guy's partner just died. If the bosses were doing anything for him, it ought to be making sure he had peer support.

No, this was unusual, and Flowers saw it for what it was. Something more was going on. He didn't know what, exactly, but it stunk. And he didn't like being kept in the dark about it, either.

Pomeroy didn't answer his front door. The house was still. No TV, no music. A small light was on in the kitchen, probably the one above the stove, Flowers guessed. Otherwise, the house was dark.

Flowers rang the doorbell multiple times and pounded on the door. No answer. He peered through the small window in the door, looking to see if he could spot Pomeroy. Maybe he'd been drinking and passed out. Some people were hard as hell to wake from that kind of stupor. As far as he could tell, though, Pomeroy wasn't crashed out in the living room. Maybe he made it to his bed.

He considered his options. Farrell had been very clear about bringing in Pomeroy. No questions, no talking, no one else was to know. Bring him to the detectives' division so they could talk to him. By "they," Flowers assumed he meant the captain and Clint, because they sure as hell weren't including him in their little shadow investigation, whatever it was.

Flowers knocked again, then hit the doorbell in frustration. Almost on a whim, he tried the door handle and found it unlocked.

That was weird, Flowers thought. Cops never leave their doors unlocked. If Pomeroy was on a bender, that would explain the oversight. He hesitated before going inside, not wanting to get mistaken for an intruder and shot. In the end, he swung the door open and called out to Pomeroy.

"Justin! It's me, Dan. Your lieutenant. Don't shoot me. I'm coming in."

He'd barely finished speaking when the smell hit him. It wasn't overly strong, like death that had been at it for days, but the harsh, cloying smell of blood was still unmistakable.

"Damn," he muttered, and drew his gun.

He stepped inside the living room decided to clear that room and the kitchen first. "Justin," he called out again. "It's Dan. Holler if you can hear me."

In the kitchen, he saw what he knew he would find but didn't want to admit. Pomeroy sat leaning against the cupboard below the kitchen sink. His arms were at his side and a darkening pool of blood spread out from his body on the cream-colored linoleum floor. Pomeroy's fixed stare and still form left no doubt in his mind.

"Damn," he said again.

Flowers put his gun away. The gashes at Pomeroy's wrists were visible even at this distance, and there was no sign of struggle in the place. Investigators would pore over things for hours, but he knew they'd eventually arrive at the same conclusion he did.

Suicide.

His mind raced. Talbott shot, and now Pomeroy kills himself? Then there was the Ocampo killings. What the hell was going on?

Flowers let out a long, nerve-wracking breath. Then he took out his phone to call the captain with the news. Before he dialed, though, his eyes caught something. Two small packets of clear plastic in the puddle of blood next to Pomeroy. There was only one thing Flowers had ever seen packaged that way.

Drugs.

He hesitated. It only took him an instant to decide, and then he texted a detailed message to Cody Lofton first. Only after he was satisfied with that did he punch in the captain's phone number and hit send.

Chapter 50

"He's a cold, calculating son-of-a-bitch," Clint told Farrell.

They sat in the captain's office at a round table he used for small staff meetings. Farrell had been listening to Clint's account of the hallway encounter, followed by Clint's theories surrounding the entire last week's events.

"I don't get it," he said. "You told me earlier this week that you thought he was innocent."

"I was turned around. I can see it straight now. He shot Talbott."

Farrell nodded. "I think you're right. They don't have any good witnesses in that shooting, according to what I can get out of their investigators. Only one of them is even sure the shooter was black."

"We got his buddy, Derek Tillman."

"He's recanted. Says now that he isn't sure what he saw, except that the cop shot first."

Clint frowned. "He's a liar."

"Maybe but try to prove it."

"I will. He made statements to me. The prosecutor can use me to impeach his testimony."

Farrell sighed. "Yeah, maybe. You know how that usually plays in court."

"Terrible, but it's our only choice if he lies."

"That'll be up to the prosecutor," Farrell said. He leaned back and rubbed his eyes. "Let's run through it one more time before Pomeroy gets here."

"All right. I'll lay it out, you poke holes in it?"

"My specialty."

"Okay, here it is. Talbott and Garrett hook up while on SWAT, start hitting dealers. Probably with Ocampo pointing them in the right direction."

"Source?"

"Pomeroy's testimony. They bring him into their little gang, and they keep at it, living double lives and raking in drug money a few times a year. Then Garrett decides to cut them out and work directly with Ocampo."

"Source?"

"Again, Pomeroy. We could have offered Ocampo some kind of deal, too, but that's obviously not an option." Clint closed his eyes and visualized. "As retribution, Talbott and Pomeroy get Todd Trotter to lure Garrett to a traffic stop in front of the house, so they can ambush him, and cut him out of the deal instead."

"Source?"

"Supposition. I didn't get a chance to confirm this with Pomeroy before being called to the Ocampo murders. We can maybe sweat Kayla Trent, Pomeroy's girlfriend and the realtor of the house. Maybe she actually knows something, but that's likely only circumstantial. Pomeroy's the key and I'll pin him down on this when he gets in here."

"The shooting goes down, but they miss Garrett. Then what? You think they sent those two guys to attack him while he was out on a run?"

Clint shook his head. "I don't think so. I never interviewed them, and we still should follow up. The case belonged to Talbott and Pomeroy, so those interviews were theirs to do. I don't know if they ever did."

"Loose end."

Clint made a note. "I'll handle it, but my sense of it is that when the whole black-cop-shoots-white-victim bit went viral, and Garrett's address ended up on Facebook, these two thugs decided to go get some of what they believe to be justice. The whole thing was racially motivated, you ask me."

"It's convenient that Talbott and Pomeroy caught the assault case, don't you think?"

Clint wagged a finger. "Convenient isn't the right word. Fortuitous, maybe. The bigger point here is that Talbott was up on the wheel for call outs on the night of the shooting. Think about that for a second. If he and Pomeroy had been successful in shooting Garrett, he would have been investigating a murder that he and his partner committed. It's a perfect plan. Even after they messed up and Garrett survived, if you hadn't decided to make a change, Talbott still would have been the shadow, not me. That would have kept him close to Harris's entire investigation, and even given him the chance to steer it a little." Clint nodded his head with certainty. "I think they picked the night they did on purpose for that very reason."

"It was a happy accident they caught the assault?"

"Probably, but then they chose to make the best of it. Talbott planted the drugs and they slapped the cuffs on Garrett."

"Source?"

"Pomeroy, again. The rest is my own speculation, but maybe Pomeroy can confirm."

"They didn't get the paperwork done in time, though." Farrell shook his head in confusion. "That bothers me. Why go to all that trouble and then tank the paperwork?"

"They may be dirty, but they're not inept. Maybe they just wanted to shock him into playing ball and figured a night in jail was enough. Or maybe they didn't think it through and once he was in jail, they realized that he was harder to get at. Either way, I think the paperwork fail was purposeful. You told me before that it was the chief that ordered them to obtain an arrest warrant. Talbott and Pomeroy wanted to let the prosecutor push it through later on down the road."

Farrell nodded in agreement. "That's true. Source?"

"Pomeroy, with you and Flowers in support."

Farrell glanced at his watch. "Let's finish up. Flowers should be here soon."

"Okay. Garrett gets released from jail on his own recognizance. He is fully engaged in the play now, working me, working people he knows, trying to get everyone riled up that he's a victim. He gets a gun from somewhere, maybe his buddy Tillman, maybe he's always had it. Either way, Talbott catches up to him. No matter who shot first, the end result is Talbott is dead, and Garrett shot him."

"Source?"

"Tillman."

"Who is uncooperative."

"We'll impeach his testimony. The other witnesses saw Talbott shoot, right?"

"Yes, but they can't identify the other man."

"If we find the gun Garrett used, that'll link him."

"What's the chance of that?"

Clint shrugged. "I don't know. That's a tough one. I'll have to run down any place connected with Tillman, and with the barbershop owner, Oakley. Plus, his mother. Maybe he hid it somewhere in one of those places."

Farrell gave him a dubious look but didn't argue. "Then what?"

"Garrett knows that things are falling apart, therefore he goes to Ocampo's house and blows away all four people. That solves Hollander's quadruple."

"Source?"

"Nona Henry, my witness. Any DNA Hollander and Hill turn up. And the gun. Plus, Pomeroy will tie Garrett to Ocampo with his testimony."

"The DNA search is a needle in a haystack," Farrell said.

"So is the gun," Clint admitted.

"Which leaves your elderly witness and Pomeroy."

Clint nodded. "That'll be enough. Pomeroy will do the lion's share of the work, and Mrs. Henry will add credibility to it with her identification."

Farrell thought about everything they'd covered. The majority of it was weak or circumstantial, unless they discovered the gun. Pomeroy's testimony would tie it all together.

"All right," he said, "let's talk about what to offer Pomeroy. You think it'll have to be full immunity?"

"I don't like that," Clint said. "I think he'll go for much less. He's weak."

The phone on Farrell's desk rang. He rose and walked to it, snatching the receiver. "This better be you, Dan."

"It's me, Cap."

"Where the hell are you?"

"I'm...I'm up at Pomeroy's house."

"Well, bring him down here."

"I can't, Captain. He killed himself."

"He *what?*"

"He sat down on his kitchen floor and cut his wrists. Hours ago, by the look of it. I'm about to call medics and patrol."

"Oh, no," Farrell whispered.

"Do you have any orders, sir? Before I get started?"

"No," Farrell said, clearing his throat. "I'll call the chief. Keep me updated."

"Yes, sir."

Farrell hung up. He turned to Clint, who was eyeing him warily.

"What is it?"

"Pomeroy killed himself."

"*Damn it!*" Clint yelled, slapping the table in frustration.

Farrell sat down, shaking his head and trying to get his bearings before he called the chief. Finally, he looked up at Clint, whose jaw was clenching and unclenching with rage. "We have to keep this to ourselves for now," he said.

"Pomeroy," Clint said through gritted teeth. "He was the key."

"We have to figure out how to bring this forward without him," Farrell said.

"There's gotta be a way," Clint insisted urgently. "I'll keep at it."

"Until we've got something," Farrell said, "we have to keep it between us."

Clint looked at him. "I'll go interview Garrett later this morning. After they get him processed in. I'll work him for a confession. That's the best shot we have."

It might be the only shot, Farrell thought.

"Do it," he said.

Chapter 51

As he walked up the sidewalk toward city hall, Cody Lofton's head wasn't in the game.

It was still back in his apartment with Amanda Donahue where they had spent the entire night together. When the alarm on his phone signaled it was time to wake, Lofton did so with reluctance.

Since Lofton knew the mayor would expect him early, he slid quietly from under the sheet. He padded into the shower and turned on the water.

He closed his eyes and let the hot water wake him not only to the morning, but to reality.

Cody Lofton knew he had made a cardinal mistake. He'd let himself become emotionally exposed to the most powerful woman he'd ever met. It wasn't money or power she had that scared him. What scared him most was the undefinable *it*.

If she turned on him now, he was ruined. If this was a ploy to weaken his standing with the mayor, it had worked.

Everything he had strived for could be undone due to a moment of weakness. He'd never wanted a woman like this in his life nor to even come close to one. Lofton turned up the temperature even hotter until it was almost scalding. The pain was a reminder of what might be coming his way if he didn't pay attention.

The shower door clicked, and he opened his eyes. Amanda stuck her hand in the shower. "Good Lord!"

Lofton turned the temperature down slightly.

She stepped in and wetted her hair. Her mascara from the previous night ran slightly. She looked in the shower's mirror and wiped it from her face.

She faced Lofton and he stood silently.

"Aren't you going to say something?"

"I—," he started and then shrugged when he couldn't find the words.

"You knew this would happen eventually, didn't you?"

He shook his head. "Never in a million years."

"For a guy who thinks he's got his act together, you're kind of clueless."

He started to say something, but she moved forward and kissed him...

"Cody!" a woman's voice shouted, breaking his reverie.

Lofton shook the thoughts of last night from his head. He was almost to the front door of city hall when Kelly Davis, the reporter from the *Spokesman-Review*, hurried toward him.

"Got a minute?"

Lofton nodded, but realized her notebook was in her hands.

"What can you tell me about the shooting in Liberty Lake yesterday?"

"No comment."

"A detective from the Spokane Police Department is murdered and you say no comment."

Lofton stared at her.

"What about the reports that Garrett was arrested this morning on his warrant?"

"I'm unaware of that."

"Are you also unaware that there is a crime scene at a northside house, right now? Suicide victim."

Lofton shrugged. "I don't usually get briefed on suicides."

"This one is a cop."

Lofton didn't reply, keeping his expression neutral, but his mind was buzzing.

"You've got one murdered cop," Davis detailed, "one in jail for assault, and one that just killed himself. What's going on inside the police department?"

"It seems you know more than me this morning," Lofton said, pushing past Davis on his way into city hall. When he was alone, he pulled out his cell phone and saw multiple text messages from Lieutenant Dan Flowers alerting him to everything that Davis had just said.

"Damn it!" he yelled.

On the seventh floor, the mayor was waiting in the doorway of his office.

"Where the hell have you been?"

"Slow start," Lofton said.

"Where the hell is Amanda?" The mayor looked toward her desk, like he was expecting her to appear out of nowhere.

"How would I know?"

Sikes studied him, a sneer appeared for a split-second.

"Have you heard the news?" Sikes asked

"About what? The murdered detective, Garrett's arrest for his warrant, or the police officer's suicide?"

Sikes shook his head. "I'm always amazed at where you get your information."

"Don't be," Lofton said. "I was bum rushed by Kelly Davis at the front door. She's the one that brought me up to speed on everything."

"What did you say?"

"No comment."

"Seriously?"

"What else could I say? I didn't know how to respond."

"Didn't you watch the news this morning? The national coverage was horrible when they found out about Garrett's arrest."

"I didn't see it."

"Our city is under siege and you've got your head in the clouds. Just what were you doing that was so important that you couldn't pay attention to what was going on in our city?"

The elevators dinged, and Amanda Donahue walked in. Her hair was perfect and bounced slightly as she walked. She wore a basic mini-skirt and blouse. Amanda smiled broadly at

Lofton, but the smile faded slightly when she saw the mayor. "Good morning, sir."

He smiled at Amanda. "Give us a minute." The mayor then inhaled deeply and looked at Lofton. "Get in there," he said, thumbing toward his office.

Lofton stepped inside and turned around as Sikes moved toward him, his finger in his face. "Did you?"

He lifted his hands in the surrender position. "Did I what?"

"You know I was working that."

Lofton shook his head. "I had no idea."

Sikes scrunched his lips before speaking. "You know damn well. You're not stupid."

"Neither is your wife."

The mayor stared at Lofton. "Are you saying you did me a favor? Because I'm not going to fall for some stupid smokescreen like that."

"I did it for myself," Lofton said, "but don't you think we have more important things to worry about?"

The mayor shook his head and threw his hands in the air. "I just want it to all go away. Where the hell is Baumgartner?"

"You told him you were too busy to meet with him today."

"Get him on the phone, then jerk his chain and get us some updates."

Lofton stared at the mayor.

"When we get past all this," Sikes said, making a circle in the air before pointing in the direction of Amanda's desk, "we're going to deal with what's happening out there. You might have just screwed your career, buddy boy."

Chapter 52

Detective Wardell Clint sat waiting in the jail interview room, practicing the deep breathing techniques he'd learned in aikido all those years ago. He focused on the inhale. Once it was fully completed, he allowed himself a few moments to finalize his interview strategy, then focused on the exhale. Limiting his thinking about the case to a small window of time forced him to focus on strategy, facts, and details, not emotion. He couldn't afford to let emotion run this interview, no matter how deeply betrayed he felt right now.

The corrections officer that escorted Garrett was a friendly country boy nicknamed Tater. Clint had always had good interactions with Tater throughout his career, but now all he got was a cold glare and formality from the big man as he unlocked Garrett's transport cuffs.

"You are limited to thirty minutes, Detective," Tater said stiffly. "I'll be outside the door, at the end of the hall, monitoring the video feed. If either of you wish to terminate this interview, turn to the camera up in the corner and give a wave."

Clint gave him a nod of acknowledgement.

"Thanks, Tater," Garrett said.

"You bet."

Tater left, and Garrett settled onto the bench seat across from Clint, rubbing his wrists absently.

"I see you're making friends in here," Clint said.

"Tater's good people."

Clint shook his head in disbelief. Garrett was going to ride this "man-wronged" horse until it dropped.

Well, time to drop it.

He removed an index card from his jacket and read from it without preamble. "I am Wardell Clint, a police detective. You have the right to remain silent. You have the right to an attorney, and to have said attorney present during questioning. If you cannot afford an attorney, one will be appointed to you without cost. If you agree to speak with me today, be advised that anything you say may be used as evidence in a criminal proceeding. Do you understand these rights as I have read them to you?"

"Man, are you serious?"

Clint knew that the interview room was recorded. The audio feed didn't go to the guard's monitoring station, but it was retrievable upon request. He intended to make sure anything Garrett said would make it into court.

"I am one hundred percent serious," he said. Then he repeated, "Do you understand these rights as I have read them to you?"

Garrett looked at him. Blinked. Then he said, "Yeah, man. I know my rights."

"Will you agree to waive these rights and speak with me at this time?"

"I will reserve my rights," Garrett said, his tone matching Clint's formality. "But I will agree to speak with you at this time without the presence of counsel and am fully aware that I may cease to do so at any time by re-asserting my right to remain silent."

He gave Clint a smirk that said there-you-go.

Clint put the card back into his jacket pocket. Ideally, he'd have Garrett sign it but he wasn't allowed to bring a pen into the interview room. The audio and video would have to do.

"Did you plan this all along?" he asked.

"Plan what?" Garrett motioned around him. "Being in jail? Be real, brother."

"I'm not your brother," Clint said, choking back the rage that he'd been struggling with for hours now.

Garrett shrugged. "We're all brothers, aren't we?"

Clint forced himself to take a deep inhale and let it out slowly while he watched Garrett's expression. The utter calmness he saw there rattled him more than he wanted to admit. There was a confidence there that shouldn't be.

"I believed you," he said. "You played me."

"I didn't play anybody," Garrett said, but his eyes were sparkling with dark amusement. "In case you didn't notice, I'm sitting behind bars for something I didn't do."

"You did, though. We both know that your only way out is through me. Through the truth."

"The truth is all I've been telling. Somebody else is spinning lies, and I'm the one getting caught up in all that."

"This is your last real chance," Clint said, hoping he didn't sound like he was pleading. "Tell me the truth, maybe you avoid the needle. Get to see your babies grow up and have lives."

The mention of his kids seemed to stir something in Garrett. His eyes narrowed, and his jawline hardened. "You leave my family out of this discussion or we're done talking."

Clint forged ahead. "They're the only reason I'm even having this conversation. I've got enough to put you away for three life terms, and after the way you played me and the system, you deserve it. But *they* don't."

"I'm warning you," Garrett growled. "Don't talk about them."

"You shot Talbott," Clint said.

Garrett smirked. "No, I didn't."

"Witnesses put you there."

"They're wrong."

"They all say Talbott shot at you first, that you fired back in self-defense."

"That's good news for whoever he was shooting at, but it wasn't me."

"Your friend, Derek Tillman, lives right there."

"Derek's all right, I hope?"

"Stop playing this game. Help me understand what happened there."

Garrett shook his head. "Brother, you know exactly what happened."

"Don't play the brother card with me," Clint said. "I didn't see you at last Sunday dinner."

"Fine," Garrett said with a shrug. "But you know what happened. White people saw a black man and remembered me from all the TV coverage this past week, so that's who they *saw*. If it had happened two weeks ago, they'd have sworn they saw Tiger Woods."

"Tillman said you were there."

"Now, that's a lie."

"Why would your friend lie about that?"

"He didn't. You just did. And since the truth is that I was never there, there's no way Derek would say I was. Man, if you're just going to lie to me..." He shrugged and glanced meaningfully toward the camera high up in the corner near the ceiling.

Clint quickly shifted gears. "You killed Pomeroy."

Garrett feigned mild surprise. "Detective Pomeroy? He's dead, too?"

"All of these denials just make you look cold, Ty. Makes it look premeditated."

"I can't premeditate what I've never done."

"I know you killed Ocampo along with those other people in his house. Why?"

"Who are you even talking about? Ocampo?"

"He deals drugs."

"Lots of people deal drugs. This is Spokane."

"You went to school with him."

"I went to school with lots of people. I'm supposed to remember every one of them?"

"Only the ones you collude with."

Garrett stared at him with an amused expression. "Collude? Is that a fancy word for conspiracy? 'Cause you know a thing or two about that, don't you, Honey Badger?"

Clint wanted to grab him. Break bones. Smash cartilage. Make him bleed. Yet he knew better. If he did that, everything fell apart, and things would be like the arm-breaking incident at the Circle K again, only a thousand times worse.

"Where's the gun?" he asked, his voice low and tight.

"What gun?"

"The one you shot Talbott with. And Ocampo."

"You just do *not* give up. I told you, I didn't shoot Talbott, and I don't know this other dude you keep talking about."

"The gun is your only way out," Clint said. "If you give up the gun, it shows remorse. It shows cooperation. If Talbott was truly self-defense, then so be it. Maybe there was an element of self-defense at Ocampo's place, too. I'm willing to accept that, but you've got to tell me. You've got to give up the gun, to prove it's all real."

Garrett stared at him for such a long while that Clint began to wonder if he'd finally broken through to the man. Then Garrett leaned back in his chair and shook his head mournfully. "Man, you really *don't* know what is real, do you? You come in here, weaving all these wild conspiracies…I'm starting to wonder if you were in on all of it."

"All of what?"

Garrett swept his hand slowly across the tabletop. "The whole thing. Whatever it was that somebody was planning against me. The ambush. The attack by those racist rednecks. The planting of drugs in my home."

"That's crazy."

"I might have thought so, too. I see it differently now, the way you're coming at me like this. Maybe that's why you got close to me. Not to help me, but to see if the plan was working. To keep tabs on me. If that's so…" Garrett shook his head. "Well, using the fact that we're both black men to work me like that is just shameful, brother. Worse than that. Despicable."

Clint sat back in his chair, incredulous. The absolute, shameless balls on this guy, he thought.

"Keep on spinning your crazy conspiracy theories," Garrett continued. "All you do is prove my point."

Clint cleared his throat. "I have a witness."

"You said that. Your witnesses are bullshit."

"At Ocampo's. I've got a witness that saw you enter, heard shots, and saw you leave."

"Hell, you say," Garrett said, but Clint saw a flicker of concern flash across his face. It gave him heart.

He pulled out a copy he'd made of the photo montage Nona Henry had viewed to identify Garrett. He unfolded the paper, laid it out in front of Garrett and smoothed it flat.

Garrett didn't look at it right away. Instead, he studied Clint's face for a long moment. Then he leaned forward and examined the paper. It didn't take long for his concerned expression to melt away.

"That's weak," he said. "My lawyer is Pamela Wei. You know her? She'll tear that to shreds."

"It's a positive identification."

"With me in the number five position? Even us patrol mopes know that's the money spot. And those other brothers? They look nothing like me." He shook his head. "Nuh-uh. You got someone to pick out the most different looking face on the page who just happened to be perfectly placed? A face that's been all over TV for the better part of a week? Like I said, my lawyer chews that up."

"Maybe she tries," Clint said, encouraged that he wasn't denying his presence at Ocampo's anymore but attacking the identification. In Clint's experience, that was almost a tacit admission of guilt. "I've got a solid citizen who will get up on the stand and tell the world that you went into that house, blasted away four people, and walked out again. That's life without parole, *at best*. Most likely the needle."

A small trickle of sweat appeared on Garrett's scalp and ran down behind his ear. He ignored it, but Clint noticed. It gave him even more resolve.

"The only way to mitigate all that is to tell me the truth. Today. Give up the gun."

Garrett leaned forward and looked at the photo montage again. "That signature looks shaky to me. Like an old person wrote it." He looked up at Clint. "Is this really the best you've got to frame me with? A circle around a black man? Probably made by an old white lady whose generation thought the word 'Negro' was polite. I mean, normally, you would have a heyday with something like that. Now you're stuffing that in my face like it's supposed to mean something?" He shook his head in disgust. "It doesn't mean a thing, and you know it."

"You were there."

"No, I wasn't."

"Then how did you know my witness was an old woman?"

He shrugged. "I had a fifty-fifty shot. Why? Was it some old man instead? Same thing applies. You're trying to pin this on me with some weak ass evidence, and it's all lies. Listen to me." He punctuated each word. "I. Was. Not. *There*."

Clint sank back in his chair, feeling defeated. His strategy had been to go straight at Garrett, to speak to his pragmatism on the one hand and use the emotion of the children to reinforce his proposed route of confession. He had failed.

"They'll find DNA," he said, finally. "At Ocampo's."

"I doubt that, unless they do me like O.J."

Clint gaped at him. "That man was *guilty*."

"Yet they still felt like they had to plant evidence, just to make sure."

Clint didn't have a reply. He couldn't imagine a cop alive who would believe this. An instant later, he realized Garrett didn't, either. He was just running his game.

"You want to talk about things they might find," Garrett said. "What do you want to bet they find drugs when they search Pomeroy's house? I think he was dirty. He always gave off that vibe. Him and Talbott both."

Clint shook his head slowly. "You son of a bitch."

Garrett seemed to be suppressing a smile as he turned his face to the ceiling camera and waved both arms slowly over his head.

"I'm going to get you," Clint said quietly. "You know that, don't you?"

Garrett didn't reply immediately. When the lock in the door buzzed open, he stood up and proffered his wrists to Tater. He looked at Clint while the corrections officer loosely ratcheted on the transport cuffs.

"You know that, right?" Clint repeated.

Garrett affected a look of pity. "What I know is you've got to stop chasing shadows and black helicopters at the tree line, brother. Get some professional help. Or retire. Your game is getting slow."

Clint watched him go.

"You son of a bitch," he repeated.

Chapter 53

After the dressing down by the mayor, Cody Lofton decided to take matters into his own hands. He wanted to know where everything stood for himself.

He held off calling Chief Baumgartner to "yank his chain" as the mayor had requested. Instead, he tracked down the district attorney, Arthur Tuck, to ask where he stood with the Ty Garrett investigation.

Amanda sat across on the other side of his desk. Her eyes were wide, and her lips parted as she watched him. His heart raced, and he never once thought it was the look she gave anyone else. He convinced himself it was the look she gave him alone.

Lofton shook himself to reality when a voice came on the telephone.

"Arthur Tuck."

"Artie, it's Cody Lofton. How are you?"

"I'm good, my friend. How are things in your world?"

"I'm great. I just met the most fascinating woman," he said, and Amanda smiled at him.

"Cody, when *aren't* you meeting the most fascinating women?"

Lofton changed gears and asked, "Hey, Artie, where are you with the Garrett thing?"

"That's what it takes to get a phone call from you these days? Well, as luck would have it, the lead detective on that case emailed me last night. She said they were finished with their investigation and would finalize the report today. I expect to have it tomorrow."

Lofton closed his eyes and thought. He quickly opened his eyes and asked, "Do you think you could come down and give us a status on where this is at? We've taken a lot of heat over the last week and we're trying to do some damage control."

Tuck let out a small laugh. "I'll bet you are. You guys have been getting massacred in the press. I'm sure Sikes is watching his reelection bid go up in smoke."

"Something like that. You've been a big supporter of the mayor in the past. Can I call in a favor?"

"Yeah. I'll make it happen."

Amanda smirked. "What's with this meeting? There isn't anything on the mayor's schedule."

"Trust me."

Lofton then called the sheriff's department and learned that the sheriff was at a Boy Scout retreat for a four-day weekend with his son. Lofton smiled. That got him one step closer to his next goal.

He texted Lieutenant Dan Flowers a question. Five minutes later the response arrived.

Det. Cassidy Harris—509-555-2314

She answered on the third ring.

"This is Harris."

"Cassidy, you don't know me, I'm Cody Lofton. Chief of staff for Mayor Sikes, City of Spokane."

"How'd you get my number?" Her voice was full of suspicion.

"Dan Flowers gave it to me. Do you know Dan?"

"SPD Lieutenant. I know him."

"Dan's a friend. I asked him to put me in touch with you. I hope that was okay."

"What do you want, Mr. Lofton?"

"I'm sure you've seen the news coverage lately. It's not shown our city in a favorable light."

"No, it hasn't."

"Cassidy, we're trying to determine a course of action going forward and part of that is getting ahead of things. I just got off the phone with D.A. Tuck who said you're going to send your findings to him shortly."

"I'm not at liberty to talk about that with you."

"I understand. What I'd like to ask is for you to join us this afternoon for a meeting."

"I won't be swayed to change my opinion, one way or the other."

Lofton's heart raced. Did that mean she had found Garrett culpable in some manner? That would be terrible for the city and the administration. Lofton pushed on. "That's not what we're asking, Cassidy. We just want to ask some questions, so we know how to prepare for this. Artie Tuck will be there. So, will Chief Baumgartner. I wanted the Sheriff to join us but he's at a Boy Scout retreat with his son."

"Yeah, we'd heard that," Harris chuckled.

"Why is that funny?"

"I was imagining him in a Boy Scout outfit."

Lofton laughed with her even though he couldn't find the humor in it.

"What do you say, Cassidy?"

"Stop calling me Cassidy."

"I'm sorry, Detective Harris," Lofton said, hoping to save the call.

"Cassie is fine," she said. "If Artie is going to be there, I'll make the meeting. On one condition."

"Name it."

"You don't invite Wardell Clint."

Getting the chief to attend the meeting was easy.

"Artie Tuck and the county's detectives will be there," Lofton said.

"How'd you get them to attend?"

"I asked nicely."

"Sure," Baumgartner said, disbelief in his voice.

Once he got him over the hump, the chief offered up the conference room at the police station. "It will be easier for the detectives to find. Tuck knows how to get here as well."

Lofton said, "I'm all for it, chief, but let me ask you this. If I tell the mayor we're doing this in your conference room, what will he say?"

Baumgartner huffed. "He'd say change it to yours."

"Exactly. Thanks for understanding. Can I ask a favor?"

"What's that?"

"Detective Clint can't be anywhere near this meeting."

Baumgartner never asked why before agreeing.

The mayor didn't take the news of the meeting as well.

"What the hell?"

"A meeting was scheduled with the D.A. and the county detectives to get a briefing on their investigation. They're going to release their findings to the D.A. as early as tomorrow. The chief wants to get ahead of the curve."

"What is the bastard up to?" Sikes said, walking back and forth behind his desk.

Lofton shrugged.

"What time is the meeting set for?"

"Two o'clock."

Sikes sneered and put his hands on his hips. Lofton couldn't tell if the sneer was meant for him or for the chief. In the end, it didn't really matter.

"What if I already had a meeting scheduled?"

Lofton smirked. "I think your invitation was an afterthought."

Sikes' eyes widened and then he slapped his hands in anger. "I should have been his first invitation. He does know I'm the mayor, right?"

"Yes, sir, I believe he does."

"Where is this meeting taking place?"

"The conference room at the police station."

Sikes stabbed a finger at him. "No way. You make sure that meeting happens here on our turf."

"Sir, he's already got everybody coming to the station."

"I don't give a damn," the mayor yelled. "I want the meeting here. Show me you can make that happen, buddy boy. Let me know I can still place my trust in you."

Lofton nodded and walked out.

Amanda was leaning against the wall outside the mayor's office. She had listened to the entire conversation. She shook her head and smiled. "Nice work, Br'er Rabbit. I see Br'er Fox just threw you into the briar patch."

"Yes," Lofton agreed. "Now the trick is getting out."

Cody Lofton escorted Artie Tuck into the conference room on the seventh floor. Detectives Cassidy Harris and Shaun McNutt were already seated at the table. Both of them had notebooks in front of them.

Lofton turned and almost ran head-on into Chief Baumgartner. He'd brought Captain Farrell with him. Farrell commanded all SPD investigators, so it made sense to have him there, although it was starting to look like an inquisition board for the county detectives.

"Chief, can I have a moment?"

Baumgartner nodded, and they stepped off to the side.

"I'm sorry for what's been occurring lately."

The chief shrugged. "It's part of the territory. The media eats this stuff up."

"I'm not talking about that. I was referring to the political struggle that's been going on."

Baumgartner's eyes narrowed.

"The mayor has been under a lot of pressure this past week. I don't think he's handled it as well as he should."

The big man gnawed on his lip, thinking.

"I think he was tough on you several times when it was unnecessary. He had plenty of opportunities to take a step back but instead he pressed forward to the detriment of several people, including you. He put me in a position with you that I deeply regret. I wanted to apologize for that."

Amanda Donahue walked up to them but stopped several feet back out of the chief's view. She had a notebook in her hand.

Baumgartner asked, "Whatever intrigue you're trying to drag me into, Lofton, leave me out."

Lofton tilted his head. "What?"

"I know you and the games you play. You're setting me up for something and I'm not going to have it. I serve at the pleasure of the mayor—"

"The council would—"

"Those pussies won't do anything. This is the first *real* strong mayor we've had, and I support him. I know where my bread is buttered. It seems like you forgot that."

"I haven't forgot."

"I value loyalty over ambition," he said before turning. He saw Amanda, nodded and then headed into the conference room.

Amanda stepped up to Lofton. "What the hell was that?"

"I tried to mend a fence."

"Oh, Cody, that was a mistake," she said, taking his hands into hers. "Baumgartner's a big dog. His master can kick him, but he'll always stay loyal. You didn't see that?"

He shrugged, not sure if he agreed with her assessment. "I thought an apology would help."

"He's old school. What you should have done is kicked him again. That's what he understands."

Cody let go of her hand as they walked into the conference room. They sat next to each other at the table. Lofton positioned himself the furthest away from Sikes who would be at the head of the table. Baumgartner was on the other side of Amanda, putting him next to the mayor. On the opposite side of the table was Tuck, Harris and McNutt. Farrell sat at the opposite end of the table.

Underneath the table, Amanda slipped her hand in to Lofton's. She leaned toward him and whispered, "I assume we're together tonight?"

Lofton looked at her with surprise. He hadn't considered anything else. A smile grew on his face that she matched.

Just then Sikes walked in and strode angrily to the head of the table. He turned, faced the group, and put his hands on the table. "All right then, let's hear what you've got."

Chapter 54

Tyler Garrett leaned into the payphone when his wife finally picked up the call.

"Hello?"

"Hey, baby, it's me."

"Oh my God," she squealed. "Are you okay?"

He tapped his knuckles on the wall as he spoke. "I'm great, Ang. Everything is golden."

Garrett took a deep breath and looked over his shoulder. The country boy jailer, Tater, had cleared the area for him to make the call. He had a few minutes to talk with his wife alone before he had to go back to his cell.

"You actually sound good."

"That's because I am."

"The news said you were back in jail."

"I am, but don't worry, baby. It won't be for long. It's all going to work out fine."

"How do you know?"

Garrett laughed. "It's just like I told you. Wardell helped me figure it out."

Chapter 55

Mayor Sikes, Chief of Staff Lofton, and Captain Tom Farrell listened carefully as Detective Harris laid out the facts of their investigation into Officer Ty Garrett's shooting. In any other reality, Farrell might be listening with an open mind, trying to take in the big picture and understand as best he could. In this world, though, Garrett was possibly a murderer, so he listened for any evidence that would help Detective Clint prove it.

He was sorely disappointed.

"This officer has been through hell," Sikes said, when Detective Harris had finished.

Farrell felt bile in his throat. He knew he had to speak up, but he also knew that he had the smallest voice in the room, probably even smaller than the mayor's assistant. When he spoke, he had to make it count.

"I can't address that, sir," Detective Harris said. "All I can do is share the facts that we know, and those we don't."

"Is there a finding?"

Harris gave him a strange look, then glanced at Tuck.

"Typically," Lofton interjected, "the investigating agency doesn't make a finding. They submit it to Artie's office, and the D.A. reviews it."

Sikes gave Lofton a look of barely masked irritation and turned to Tuck. "So, you decide, Artie?"

Tuck nodded. "We determine whether there was any criminal culpability, or if it was accidental, or justified."

"And?"

"And...?" Tuck waved his hand to draw out more from the mayor.

"What's your finding?"

"I don't have one. I haven't reviewed the case yet."

Sikes pointed at Harris. "She just spent the last hour and a half reviewing it for you."

"I need more than just a briefing. I need to study the entire file. Consult case law. SPD policy. Garrett's training records. It can take a while."

"How long?"

"It depends. Certainly, a month. Maybe longer."

Sikes shook his head. "That's ridiculous."

"That's the process," Tuck said. "It's designed to be meticulous, full of checks and balances, and has to be able to withstand public scrutiny in a transparent environment."

Sikes cocked his head at Tuck. "That sounds like something a politician would say."

Tuck shrugged. "My position is an elected one, just like yours. I didn't win the election by being unable to string a few words together."

"I can see that but Artie…a *month*?"

"That's the process," he repeated.

"What's your initial take, at least?"

Tuck took a deep breath and let it out, considering. "I'd say that there are some unanswered questions, the largest being that Officer Garrett was ambushed, but by who?"

Sikes turned to Harris. "Any thoughts on that?"

Harris shook her head. "That avenue of investigation has been a dead end. But ultimately, our job was to investigate the death of Todd Trotter and Officer Garrett's actions in causing that death. The fact is, he was ambushed. Regardless of who shot at him, he took fire and his actions have to be examined within that context."

"What's your take on it, Detective? Unofficially, of course."

Harris cast an uncomfortable glance at Tuck, but the D.A. did not object to the question. Carefully, she adjusted the file in front of her. Without looking at the mayor, she said, "Based on all of the evidence Detective McNutt and I examined, if it was my role to determine a finding on this investigation, I would lean toward justifiable homicide."

Farrell felt his heart sink at those words. Maybe she was right, but everything Garrett did after that night tarnished even a righteous act for him.

Sikes snapped his fingers and looked at Tuck. "There you go. And she's the expert."

"She's an expert investigator," Tuck corrected him. "She's not an expert legal analyst. That's my job."

"What if," Lofton suggested, "your office were to say something along the lines 'Our preliminary view of this tragic incident is that Officer Garrett's actions appear justifiable within the context of the events he faced.' Would that work?"

Tuck opened his mouth to answer but Baumgartner interrupted.

"Say 'justifiable, given the totality of the circumstances,' instead," the chief said. "Use the language of the law."

Farrell winced slightly. He could see where this was going. They were trying to hang armor on Garrett.

"I'm not entirely comfortable with that," Tuck said.

"Look," Mayor Sikes growled, "we are in a Gong show here. Public opinion is wavering, and I'm talking about our base here, not the sizable chunk of people who have already turned against us on this. We need to get back in front of the situation and salvage it before they show up at city hall with pitchforks and torches."

"That's a little dramatic, don't you think?"

"If you need me to be more literal, Artie, then think of the pitchforks and torches as vigils, protests, and riots, followed by election recalls. It is surprisingly easy to kick a mayor out of office in this city." He paused, then added, "Or a district attorney."

Silence hung in the air for a few seconds, though it seemed much longer to Farrell. He silently hoped the D.A. would stand his ground. If he waited to rule on the Garrett shooting, and slowed down this whitewash train that the mayor seemed determined to push down the track, maybe Clint could find something more tangible in the meantime.

"All right," Tuck said. "I'll agree to a preliminary statement along the lines you've suggested, but I am including a clause that reads 'pending a full review.' That's the best I can do."

"That will work," Lofton said. "Thank you."

Sikes shot Lofton another glare, then turned to Tuck. "Yes, Artie, thanks for seeing things so reasonably. I knew I could count on your integrity, as always."

Tuck didn't reply.

"I know we all have a few more things to discuss, but I believe we can continue without the detectives. I know you're both busy, and we've already monopolized enough of your time."

The dismissal was clear, and both Harris and McNutt seemed almost relieved to hear it. Harris gathered her notes, closed her file. The others remained silent while she did so, watching until she and her partner rose as one and left the room.

As soon as the door closed, Sikes turned on Baumgartner. "What the hell is going on in your police department, Bob?"

Baumgartner flushed slightly. "It's been a bad week. But—"

"But nothing! One of your officers gets ambushed, then is the victim of a racially motivated attack. Another one is dead in a separate jurisdiction, and then a third kills himself in his own kitchen. Meanwhile, you decide that's a good time to head off to the coast to dip your wick?"

An uncomfortable silence followed while the mayor glared at the chief and the rest of the room watched. Artie Tuck shifted uneasily in his chair.

"Sir," began Baumgartner, "this has been a worst-case scenario of events. It looks bad in its totality but—"

"You already used that magic word earlier," Sikes sneered. "*Totality*. It doesn't make you seem smart, Bob. Not from where I sit."

Farrell felt a stab of pity for Baumgartner and considered rising to his defense. Unfortunately, the only information he had to share wasn't going to make things any better for his chief.

Now is not the time, he told himself. Wait for the right moment.

Tuck cleared his throat. "Perhaps someone could bring me up to speed on current events?" he asked, clearly trying to be the peacemaker. "All I know is what the news is reporting."

"That's the problem," Sikes snapped. "That's all anybody knows, and it is hurting us in a big way."

Somehow, Baumgartner seemed to keep his cool. He glanced at Farrell, as if considering turning the floor over to him, but didn't. Farrell had briefed him earlier on the official, established events, holding back on what he and Clint believed about Garrett until there was enough evidence. By doing that, Farrell knew he was protecting the chief, but he also knew he was putting himself in a precarious position. The only way he could share what he knew now was if he and Clint found concrete evidence. Otherwise, what he had to say would fall on deaf ears, and the fact that he'd held it back would spell the end of his career.

What a tangled mess of lies, Farrell thought, hating himself for it, even if it was for a greater good.

"I can fill in some of the gaps," the chief said. "Let's start with the attack on Garrett. That appears to be unrelated to any of these other events."

"How do you know?"

"One of our detectives reviewed Talbott's case notes a couple of hours ago. He and Pomeroy were assigned the investigation of the assault."

"Notes?" Sikes asked. "There's no official report?"

"Detectives often take extensive notes on a case and then compile a report later. It's pretty standard, especially if they're working a case actively."

"Fine, but were they investigating the assault *or* the drugs they found in Garrett's house?"

"Both," Baumgartner answered. "Early on, they interviewed the men who attacked him while they were still in the hospital. From what our detective can make of their notes, these two both initially tried to say they were just on a drive and that Garrett tricked them into stopping and then attacked them."

"What about the video that the Mexican woman took? Alzado?"

"Alvarado, sir," the blonde assistant corrected gently.

"Whatever," Sikes said, ignoring her. "No one has bothered to brief me on what the whole video shows."

"She was originally filming a dog crapping on her lawn. She's been having some trouble with a neighbor and wanted to get some proof. Her camera pans up to show the two men pull to a stop, get out and aggressively confront Garrett," Baumgartner said. "One of them has a club."

"Can we legitimately say that Officer Garrett acted in self-defense?"

Baumgartner shrugged, and motioned toward Tuck. "I say yes, but it's not my call."

Sikes turned on Tuck. "Artie?"

Tuck considered. "The video I saw on television is pretty brutal, and Garrett appears to be the aggressor. If these other two instigated the encounter and threatened him, his actions could be construed as self-defense. Especially when you factor in that it was a two-on-one scenario in which one of the attackers was armed with a deadly weapon."

"Just because you lose the fight," Baumgartner added, "it doesn't make you a victim."

Sikes nodded, seemingly delighted. "Good. Then we're clearing Garrett on the shooting and the attack. How about the drugs?"

Baumgartner shifted uncomfortably. "That's tough. The drugs were under his sink, in his house. There's no getting around that."

"There's a lot of shadows surrounding that entire event, Bob. Do we even know that the drugs were Garrett's? Could they have been planted?"

"By who?"

"You tell me."

Baumgartner stared back at the mayor, bristling. Farrell knew the quandary the chief faced. Either one of his patrol officers was dealing drugs, or one of his detectives had planted drugs. He was screwed either way.

Farrell found his voice finally and spoke. "Maybe we shouldn't be so quick to clear Garrett," he said carefully. "With so many unknowns."

Sikes snapped his gaze to Farrell. "Those unknowns are your responsibility, *Captain*. I'm more concerned with what I *do* know. I know that we're talking about a top-flight officer who was ambushed *twice*, for either wearing a badge or being black, or both. From where I sit, that makes him a victim. The drugs? I don't know about that, but I do know it isn't clear-cut. Maybe your detective, the one who was shot?" He looked to the chief with impatience. "What was his name?"

"Talbott," Baumgartner said.

"Maybe Talbott put the drugs there for some unknown reason. Maybe that's what got him shot. Maybe that's why his partner killed himself."

"That's no true!" Baumgartner interrupted. "You can't slander my men that way. I don't care who you are."

"You better care who I am!" the mayor roared. "Because I can end you."

The threat hung in the air. The mayor glared hotly at the chief, who returned the stare with equal intensity. Farrell could feel the wheels coming off of this meeting and wondered crazily if it was about to devolve into a fistfight. In that event, at least, he knew his chief would win.

"Let's take it down a notch," Artie Tuck said quietly. "We're not accomplishing anything with this in-fighting."

The mayor didn't respond, and Farrell knew good and well that Baumgartner wouldn't blink, either. He saw his opportunity and took it.

"We don't know enough to answer all these questions yet, sir," Farrell said evenly. "And we don't know for sure about Garrett. What if he's the dirty one? What if we find out that he was dirty all along, and is involved in more than just this shooting?"

"Like what?" Sikes snapped.

"Any of it. Talbott's death. Pomeroy's suicide. The quadruple homicide up north."

Baumgartner broke away from staring at the mayor and turned to Farrell, shocked. "Christ, Tom. You're starting to sound like Ward Clint, spouting conspiracies."

"I'm only saying—"

Baumgartner jabbed a finger in the mayor's direction. "*He* wants to make villains out of Talbott and Pomeroy and *you* want to make a villain out of Garrett," he thundered. "What the hell is your problem?"

Farrell swallowed. "My point is just that we should let the state finish their investigation of Detective Talbott's death and wait until they have some concrete results. Same thing with Detective Pomeroy's suicide and then—"

"Is it true that Detective Pomeroy was found with drugs…on his person?" Lofton asked quietly.

Farrell was surprised by the question. "Where did you hear that?"

"Is it true?" Lofton repeated.

Reluctantly, Farrell nodded.

"Will you be able to tell whether it was related to the drugs found under Officer Garrett's sink?"

Again, Farrell nodded. "Not definitively, but close enough."

Lofton glanced at the mayor. "Maybe you've got a couple of dirty cops—"

"You don't *know* that," Baumgartner snapped.

"No, I don't," Lofton admitted, "but it seems to me to be every bit as possible as the idea that the drugs were Garrett's. Talbott was killed under suspicious circumstances, and then his partner decided to kill himself shortly thereafter and is found with drugs. Those two seem related to me. It reeks of corruption, and that is most certainly how it will play in the public eye."

"Screw the public eye," Baumgartner said. "We need to find the truth."

Sikes shook his head. "That attitude is why I'm starting to wonder if you're still the right fit for the chief's job, Bob. Public opinion *is* reality. It *is* the truth."

"No, the truth is the truth."

"Maybe the truth is what we say it is," Lofton said.

"I'm not comfortable with that," Tuck said immediately.

"Me, either," Baumgartner agreed just as quickly.

"I'm not talking about lies, gentlemen," Lofton assured them. "I'm talking about presentation, that's all."

Farrell felt the momentum of the meeting shift. He had one card to play, and he knew he had to play it soon, or be lost. "We need to complete all investigations first," he began. "The state has to finish theirs, we have to complete ours. Pomeroy's suicide, for starters. Then we need to launch an internal investigation of Talbott, Pomeroy, and Garrett to see—"

"You are clearly not listening to me, *Captain*," the mayor said through clenched teeth. "I want this resolved tonight."

"That's not possible, sir."

"It is possible, and we are going to do it. Now—"

"Mr. Mayor," Lofton interrupted. "The captain has a point. If there's still doubt as to Garrett's innocence, we might want to be careful about getting behind him. If it comes out later, it won't just look bad for you, it might even appear corrupt."

"You flip-flop a lot, Cody," the mayor said derisively.

"I'm not flip-flopping, sir. I'm saying we can strike a middle ground here."

"If you walk down the middle of the road," Sikes said forcefully, "you get hit by traffic from both lanes. No, we are going to make a definitive move here, and put this behind us. We don't have the luxury of time."

"I'd advise against that approach, sir," Lofton said evenly.

"Losing your stomach for the game, buddy boy?" Sikes turned to Baumgartner. "Is there any evidence that those drugs belonged to Officer Garrett?"

"Other than the fact that they were found in his house?"

"Don't be a smart ass."

Baumgartner looked at Farrell, who shook his head. "No," the chief said.

Sikes turned to Tuck. "Is your office willing to prosecute Garrett for possession of drugs, Artie?"

Tuck shifted uncomfortably. "The case is problematic," he admitted. "The key witness would be Talbott, who can longer testify. Pomeroy, a secondary witness, is gone. Who does that leave?"

"Lieutenant Flowers," Baumgartner said.

"All he can say is that Talbott showed him the drugs under the sink?" Tuck shook his head. "While I believe your arrest based upon probable cause was solid at the time, there's no way I can prove this case in court beyond a reasonable doubt. If I don't have a reasonable belief that I can do that, professional ethics dictate that I don't charge in the first place. Doing so would be considered merely punitive."

"There go both criminal charges," Sikes said, clearly on a roll. "Now for the perception issues." He turned back to Baumgartner. "Do you have any proof that some thug like the ones who attacked Garrett didn't break into his home and plant those drugs?"

"Excuse me," Tuck said, "but that's a little far-fetched, don't you think? You're saying that an unknown party planted the drugs in Garrett's house, right where Detective Talbott happened to find them?"

"I'm not asking you to solve the case, Artie. In fact, I think we've just about covered everything on the agenda that relates to your office. Thank you for your support and your integrity. I'm sure both will ensure your re-election next year, the same as my own."

Tuck took the obvious dismissal with a pinched expression. He rose from his seat and addressed the mayor. "Drew, I'll keep my word on the things we've agreed to here, but I'm throwing up a Chinese wall on the rest. Anything else you decide, you keep me out of it." He glanced around the table. "All of you. Contact me in an official capacity only, and I will reply in the same fashion." He returned his gaze to the mayor. "I'm not getting caught up in your dirt."

The mayor didn't reply. Tuck turned around and briskly strode out of the room.

Once he was gone, the mayor resumed his line of questioning. "Is there any evidence the drugs weren't planted by a third party?"

Baumgartner spread his hands. "I can't prove a negative."

"Then it is clear to me that Officer Tyler Garrett is a victim. More than that, he is a hero, the first of two officers attacked in this community. We are going to go out into the world and tell them that. Moreover, we are going to apologize for his arrest—"

"Apologize?" Farrell said, choking out the word.

"Yes!" The mayor nodded decisively. "We're going to apologize to him, and we're going slap that life-saving medal on his chest just like we already should have done. And then I am going to get the city attorney working with his lawyers on a damages settlement to protect us from a future lawsuit."

"Sir—" Lofton began, but Sikes ignored him.

He pointed directly at Baumgartner. "If you are still chief after that, you can oversee whatever internal investigation you want. If you want to sully the reputation of a slain officer like

Talbott or further victimize a hero like Garrett, you go right ahead. You want to turn the tragedy of a depressed man succumbing to the stresses of this noble profession, you go right ahead. If it were me, though, I think I'd realize that the facts in that case are inconclusive."

A heavy silence fell over the room. Sikes looked at the faces around the table as if gauging the resolution of each person there.

Farrell's mind was whirring. What did he have? In the end, what did he *really* have?

Not much.

The only solid piece of evidence that Clint could point to was Nona Henry's identification. That was it. An eighty-year-old woman identifying a black man from two houses away, and then picking out of a photomontage the one black man that had been plastered all over television screens for the past week.

Clint was right. It wasn't enough.

Everything else was tainted, or inconsistent, or circumstantial. Once the mayor put through this plan of his, any of that weak evidence would be rendered even weaker, or useless. Once Garrett was painted as a victim and a hero, only a smoking gun could change that.

Even so, when the mayor's hard stare landed on him, Farrell felt the urge to speak up. He could share the revelation of Nona Henry's shaky identification and cast some doubt in the minds of the men present. From the way the conversation had gone, he believed Lofton might back him. Normally, that might be enough, but it was clear that Lofton was currently not in the mayor's good graces.

Baumgartner would be enraged at him, of course. Keeping his chief out of the loop was inexcusable. There would be severe consequences. The chief had the power to reduce him back to lieutenant, and stick him in some administrative, nowhere job. Janitorial services, or something equally as dead end. He might have been able to survive the transgression if he had something substantial when he finally came forward but everything Farrell had was falling away fast, like paper in fire.

The mayor's eyes narrowed, as if he sensed the conflict in Farrell's head. Under that gaze, Farrell saw how committed the mayor was to his chosen path. If someone stood in his way, the mayor would likely destroy that person. If Farrell spoke up now, both Baumgartner and Sikes would become his enemies.

Am I really willing to sacrifice my career just to be on the losing end?

Farrell's lips parted, but no words came.

The moment passed, and Sikes moved on to Baumgartner.

"We do it your way," Baumgartner said, resigned.

"Of course, we do," Sikes replied, slapping the table. "Because I'm the damn mayor."

Farrell hung his head and stared down at his shoes. Waves of shame rolled over him, but if he was being honest with himself, part of the shame he felt was because it was accompanied by a strong sense of relief.

"Let's get this done," the mayor said, "and then let's put it behind us."

FRIDAY

*A deception that elevates us is dearer
than a host of low truths.*
—Marina Tsvetaeva, Russian poet

Chapter 56

"All rise," the bailiff intoned, and everyone in the small hearing room obeyed. The judge made her way to the bench and took a seat, and the rest followed suit.

The court clerk quickly read the criminal complaint number and charge, and then she sat down as well.

"This is strictly a bail hearing," the judge said. "The defendant will have the opportunity to enter a plea once these charges have been formally laid before the court. This is the second time the court has heard arguments regarding this matter. Mr. Garrett was booked previously on the probable cause of police detectives, but no affidavit was filed. He is currently before the court because the prosecutor obtained a warrant for his arrest."

"Your Honor, if I may?" Pamela Wei stood respectfully.

"Ms. Wei," the judge acknowledged.

"Your Honor, not only do all of our previous arguments to release Mr. Garrett on his own recognizance apply in this case but this second arrest is beginning to appear almost punitive in nature. Only last night, the mayor of Spokane and the chief of police held a news conference and formally apologized to my client. They *apologized*, Your Honor! This is an admission of wrongdoing in this case, of persecution of my client. This morning, I have already been contacted by the city's civil attorneys to negotiate a settlement to avoid a lawsuit."

"This is a criminal court, Ms. Wei, not a civil one."

"Yes, Your Honor, but the city's action bears upon this criminal case. If the mayor and the chief of police are apologizing for arresting my client, how can the prosecuting attorney even be remotely considering charges in this matter? It's unconscionable."

"Please keep your editorial remarks in check, Ms. Wei. This is a court of law, not a media scrum. We discuss facts in this courtroom."

"Yes, Your Honor. I apologize."

The judge turned her attention to the prosecutor, a gangly man who sat scrunched in his chair like a dog who had been repeatedly whipped and knew another beating was imminent. "Mr. Carver?"

Carver rose reluctantly. "Your Honor, I've been informed by District Attorney Tuck that this case will be dismissed without prejudice due to extenuating circumstances."

"Those circumstances being?"

"In the charges of assault, the district attorney does not believe it is likely the state can overcome the assertions of self-defense made by the defendant in this matter to the required burden of proof of beyond a reasonable doubt." Carver swallowed and continued. "Furthermore, the state is unable to materially pursue the second charge, possession of a controlled substance, due to the fact that the key witness in this case has, tragically, passed away. The state is unlikely to meet the required burden of proof of beyond a reasonable doubt without the testimony of this witness."

The judge eyed Carver dangerously. "If this is the state's intent, Mr. Carver, please explain to me why Mr. Garrett spent last night in jail and is currently standing in my courtroom?"

Carver licked his lips nervously. "These determinations were made very recently, Your Honor."

"How recently?"

"I was only informed shortly before this hearing, Your Honor."

The judge gave Carver a withering look but said nothing.

Pamela Wei rose. "Your Honor, in light of what the counsel for the state has said, I would respectfully request that my client be released from custody immediately."

The judge didn't hesitate. "Your request is granted." She banged the gavel. "See that he is out-processed from jail, Mr. Carver. Rapidly."

Chapter 57

Ty Garrett stood at the out-processing counter waiting for Deputy Rob Utley to return with his bag of personal items.

Garrett looked around, taking it all in. He studied the agency-sponsored posters on the wall advocating various types of treatment. Each of them was loaded with contact information. *Spousal Abusers Seek Counseling Now! Drug Abusers Call Today for Treatment! Learn to Control Your Violent Impulses!* Garret shook his head. His attention was then attracted to the wooden bench attached to the wall. It was littered with hand-written graffiti.

He sat on the bench and let his eyes scan the various tags and monikers that had somehow made their way onto the wood. His fingers ran over the letters and he looked around for a pen, wondering how they'd made their way on to the bench over the years.

Deputy Utley returned to the counter, a brown paper bag in his hands. His bald head gleamed under the building's fluorescent lights. The heavyset man gently placed the bag onto the counter. "Here you go, Ty," he said.

Garrett stood and walked over to the counter. He opened the bag as Utley ran down the list of clothing. "Green T-shirt, green sweats, socks—"

"Yeah, yeah," Garrett said, waving at Utley to give him the clipboard and pen. "I know the stuff inside." He quickly signed his name but held on to the clipboard.

"I'm glad things worked out for you," Utley said.

"Really?

Utley looked confused. "Of course."

"That's funny because you were a dick to me the first time I came through."

The big man swallowed.

"I'm the same man I was before. I was innocent then just like I am now, but you already judged me. Why the change in attitude, man?"

"I'm sorry," Utley muttered. "I didn't mean nothing by it."

Garrett smiled. "Yeah, I figured. That's how most racists play it. Puss out when confronted."

Utley's face went flat. "What?"

"You heard me."

Garett tossed the clipboard on the counter and grabbed the bag.

"You're an asshole," Utley said.

"You're the asshole!" Garrett yelled as he walked into the bathroom to change.

It only took Garrett a few minutes to put on the green sweats and T-shirt he'd purchased from Walgreens. When he stepped out of the bathroom, he checked for Utley. He wasn't behind the counter. Since most prisoners come from a separate hallway that Utley would see, he wouldn't have expected Garrett to come back.

Garrett walked over and sat on the bench. With the pen he'd kept from Utley, he quickly scratched his initials into the wood.

When he was done, he stood and smiled at his work. He then tossed the pen over the counter and left the building.

Chapter 58

The Maxwell House Tavern sat in the midst of an old school West Central neighborhood. Working cops had always liked the tavern's perfect proximity to the Public Safety Building— far enough away to avoid the fancier locales that the judges and lawyers and white shirts frequented, but still only a short drive away for cops just getting off shift. For years, it served as something more than just another neighborhood bar in a rough and tumble part of town, but something less than a flat-out cop bar. It was a place where cops were seen in the same light as plumbers and mechanics, grocers, and steelworkers.

Or it used to be, when Farrell was coming up. His probation party had been at the Maxwell House, and so had several of his promotion celebrations. Things changed, and people did, too. Now, only his generation of cops frequented the place. Anyone with less than fifteen years on the job associated the Maxwell House with the old guard. They chose trendier spots up north, or in the Valley, and the number of cops warming barstools at the Maxwell House dwindled.

He'd come in plain clothes, and taken a corner booth, well away from the bar. While Travis Tritt competed with Lynyrd Skynyrd and Marvin Gaye on the antiquated jukebox that didn't even accept bills, much less a credit card, Farrell sipped his beer. He'd downed the first shot of whisky as soon as he came in, right at the bar, and chased it with the beer. Now that beer was half empty, and another empty shot glass sat upside down on the table next to it. He was preparing to order a third when Wardell Clint entered through the front door.

That door was another thing Farrell always liked about the Maxwell House. It opened big and wide and showed everyone in the place who was coming in before that person could get a bead on anyone sitting inside. The whole set up was perfect. He couldn't understand why the younger set was abandoning it.

Clint spotted him after a couple of seconds and made his way to the booth. He slid into the seat across from Farrell.

"I'm about to order another shot," Farrell said, feeling the slight thickness in his speech already. "You want one? On me."

Clint shook his head. He took off his glasses and wiped the lenses with a small white cloth. "I will have one of those beers, though, since you're buying."

Farrell caught Margie's attention at the bar with a wave and pointed to his shot glass and his beer.

Clint put away his cloth and returned his glasses to his face. "Exactly how screwed are we, Captain?"

"I was going to ask you the same question."

Clint snorted. "You're the one with the inside access."

"Nothing but poison on the inside," Farrell told him. "Believe that."

"You don't have to convince me. I've been saying it for years. Power corrupts, and the more power, the more corruption."

Farrell sipped his beer. "Garrett's out by now."

"I figured. What were they going to hold him on? The assault was self-defense, and the D.A. isn't going to file on drugs, so he skates."

Farrell let the words burn in his ears for a few seconds before replying. "You read Talbott's notes on the interview with those rednecks. You believe that attack was random?"

"I do."

"And the drugs?"

Margie arrived with a shot glass and a beer. She put them both in front of Farrell and picked up his empty. She glanced over at Clint expectantly, her expression sour, but when Farrell slid the full beer across to him, she turned and walked away without a word.

"What's that about?" Farrell asked. Margie was usually pleasant.

"Old business, forever ago. Don't worry on it." Clint took a swig of the beer. "You asked about the drugs. Truth is, I don't know. Maybe they were Garrett's and Talbott found them, or maybe he brought them along and planted them. It doesn't matter now, does it?"

"I suppose not."

"I'll tell you one thing. You can bet those drugs and the one's found next to Pomeroy will be from the same batch."

"That's not exactly a news flash."

"If I keep digging at this, Captain, there's a good chance I'm eventually going to find a connection between Trotter and that dealer, Ocampo."

"That's good. It'll tie in Garrett."

Clint shook his head. "No, it'll tie in Talbott and Pomeroy. Marty Hill found drugs under a cushion in Ocampo's house. Packaged for individual sale, just like the ones Pomeroy had. If we test those..." He gave Farrell a meaningful look.

Farrell finished the thought. "You think they'll match."

"I know they will."

Farrell sighed. It was one more link between Talbott, Pomeroy, and Ocampo. "No connection to Garrett in all of this except what? The ID from Nona Henry?"

"That, and the location of Talbott's shooting. It happened outside Derek Tillman's condo. He's friends with Garrett."

"And he's not saying diddly."

"Probably won't ever," Clint agreed. "Even if he did, or a good witness materializes out of thin air, so what? It sounds like Talbott really did fire first and Garrett fired back in self-defense. What do we get Garrett and Tillman on? Garrett for defending himself and Tillman for interfering with a police investigation because he lied?" Clint made a *psshhh* sound and took a drink of his beer. "It's not even our investigation."

"Then there's nothing else we can do now. Any internal investigation is going to get stymied by the chief. He's too loyal to the mayor not to go along with the city hall whitewash, especially since breaking ranks means he loses his job and makes a whole bunch of cops look bad."

"Some of them are bad. Or were."

"That doesn't seem to matter these days."

"And exactly which days did it matter?"

Farrell lifted his whisky and downed it. Clint watched him as he chased it with beer. Farrell enjoyed the spreading warmth in his stomach, then asked, "How does this happen?"

"The world is a dirty place. You ain't figured that out yet?"

"No, I mean Garrett. How's that…happen?"

Clint shrugged. "His pops died young. There's a hole there that even the best mama in the world can't fill."

"Clara Garrett was a pretty good mom," Farrell said.

"Was she?" Clint asked. "She was a great council president, I know that. I don't have any idea what kind of mom she was. Her son would have been exposed to all the nastiness of Spokane politics at a young age. Maybe he just decided, hell with it, I'm gonna get mine."

"You think so?" Farrell asked doubtfully.

"You don't?"

He considered, then shook his head. "No, I think it's classic Noble Cause Corruption. Cops shave corners to put bad guys in jail. End justifies the means, but it's a slippery slope. They start out small, massaging facts in reports, maybe planting evidence on a guy they know is guilty. Then one day, they're hitting a drug dealer's house and taking thirty grand from the safe and splitting it with their partner."

Clint scoffed lightly. "Some Ph.D. came up with that nonsense for his doctorate."

"It happens."

"So, do solar eclipses. Just not that often." Clint took a swig of beer. "He's probably just a classic sociopath."

"Those are rare, too."

"Not as rare as an eclipse." Clint sighed heavily. "Forget the why. What really grinds me is to see him getting away with it all, being hailed as a hero."

"You want to give up?"

"Hell, no. Not a chance. He dirtied the badge."

Farrell nodded in agreement.

"Not only that," Clint said, an edge in his voice. "He made it harder for any black man to carry it. He played me for a fool along the way. *That cannot stand.*"

For the first time, Farrell thought maybe he truly understood Wardell Clint. Perhaps not all the wild conspiracies, maybe not even everything Clint believed about Garrett, but Farrell now had an inkling of exactly who the man across from him was truly. What he saw was someone much braver than he would ever be.

"You think you stand a chance?" he asked.

"He'll make a mistake. Sometime. Somewhere."

"I hope so."

"What's next?" Clint asked.

Farrell snorted. "The world turns. Sikes gets re-elected. Baumgartner brushes away all the shadows of this case, makes a hero out of Garrett, and probably Talbott and Pomeroy, too. Garrett gets a settlement and his job back, and the other two get bagpipes and a seven-gun salute at the funeral. For my part, I'm going to sit here and get soundly drunk. Maybe look into retiring my way out of this mess. What are you going to do?"

Clint gave Farrell a flat stare, but his eyes burned with anger. "I'm going to bury that traitor the first chance I get."

Farrell smiled at that. He raised his beer and clinked Clint's glass. "*Buona fortuna,*" he said. "You've got the weight of the world lined up against you on this one, Wardell."

"Same as always," Clint agreed matter-of-factly, and they both drank.

Chapter 59

Cody Lofton brushed several strands of hair away from Amanda Donahue's eyes. She had lain her head in his lap while they rested on his couch. She was wearing a pair of white shorts and a Mariner's jersey. They had huddled together to watch the fallout from Garrett's release following the mayor's poorly handled press conference the night before.

A half-eaten pizza and two glasses of wine sat on the table in front of them.

Lofton's mind drifted to the hastily scheduled press conference the mayor made him call after the conference room meeting. The mayor stood in front of a small group of press and announced to the world that the city of Spokane was "one hundred percent behind Officer Garrett" and, indeed, issued an apology for how he was treated. Sikes even made the announcement that he would seek to meet with Garrett's attorney to discuss a financial damages package for him. It didn't take long for that story to go viral. As the day spun out of control, the mayor went into hiding. No one could find him, leaving Lofton to field calls from city council members, the press and irate citizens throughout the day.

Everything Sikes did during the past week showed him to be a man in a position he wasn't suited to serve. A nagging thought had plagued Lofton since the meeting late yesterday afternoon.

"I can't believe Sikes," Amanda said, absently.

Lofton watched the silent footage of the press conference being aired on *The Rachel Maddow Show*. Sikes had a big smile during the conference, proud of himself for taking control. Chief Baumgartner stood behind him, nothing more than well-uniformed window dressing, a puppet with a badge.

Earlier, Maddow had torn Sikes apart for announcing the backing of Ty Garrett before the district attorney's office could officially announce their findings. This was after Sean Hannity had ripped Sikes apart on FOX News for the same thing. Hannity went so far as to call Sikes a moron for announcing his intention to offer damages *before* an attorney for Garrett made any threat of litigation. Both sides of the media had rallied against the city and everyone was crying foul. The common consensus was something stunk in Spokane and no one was looking at Garrett. The day had started out at a simmer. The national fervor was now at full boil.

"I'm going to quit," Amanda said.

"Me, too," Lofton whispered, finally addressing the nagging thought in the back of his mind. "I realized that after the meeting in the conference room, yesterday. I guess today was the topper. When he vanished, leaving me to take the heat, it made me realize that I don't believe in him anymore."

She turned her head and looked up into his eyes. "What are you going to do?"

Lofton shrugged, his eyes still on the TV. "I don't know. Brush up my resume, I guess."

Amanda sat up, turned to him, and crossed her legs. Her eyes were wide, and her lips parted. "I know what you have to do."

Lofton smiled. His problems melted away in her eyes. Everything was clear to him now. He leaned over and kissed her.

She quickly pushed him back. "No, this is serious."

"Oh, I thought…"

"They'll be plenty of time for that. This is about our careers."

Lofton focused on her. "Okay, what am I missing?"

Amanda pointed at the TV. "What do you see?"

Lofton turned to the screen and watched. "A city still under siege by the media. A mayor who clearly can't pull his head out of his own ass. What? What should I be seeing?"

Amanda thrust her finger at the TV twice. "Opportunity."

"What?"

"I know you want to do it. Everyone knows. It's not a secret."

Lofton studied her until he understood what she was saying. When he turned to look at the TV again, he saw it with new eyes. No more was it ugly and depressing. Instead, it was beautiful and hopeful. A smile grew on Lofton's lips.

Amanda climbed into his lap and took his face in her hands. She studied him. "It's time you announce your candidacy for mayor. Let's kick Sikes in the balls. It's time to remake this town in *your* image."

Cody Lofton laughed and then kissed her.

EPILOGUE

To betray, you must first belong.
—H.A.R. (Kim) Philby, British traitor

Tyler Garrett pulled to the curb and parked his Nissan Murano. He climbed out and smiled. His Roka Aviators protected his eyes from the sun. He loved being in his old neighborhood, especially when he wasn't working.

A little more than a month had passed since the shooting of Todd Trotter and he'd been reinstated. Initially, the administration assigned him to a desk until the media storm died down. It took only a week and a school shooting in Alabama to divert the press's attention. Once Garrett was yesterday's news, he was back on the street.

Angie and the kids had returned from Kennewick after his release from county jail. Life struggled to get back to normal. Angie looked at him slightly different, but he believed time would heal all wounds with her.

Garrett walked the half block, enjoying the sights and smells of his neighborhood.

He pulled open the door to Oak's Barbershop and stepped in.

Son Seals' "I Believe to My Soul" played through the speakers in the shop. Delmar Oakley sat in the corner with his eyes closed, bobbing to the song.

Garrett removed his sunglasses and watched his friend enjoy the music.

As the song faded out, Oakley opened his eyes and focused on the young man. The joy in his eyes faded. He slowly stood and turned down the volume before the next song could start.

"Hey, Oak. How you been?"

The old man nodded.

Garrett ran his hand over the top of his head. "Been some time and I'm looking a little rough. You think you can fit me in?"

"I'm full up right now, kid."

Garrett looked at the empty chairs and then back to old man. "What gives?"

Oakley slowly walked to the front door and flipped the sign to *Closed*. He turned back to Garrett. "We have some unfinished business."

"What's that?"

"My gun. You took it and never brought it back."

Garrett nodded, then ran his tongue over his top lip. "I'll get you a new one, Oak."

"Don't want a new one. That old one has special value to me."

"Yeah? I didn't know that. What value does it have?"

"It proves you're innocent."

Garrett pursed his lips.

Oakley walked past Garrett and leaned on one of the barber chairs. "You remember that crazy-eyed brother that you called here when you were trouble?"

"Clint," Garrett said with a sneer.

"Right. He came by the shop a couple weeks back."

Garrett's eyes widened for just an instant, but he quickly recovered. "What did he want?"

"He came spinning a story of how maybe you shot that man in the back on purpose."

"That's a lie. I was ambushed. Even the district attorney cleared me of the shooting."

"That's what I said, but Clint said to listen to his story. He can be very convincing when he wants to be. He said you were caught up in some drug dealing with a couple of dirty cops."

Garrett looked away from Oakley, anger flashing across his face.

"He told me how one of those cops ended up shot to death. He thinks you did that. Then four people were murdered in connection to some drugs, and he seems to think you're responsible for that one as well. The one I didn't get was how you convinced a man to kill himself, but that four-eyed bastard seems to think you managed that as well."

Garrett looked at the ground, his jaw flexing.

"How many is that? Six? That's a lot of people in the ground, son. He kept trying to pin that all on you. I told him he was full of it."

The younger man lifted his head, looking at Oakley.

"He then tells me he found a link between the man you shot in the back and the drug dealer that was murdered. He believes you shot that man on purpose. He's not sure why, but he says he's still working on that angle."

Garrett shook his head.

"Then you know what the crazy son-of-bitch said?" Oakley said. "He said, the one thing he couldn't figure out was where you got the gun to do all them killings."

"I didn't shoot anyone, Oak. Clint is just lying to stir the pot. He's upset about the two detectives and thinks I'm part of it. Those guys were his friends."

Oakley shook his head. "See, that's a lie. I could always tell when you were lying, son."

Garrett stared at him.

"Looks like the only one telling the truth around here is Wardell Clint."

Garrett raised an eyebrow.

Tears filled the old man's eyes. "I dirtied my soul by lying for you. I don't know if I'll ever get that lifted. I love you like a son, Garrett, and I wouldn't give that man what he wanted to know." Oakley wiped his eyes with the back of his hand. "I need you to go. You're not welcome here no more."

"Oak…"

The old man held up a hand and walked over to the stereo, turned up the music and sat back in the corner chair. Little Milton's "I Play Dirty" popped through the speaker. Oakley closed his eyes and started bobbing his head to the music.

Garrett watched him, expecting him to talk to him further. When he didn't, Garrett finally turned and left.

He stood on the sidewalk, looking up and down the street, taking it all in.

A car honked, and the driver stuck his finger out the window at another car. A pregnant young woman with tattoos on her arms pushed a baby stroller while a Rottweiler trotted alongside her. Across the street, a large black man argued with a skinny Hispanic woman. Without warning, he slapped her across the face. When he turned to walk away, she trotted behind him, yelling "I'm sorry."

Garrett took it all in before laughing.

He put his sunglasses on and lifted his face to the sun. Then he turned and strutted to his car.

Acknowledgments

The authors wish to thank those essential first readers who helped make *Charlie-316* the best novel it could be: Dave Mather, Melanie Donaldson, C.W., Judy Orchard, Brad Hallock, John Emery, Cheryl Counts, David Conway, and Kristi Scalise.

About the Authors

COLIN C ONWAY is the author of the 509 Crime Stories, a series of novels set in Eastern Washington with revolving lead characters. They are standalone tales and can be read in any order. He served in the US Army and later was an officer of the Spokane Police Department. He's a commercial real estate broker/investor, owned a laundromat, invested in a bar, and ran a karate school. Colin lives with his beautiful life partner, their three wonderful children, and a crazy, codependent Vizsla that rules their world. Find out more about him at **ColinConway.com**.

FRANK ZAFIRO was a police officer in Spokane, Washington, from 1993 to 2013. He retired as a captain. He is the author of numerous crime novels, including the River City novels and the Stefan Kopriva series. He lives in Redmond, Oregon, with his wife Kristi, dogs Richie and Wiley, and a very self-assured cat named Pasta. He is an avid hockey fan and a tortured guitarist. You can keep up with Frank at **FrankZafiro.com**.

Are You Ready for the Next Book in the Charlie-316 Series?

NEVER THE CRIME

The Tyler Garrett Saga Continues…

Spokane Police Officer Tyler Garrett is a man of many different images. To the public, he is a once maligned and now redeemed cop, the victim of public prejudice and city politics. To the Chief of Police and the Mayor, he is a good cop, falsely accused and thankfully back to work. To his wife, a man she no longer knows. And to those who know his secret, he is the most terrible thing any police officer can be—a traitor to his badge.

Clear of the controversy that surrounded him less than two years ago, Garrett is moving on and getting his life back in order. Meanwhile, Detective Wardell Clint remains on the hunt for any evidence against him that proves what Clint already knows—that Tyler Garrett is dirty. Clint has vowed to stop at nothing to bring down Garrett once and for all.

In the midst of Clint's efforts, a rash of new city hall scandals break out, including a suspicious death, and Tyler Garrett inserts himself into the investigation. But he isn't the only one. No one seems immune to being drawn into the web of dirty politics. Officer Gary Stone, assigned as a liaison to city hall, finds himself thrown into the midst of this maelstrom, struggling as his loyalties and ethics are challenged. The mayor, the chief, councilmembers, police captains, and news reporters all square off, each with their own agenda.

Before it ends, everyone will learn that it's never the crime that causes downfall, but the following cover-up.

Made in the USA
Monee, IL
22 May 2021